Cast-Iron Cooking

for **dummies®**
A Wiley Brand

Cast-Iron Cooking

2nd Edition

by Antwon Brinson

A Wiley Brand

Cast-Iron Cooking For Dummies®, 2nd Edition

Published by: **John Wiley & Sons, Inc.**, 111 River Street, Hoboken, NJ 07030-5774, www.wiley.com

Copyright © 2024 by John Wiley & Sons, Inc., Hoboken, New Jersey

Published simultaneously in Canada

For general information on our other products and services, please contact our Customer Care Department within the U.S. at 877-762-2974, outside the U.S. at 317-572-3993, or fax 317-572-4002. For technical support, please visit https://hub.wiley.com/community/support/dummies.

Wiley publishes in a variety of print and electronic formats and by print-on-demand. Some material included with standard print versions of this book may not be included in e-books or in print-on-demand. For more information about Wiley products, visit www.wiley.com.

Library of Congress Control Number: 2023948980

ISBN 978-1-119-88813-0 (pbk); ISBN 978-1-119-88814-7 (ebk); ISBN 978-1-119-88815-4 (ebk)

SKY10059605_111023

Contents at a Glance

Recipes at a Glance

Vegetables

Cornbreads

Biscuits

Other Breads

Pancakes

Muffins

Desserts

Campfire Cooking

Tailgating

One-Pot World Favorites

Table of Contents

Introduction

The importance of cast iron in your life may vary depending on where you live. The process of casting metals has played a vital role in shaping today's world. Without this incredible discovery, civilization would have developed differently.

In this book, I guide you on a captivating exploration where you discover (or rediscover) the timeless art of cast-iron cooking. Throughout this journey, you uncover the remarkable influence that cast iron has had, and still maintains, in kitchens all around the globe.

Whether you find yourself cooking al fresco over an open flame or stumbling upon the historical value of a vintage cast-iron skillet hanging on the wall at your grandparents' house, my goal is for this book to inspire you. Through its pages, I motivate you to venture into uncharted culinary territories, uncovering new recipes, acquiring novel techniques, and above all, immersing yourself in the age-old mysteries of cast iron that have left an indelible mark on how food is perceived today.

About This Book

For many people cast-iron cooking sounds historic. You may have heard stories about delicious dishes that remind you of your elders, and beautiful cakes, fried chicken, and baked dishes that allow you to live vicariously through their nostalgic memories. The thought of re-creating these dishes seems impossible and impractical because these memories didn't come with instructions.

Fear not! This book is designed to be your step-by-step guide to successful cooking in cast iron. I break down those mental barriers that have prevented you from taking that leap of faith. I include tips, tricks, and tons of information to help you gain the confidence you need to cook your favorite dishes in cast iron. I recommend taking your time reading these pages and don't just skim.

Consider this book a relationship-building tool for you and your cast iron. Like any good relationship, it takes work. Until now, you may have had troubling relationships with your cast iron. They heat up too quickly and burn your food, they cool down too quickly and steam everything, or everything sticks to the pan creating a logistical nightmare. If you follow the advice in this book, cast iron can help you take your relationship with cooking to the next level.

This new edition of the book includes the following info:

>> Everything you need to know about the different types of cast iron, including minis

>> More than 50 new recipes and dishes from around the world, adding culture and new flavors to your recipe repertoire

>> Ways to season and cook fresh vegetables as sides and main dishes that make use of your local farmers' market

Each recipe indicates a size and the type of cast iron to use. But because cast iron is so versatile, you can use just about any cast-iron pan that you have on hand. Just keep the following in mind:

>> Make sure the pan that you use is suitable for the task at hand. If the recipe calls for deep-frying, for example, a skillet won't do because it isn't deep enough, but a Dutch oven will work fine.

>> If the pan that you use is larger or smaller than the one specified in the recipe, especially for baking recipes, such as cakes, you may have to adjust the cooking time. Baking a cake in a 10-inch skillet, for example, takes longer than baking a cake in a 12-inch pan.

So feel free to use whatever cast iron you can. Some good candidates for swapping are as follows:

To Do This		Use Any of These Pans
Roast	Meats	Deep fryer, Dutch oven, fry pan, deep-sided skillet
	Vegetables	Dutch oven, any skillet, casserole dish
Deep-fry		Deep fryer, Dutch oven, fry pan
Pan-fry		Dutch oven, fry pan, skillet
Bake	Cakes, pies	Skillet, Dutch oven, specialty bake pans

To Do This		Use Any of These Pans
	Muffins, cornsticks	Muffin pan, cornstick pans, divided cornbread skillet
	Loaf breads	Loaf pan, Dutch oven, skillet
	Rolls	Dutch oven, skillet, griddle
	Biscuits, cornbread	Skillet, drop-biscuit pan, Dutch oven, cornbread skillet
Simmer soups or stews		Dutch oven, deep fryer, deep saucepan
Sear meats		Skillet, griddle
Stir-fry		Skillet, wok

One of the fun things about cast-iron cooking is that it's as much an art as a science. Many older cast-iron recipes have been handed down from one generation to the next and passed from cook to cook. Many recipes have made it to this book in just that way. So, you're getting authentic cast-iron recipes that have stood the test of time.

Another typical characteristic of these types of recipes is that they often don't use precise measurements or give specific time guidelines. Instead, they tell you to "Add just a smidgeon of salt," or "Simmer the sauce until it's nice and thick." So that anyone from the culinary novice to the seasoned cast-iron cook can have success with the recipes in this book, the impreciseness is kept to a minimum:

>> **Measurements:** The recipes largely give precise measurements (a half teaspoon of this or 1½ tablespoons of that, for example) or indicate a range (½ to 1 teaspoon, for example).

>> **Times:** The recipes also indicate approximate prep and cooking times and times for the tasks within individual recipe steps.

But, at the end of the day, to be true to cast-iron's heritage, some ingredient amounts are occasionally left to your cooking judgment. (Don't worry, I'm talking about things like salt and pepper.) Continuing a long-standing kitchen tradition, as soon as you make a recipe, that recipe becomes yours to do with as you please. Take advantage of this flexibility and feel free to adjust any of these recipes to suit your own tastes and cooking style.

The recipes in this book are complete, but they may not spell out every detail of prepping and cooking the food. For example, certain steps and techniques in cooking are standard no matter what you're preparing. In addition, I require specific types of ingredients and also want to make sure that you adhere to a few of my other cooking preferences. Take a quick look at the following list for points that apply to all the recipes:

>> Fruits and vegetables are washed under cold running water before using.

>> Pepper is freshly ground pepper. Invest in a pepper mill and give it a few cranks when you want pepper bursting with flavor.

>> Fresh herbs are specified in many of the recipes for their bright, authentic flavor. But you can still make a recipe if you don't plan to use these by substituting dry herbs, using one-third the amount of fresh.

>> Dairy products are lowfat.

>> Eggs are large unless otherwise indicated.

>> Olive oil is mild unless otherwise indicated.

>> All onions are sweet unless otherwise indicated.

>> Water is filtered water.

>> All temperatures are Fahrenheit.

>> Keep pots uncovered unless I tell you to put on the lid.

Foolish Assumptions

In the writing of this book, I make some assumptions about you:

>> You found yourself the proud owner of cast iron, but you aren't quite sure what to do with it.

>> You've had cast iron for a while and are looking to expand your repertoire of cast-iron recipes.

>> You've had bad experiences with cast iron but are willing to give it another go.

>> You don't own a lick of cast iron, but you've been hearing so much about it (or you've tasted something cooked in it), and you want to give it a try.

>> You don't have time for long treatises on the joy of cast-iron cooking and just want practical cooking tips and cut-to-the-chase directions.

If any of the preceding assumptions describe you, you have the right cast-iron cookbook in your hands.

Icons Used in This Book

The icons in this book help you find particular kinds of information that may be of use to you:

TIP

You'll see this icon anywhere that I offer a suggestion or a bit of practical, advice — such as how to save time or what special tool to use — that can help you with the task at hand.

REMEMBER

This icon points out important information about cast-iron cooking or care that (surprise, surprise) I don't want you to forget.

WARNING

If something can ruin your cast iron, mess up your meal, or prove hazardous to your health, you'll find it highlighted with this icon.

TECHNICAL STUFF

This icon appears beside information that explains the finer points — the technical details (such as how cast iron is made or why yeast works) — that you may find interesting but that you don't need to know to get a handle on cast iron. Feel free to skip this information at will.

Beyond This Book

This book is full of tips and other pieces of helpful advice you can use as you're cooking with cast iron. In addition, check out the book's Cheat Sheet at `www.dummies.com` and search for "Cast-Iron Cooking For Dummies Cheat Sheet" for information to reference on a regular basis.

Where to Go from Here

This book is organized so that you easily find whatever you want to find. Have some potatoes that you need to use and want some recipe ideas? Head to Chapters 17 and 18. If you're interested in outdoor recipes, because a campout is coming up, go to Chapter 22. You can use the table of contents to find broad categories of information, the index to look up more specific items, or the Recipes at a Glance section at the front of this book to find the right recipe.

What's great about this book is that *you* decide where to start and what to read. It's a reference that you can jump into and out of at will.

If you don't currently have any cast iron or you're not sure how to cook with cast iron, you may want to head to Part 1. It gives you all the basic info that you need to get started. After you've digested the tidbits in Part 1, you can go anywhere your heart — or your taste buds — takes you.

1

Getting Started with Cast-Iron Cooking

Chapter **1**

Welcome to the World of Cast-Iron Cooking

n today's world, you're no longer limited by the few select materials needed to create good cookware. Just search online for the best pans, and you'll populate hundreds of options. Unless you're a trained professional chef or have time to sift through webpages or blogs or watch hundreds of YouTube videos, buying a good quality pan can be daunting. This chapter serves as a launching pad to this book where I break down some of those barriers and help you achieve your aspirations and goals in the kitchen through cast iron.

Easy to use and easy to care for, cast iron lasts practically forever, and you can use any cooking method to cook anything in it. And most cast-iron cooks will tell you that food cooked in cast iron tastes better than food cooked in anything else. But like any well-crafted cookware, cast iron does require some care, and what you cook in it can turn out better if you know a few tricks.

Here I introduce you to basic information about cooking in cast iron, explain its benefits, and tell you what you need to know to use it successfully.

Understanding the Benefits to Cooking with Quality Cast Iron

Most modern-day cooks have never cooked in cast iron, many have never (knowingly, anyway) tasted a cast-iron dish, and even fewer have probably ever cared for a cast-iron skillet — beyond hanging it on the kitchen wall and dusting it periodically. If this sounds familiar, chances are, you don't even realize the culinary adventure you're missing out on.

REMEMBER

So what's so great about cooking in cast iron? Plain and simple, cast iron is a great cookware. Cast iron has much to offer in terms of heating properties, economy, usefulness, and health benefits (yes, even health benefits). And that list doesn't even begin to touch on the area of taste! Cast iron, with the proper seasoning and care, offers all the same benefits — and then some — that more modern cookware offers, and it has a history and longevity that these others lack.

Durability and longevity — A pan made to last

Cast iron isn't just a descriptive term. These pots and pans are actually made from iron that has been melted and formed in pan-shaped molds or casts. (If you're interested in the details of how cast-iron pans are made, see the nearby sidebar) Made from the same base material that's used in engine blocks and building girders, cast-iron pans can last forever. Well, maybe not forever, but pretty darn close.

REMEMBER

Cast iron's longevity is one reason why it can be so easy to find and relatively inexpensive. You don't have to buy it new. Many people inherit their cast iron or buy it at garage and yard sales. Even old pans that have been abused can be reborn with a little work. (Chapter 4 tells you how to save a worn cast-iron pot.)

Cast iron is extremely tough and can last generations if cared for properly. It won't scratch, chip, or melt. (Well, at least not below 2,500 degrees. And I'm guessing you're dealing with temperatures slightly below that mark.) The handles don't fall off, and cooking in it won't kill your pet parakeet.

Another great quality about this pan is that you can change between cooking surfaces. Cooking on the stovetop and want to finish in the oven? Go for it! Cooking in the oven and want to finish on the grill? As chefs say in the kitchen "Yes, Chef!" You don't have to worry about plastic handles melting or the loosening of screws; this pan is made to last and can adapt to almost all cooking environments.

THE ESSENTIAL UTENSIL — UNTIL 1940

People have been using cast iron for more than cookware since the 1600s. They also used it to dip candles, dye fabric, make soap, and wash clothes. During the California Gold Rush, folks panned for gold using small cast-iron skillets. Keep reading for more cast-iron trivia tidbits:

- Many people credit Paul Revere with being the creator of the Dutch oven — a fact that the Dutch are none too happy about.
- George Washington's mother bequeathed her cast iron in her will. You can still see some of the selection on display in the National Museum in Washington, D.C.
- Lewis and Clark listed their Dutch oven as one of the most important pieces of equipment that they took with them on their exploration of the Pacific Northwest in 1804.
- Cast-iron cookware remained popular in the United States until the 1940s, when lighter, shinier aluminum cookware was introduced.
- The Dutch oven is the official cookware of the states of Texas, Arkansas, and Utah.

Few things can harm a cast-iron pan. What are the two biggest dangers of cast iron? Cold water on a hot pan and a trip through the dishwasher. Head to Chapter 4 for care instructions.

Timeless beauty — Aging with grace

If you've ever found yourself examining (and cursing) the bottom of a nonstick pan for scratches and peels, you may come to appreciate that cast iron doesn't wear out with age; it gets better. The reason is that every time you cook in the pan, you're actually seasoning it again, filling in the microscopic pores and valleys that are part of the cast-iron surface. The more you cook, the smoother the surface becomes until you have a pan that's the envy of cast-iron cooks everywhere.

New cast iron is gunmetal gray. This color darkens with the initial seasoning. (See Chapter 3 for seasoning instructions.) It grows darker with every use until you reach the *patina* (the dark color and slight shine cast iron develops over time). That's the mark of well-used and well-seasoned cast iron. (See Figure 1-1.)

Of course, not all old cast iron has been taken care of, and some old pans look their age. Your cast iron may have enough rust spots, cooked-on gunk, and pitted surfaces to earn a place on the junk pile.

FIGURE 1-1:
New cast iron (front) is relatively light. Older cast iron (rear) has a satiny patina.

Photograph by Tracy Barr

TIP

Keep in mind, however, that looks can be deceiving. Many battered and beaten cast-iron pieces can be reclaimed, rejuvenated, and restored to life (Chapter 4 provides details). With a little work, you can restore most old cast iron to cooking condition. And many consider cast iron to be a collectible, so you could end up with a pan that has value beyond how well it bakes biscuits. (For a word or two about collectible cast iron, see Chapter 2.)

Making dollars and sense

Cast iron is known to be rugged and heavy. Traditionally there was one standard look, nothing fancy, and it definitely didn't lend itself to a themed kitchen where everything matched, including your cookware. Well . . . welcome to the future! Nowadays, you can buy enameled cast-iron pieces that come in a variety of colors. Companies are making metallic-finished cast iron with brass, bronze, copper, and even silver. This section takes a deep look at some of these varieties and explores the pros and cons.

The world of cast iron has definitely evolved over the years, and so has the cost. Table 1-1 gives you an idea of the cost difference between traditional, modern, and other nonstick cookware. As you read this table, keep the following in mind:

>> The prices are approximate. You may pay more or less, depending on whether you buy your cookware from a retailer or the manufacturer or order it from a third party that's offering discounts.

>> All the non-cast-iron items listed come from nonstick product lines. When seasoned properly, cast iron has a nonstick surface, so I include only comparable surfaces.

TABLE 1-1

Cost of New Cast Iron versus Other Cookware

	10-inch Skillet	12-inch Skillet
Cast Iron		
Natural finish	$25	$30
Preseasoned	$34	$50
Enameled	$70	$90
Carbon Steel	$45	$50
Nonstick Cookware		
All Clad	$100	$120
Calphalon	$60	$80
Cuisinart	$40	$60
Le Crueset	$120	$130

Over the past two decades, new producers of cast iron have been emerging across the United States. Lodge Manufacturing previously held a monopoly as the sole domestic producer of cast iron for many years. However, the landscape has evolved, and today, several other American brands have entered the market. Here is a list of some of these brands made in United States:

» American Skillet Co. — made in Wisconsin

» Appalachian Cast Iron Co. — made in Tennessee

» Borough Furnace — made in New York

» Butter Pat Industries — made in Pennsylvania and Maryland

» Field Company — made in Illinois, Indiana, and Wisconsin

» Finex — made in Oregon

» Fredericksburg Cast Iron — made in Texas

» Grizzly — made in North Carolina

» Lancaster Cast Iron — made in Pennsylvania

» Lodge Manufacturing — made in Tennessee

» Marquette Castings — made in Michigan

» Nest Homeware — made in Pennsylvania and Rhode Island

>> Smithy Ironware Co. — made in South Carolina

>> Stargazer Cast Iron — made in Wisconsin, Ohio, and Pennsylvania

Although I primarily focus on traditional cast iron in this book, it's important that you're aware of the alternatives. Every pan has its pros and cons, with two of the major factors being cost and time. Most nonstick pans have an expiration date, meaning at some point they'll start sticking. Investing in cast iron is a long-term investment. If maintained properly, your investment will far outperform all other nonstick cookware.

Aside from the great return, cast iron is also economical. Cooking with cast iron uses less heat. Cast iron absorbs and retains heat so efficiently that you use less fuel when you cook with it. On the flip side, because it retains heat well after you put it off the stove or take it out of the oven, you don't have to worry about your food cooling down right away, which makes it great for family style meals. Chapter 5 explains the heating properties of cast iron and how these affect the way you cook in more detail.

A PAN IS BORN

The process used to make cast-iron cookware, *sand casting,* has existed for many centuries, and the basic technique is still pretty much the same as it's always been: Take a mold shaped in sand, pour in molten iron, let it cool, chip away the sand, and there you go.

Of course, the actual process is a little more complex than that. Lodge Manufacturing mixes and melts pig iron (basically iron ore) and scrap steel (the leftovers from the manufacture of electric plates — the cleanest scrap steel available) together in a 2,800-degree furnace. After slagging off the impurities, which rise to the top, Lodge tests the molten iron to make sure that it meets quality and safety standards.

Then the molten iron is poured into the *cast,* a sand-clay mold. After it cools, the mold is dumped onto a vibrating conveyor belt that shakes the sand mold loose from the cast-iron product. The cast iron is then shot blasted with millions of tiny BB's to remove any crusted sand that remains. Rough or sharp edges left over from the molding process are ground by hand, and the pan is literally stone washed to remove any remaining dust and smooth the pan's surface.

Lastly, the pan is dipped in a food-grade, FDA-approved wax dip to protect it from rust during shipping. One final quality control check looks for imperfections or flaws, tossing out any cast-iron products that don't meet the standards before packaging and sending the product to destinations around the world.

Offering versatility and variety

As plain as it looks, cast iron offers plenty of variety regarding what you cook and how and where you cook it:

>> **The selection is huge.** Cast iron comes in just about any kind of pan, pot, and cookware shape you can think of. In addition to fry pans and skillets, you can find cast-iron griddles, grill pans, serving pots, Dutch ovens, pizza pans, melting pots, kettles, casseroles, loaf pans, muffin pans, woks, minis, and more. For information on selecting your cookware and specialty items, head to Chapter 2.

>> **A single pan covers a multitude of dishes.** Just because you can find all sorts of different cast-iron products doesn't mean that you need to have them to have a well-stocked kitchen. You can use a single cast-iron skillet for just about any cooking task: Bake a cake (Chapter 11), sear a filet (Chapter 6), roast a chicken (Chapter 7), fry potatoes or stir-fry vegetables (Chapter 9) — one skillet is all you need. But if, like me, you discover that cast-iron cooking is loads of fun and makes the food you cook in it taste great, you're probably going to want more than a single skillet.

REMEMBER

>> **Cast iron isn't particular about where you cook.** With cast iron, you begin a recipe on the stovetop, for example, and then move it to the oven to finish. In fact, many recipes in this book instruct you to begin the dish in one place and then transfer it to another. You can even take your cast iron outside to cook under the sun or stars.

This one probably goes without saying, but you *cannot* use cast iron in your microwave. If you do, you'll ruin your pan and your oven, and the fireworks display won't be worth the cleanup and replacement costs.

WARNING

>> **You can use it for most cooking tasks.** Cast iron is great for baking, simmering, braising, roasting, frying, grilling, and more. Really, the only thing that you don't want to do on a regular basis with your cast iron is boil water in it. (Water breaks down the seasoning and can cause your cast iron to rust; head to Chapter 4 for information on caring for your cast iron.)

>> **You can cook almost anything in it.** Although cast iron made its reputation as the cookware to use for good, ol' fashioned cooking, don't let this reputation limit you as to how you use it. Because of its heating properties, its nonstick surface, its ability to withstand high temperatures, and the fact that you can use it both in the oven and on the stovetop, you can cook just about any food in it. Of course, some rules exist for what you can cook in cast iron and how you should cook it. Chapter 5 includes all the cooking tricks and techniques that are an important part of successful cast-iron cooking.

>> **It's cookware and serving ware all rolled up in one.** Regardless whether you're a novice home cook or a seasoned professional, cast iron is the perfect backdrop to accentuate your culinary masterpiece. Over the years, various companies have emerged, offering diverse, eclectic cast-iron pan lines catering to different cultures and cuisines. Nowadays, you can find everything from woks to giant paella pans and even small cast-iron minis used for individual portions. The possibilities are endless! Check out Chapter 2 for more about different types of cast iron.

Here's to your good health

The evolution of food, science, and technology has transformed people's perceptions of how they eat, what they eat, and how much they eat. Unfortunately for many, when they think about cast-iron cooking, thanks to brand recognition, they think of fried chicken, fried fish, buttery cakes, and a list of many other comfort foods that are sure to shorten your life span.

I challenge you to think differently and cook healthier. Food can be delicious without all the extra fat. As I share with the recipes in Part 4, flavor can be extracted, infused, and enhanced in so many ways.

TIP

Well-seasoned cast iron is virtually stick-free, requiring less or no oil — a characteristic of many heart-healthy recipes. You can cook any of the dishes that you would normally cook in any other nonstick pan in a cast-iron skillet. Cast iron isn't just good for heavy comfort foods; you can also use it to cook healthier, lighter fare. The trick is to keep your cast iron well-seasoned. (Chapter 3 tells you how.)

Cooking in cast iron also boosts your iron intake. Trace amounts of iron get absorbed into the foods you cook.

TECHNICAL
STUFF

The World Health Organization (WHO) considers iron deficiency to be the most prevalent nutritional disorder in the world, being one of the major contributing factors to anemia. People at high risk of iron deficiency or anemia include women of childbearing age, pregnant women, older infants and toddlers, and teenage girls. Also at risk are those who suffer a significant or ongoing blood loss due to a trauma or a disease. After you're diagnosed with an iron deficiency, you can't take in enough iron from the food that you eat to make up for the iron you lost.

Showing Special Consideration to Your Prized Possession

By design cast iron is made to last. It's tough enough to withstand plenty of rough treatment. You don't have to worry about scratching it, so feel free to cook with everything from your favorite wooden spoon to that beautiful bubble whisk for sauces or maybe that metal spatula that flexes just right in the pan. Unlike with nonstick coating in your other pans, pretty much anything can be used in cast-iron pans. Despite how tough and versatile it is, preserving the longevity does require some special care:

>> **You have to season it.** Seasoning is the key to cooking in cast iron. Without the proper seasoning, food will stick and taste metallic, and your pan is more susceptible to rust. Seasoning isn't difficult, but it does take a little time. For information on how to season or reseason a pan, skip to Chapter 3.

>> **The dark patina takes a while to achieve.** Cooking with your pan frequently can help your pan along; washing and storing it as described in Chapter 4 also helps, but a new cast-iron pan takes a while to break in. After it's broken in, though, you're going to have a hard time finding another type of pan that beats it for usefulness and flavor.

TIP

If you can't stand the idea of seasoning a pan yourself or you want the instant gratification of a pan that's already been seasoned before you lay hands on it, consider wheedling Grandma out of her cast iron or buy preseasoned cast iron, which is now available.

>> **To preserve your pan's seasoning, be careful when cooking certain types of foods.** Acidic foods, such as tomatoes or citrus products, can react to the iron and mess up your seasoning. So as a rule, avoid cooking these types of foods until your pan is well seasoned. Chapter 5 explains this and other cooking techniques that you need to know.

TIP

>> **Cooking successfully in cast iron requires certain techniques that may be unfamiliar to you.** Did you know, for example, that before you pour batter into a cast-iron pan, you should preheat the pan? You'd be surprised at the difference this little trick makes to the consistency and flavor of your foods. You can find other successful tips like this in Chapter 5.

>> **You have to follow a few cleaning and storage rules.** These rules keep the seasoning intact and help you avoid rust. But don't worry, they aren't difficult to follow: Don't use soap; don't put it in the dishwasher; store the cookware in a cool, dry place, and so on, but they may be different from what you're used to. Head to Chapter 4 for cleaning and storage instructions and Chapter 25 for some do's and don'ts.

>> **Cast iron weighs a ton.** You can look at this as a good thing: Because of its weight, it's sturdy, and it'll help you stay buff. Or you can look at its heaviness as a negative: Heaven forbid that you should try to anchor it on the drywall in your kitchen.

Before you throw up your hands and proclaim that cast iron isn't worth the effort, try to keep a little perspective: These care instructions aren't much different from the instructions that come with fancier and more expensive cookware. Various manufacturers include the recommendation that you not wash their cookware in a dishwasher. (The detergent is too abrasive and can mar the surface.) And you're likely to find added warnings: Don't use high heat, or you void your warranty; don't use metal utensils, or you run the risk of damaging the nonstick surface and ruining your pan.

REMEMBER

If you don't follow the care and cleaning instructions with cast iron, what you run the risk of ruining isn't the pan; it's the seasoning. It's a hassle, but you can fix that.

Chapter 2

Selecting Cast-Iron Cookware

The evolution of cast iron has transcended the perspective of food both culturally and conceptually. Whether you're whipping up a family-style meal at home, camping for the weekend, or looking to elevate a dish, the adaptability of cast iron allows you, the cook, to shine. On your journey to discovering the right cast-iron pan, consider a few things before investing your money. Like in life, you always want to start with a goal: What are you hoping to achieve? For example, if you're beginning, you may only want to invest in a standard 10-inch pan to get a feel for cooking. If you're an avid camper, you may want a Dutch oven, which is excellent for stews and chilis. If you're like me, a professional chef, you may want a griddle or a wok. You may want a grill press for your meats or cast-iron minis, which are great for sides. No matter where you are on your culinary journey, cast iron can meet you in the middle.

Chapter explains the different cast-iron pieces and accessories available and tells you what to look for when you're shopping for cast iron (quality matters because you want cast iron that's safe, easy to use, and durable), whether you're buying it new or used. And for those just beginning their cast-iron cooking adventures, this chapter also advises you on essential cookware.

When you're looking to add cast iron to your kitchen, you can find both new and used cast-iron cookware in a variety of shapes and sizes. Depending on where you are on your culinary journey, your aspirations may be different. The most popular pieces are the skillets and Dutch ovens, but you can find all sorts of other basic pans and pots, too, as well as specialty items. Keep reading for an explanation of the different kinds of cast-iron products and the types of food that you can cook in them.

THE EVOLUTION OF CAST IRON: CLASSICS VERSUS MODERN

From the discovery of fire to earthenware, copper, and cast iron, it's pretty remarkable that all of these materials have stood the test of time. Cast iron, in particular, has evolved and continues to diversify its value in many ways.

Hands down, when you look at the early cast iron produced in the early 1700s there is just something special about the way they made pans back then. In the early 1700s Abraham Darby patented a method for casting iron into relatively thin pots, making them cheaper to produce.

Personally, I love super smooth interior surfaces and deep sides. It feels like you're cooking on a glass pan. They're easy to clean and even easier to use. What I don't like about the antique pans is the thin bottoms. Unlike modern cast iron, where it's usually the same thickness from the bottom to the sides, traditionally, the bottoms were made thinner so that they would heat up quickly. On the one hand, that's great as your food gets hot faster, but on the other hand, it means you need to watch your heat on the pan because it easily burns or scorches food.

When you're looking at a modern pan, the first thing to notice is that the surface is rougher. Now over time, it will become somewhat smoother, but it will always remain bumpier than your antique pan. Modern pans also have an assist handle in the back, which is great when you need to move the pan. Another great addition is the side spout, which is fantastic when you need to strain off fat, stocks, or sauce from a pan.

REMEMBER

When you talk about cast iron, you have to talk about *versatility*. Although some items are designed with a special purpose in mind (the camp oven, for example, is designed for use outside), you can use cast-iron cookware in a variety of ways and for several different purposes. Use it indoors or out. Put it on the stove or in the stove. Bake a pie in a Dutch oven or roast a chicken in a fry pan. I explain what these pans are *generally* used for. How *you* use them depends on your own cooking style, need, and imagination.

For information about where to go to buy cast iron and how to recognize well-made cast iron, head to the section "Buying the Right Cast Iron" later in this chapter.

Skillets

Cast-iron skillets (see Figure 2-1) come in a variety of sizes, from very small (approximately 6 inches in diameter, some less) to very large (more than 15 inches in diameter). With average depths between 1¼ inches and 2½ inches (depending on the size of the pan), skillets are great for a number of cooking tasks, on the stove or in the oven:

>> Baking

>> Braising

>> Broiling

>> Pan-frying

>> Roasting

>> Simmering

>> Stir-frying

The size you need depends on how you plan to use your skillet and how many people that you need to feed. The smaller skillets are great for making great one- or two-serving meals and side dishes. The medium-size skillets (9 to 11 inches) are good for feeding average-size parties and baking cakes, breads, and biscuits. Reserve the larger pans for when you need to feed a crowd.

In addition to the standard round skillets, square skillets are also available (see Figure 2-2), and you can use them in the same way that you use the round skillets. Some — particularly the smaller ones with shallow sides — can function as mini-griddles (see the "Griddles and grill pans" section, later in this chapter). These are ideal for grilled cheese sandwiches or pancakes if you want to make one or two at a time.

FIGURE 2-1:
Cast-iron skillets
are good,
all-purpose
cooking utensils.

Photograph courtesy of Lodge Manufacturing Co.

FIGURE 2-2:
You can also find
square skillets in
different sizes.

Photograph courtesy of Lodge Manufacturing Co.

TIP

Two dishes that, hands down, are better when cooked in a cast-iron skillet? Cornbread and Pineapple Upside-Down Cake. (See Chapter 19 and 21 for great cornbread and cake recipes.) Many southern cooks, in fact, will tell you that they keep one skillet reserved solely for cornbread. Just as many will say that making Pineapple Upside-Down Cake in anything other than a cast-iron skillet is tantamount to heresy

Fry pans

Fry pans (refer to Figure 2-3) are similar to skillets except that the sides of fry pans are deeper (usually 3 inches or deeper) so that the grease doesn't splatter as much when you're frying. You can perform many of the same cooking tasks in these pans that you can in the skillets. Because of the depth of the pan, you can also use fry pans to do the following:

>> **Deep-frying:** When you deep-fry, you submerge the food completely in hot oil instead of cooking the food a side at a time as you do when pan-frying.

>> **Simmering stews and soups:** Whereas shallower pans tend to expose too much of the soup's surface to evaporation, fry pans are deep enough to give you a nice slow simmer without drying out the broth.

>> **Slow-cooking foods on the stovetop or in the oven:** If you have a lid or want to cover the top with aluminum foil, you can use a fry pan in the same way that you use a Dutch oven. See the section "Dutch ovens," later in this chapter.

FIGURE 2-3:
The deeper sides of a fry pan mean less splattering and less mess.

Photograph courtesy of Lodge Manufacturing Co.

Griddles and grill pans

Griddles (refer to Figure 2-4) can be round, square, or rectangular (long enough to fit across two burners on your stovetop), and they come in various sizes. The smooth surface and shallow sides (usually ½ inch or less) are perfect for making pancakes (see Chapter 10) and hot sandwiches; frying eggs, bacon, and anything else; roasting vegetables (Chapter 9); and making great foods of the hand-held variety (see Chapter 23).

FIGURE 2-4:
A sampling of
griddles.

Photograph courtesy of Lodge Manufacturing Co.

Grill pans (see Figure 2-5) are exactly what they sound like: Pans that you use to grill food (vegetables, seafood, poultry, meat, and so on), either on the stovetop or over a campfire. The ribbed bottom keeps the food out of the drippings and leaves nice sear marks, much like you'd get from cooking on an outdoor grill.

FIGURE 2-5:
The ribbed
bottom of a grill
pan keeps your
food up and out
of any drippings.

Photograph courtesy of Lodge Manufacturing Co.

REMEMBER

Because of the ribbed bottom, grill pans aren't suitable for anything other than grilling. If you don't believe me, try stirring a stew or getting cornbread to pop out.

Dutch ovens

Dutch ovens are deep-sided pots with lids that you can use on the stovetop or inside the oven. They're the original slow cookers. Put in the food, slap on a lid, set the oven to a low or medium temperature, and then come back a few hours later to a tender, delicious meal. But you can use your versatile Dutch oven for more than slow cooking. You can also use Dutch ovens for

>> Baking

>> Braising

>> Deep-frying

>> Pan-frying

>> Simmering

You name it; a Dutch oven can probably do it.

Staying inside or getting outdoors

If you go looking for a Dutch oven, keep in mind that they fall into two categories: those designed primarily for indoor cooking and those designed for outdoor cooking (see Figure 2-6). The differences between the two are as follows:

>> **The lid:** An indoor oven has a domed lid. The lid of an outdoor oven is generally flatter and is *flanged* (has a lip around the rim) so that you can put coals on the top.

>> **The bottom:** Indoor Dutch ovens have flat bottoms; outdoor Dutch ovens have three short legs to keep the oven above the heat source.

>> **What they're called:** Indoor Dutch ovens are called *Dutch ovens*. Some people call them *bean pots*. Outdoor Dutch ovens are called *camp ovens* or, less frequently, *cowboy ovens*. You, however, may call yours anything you want.

For more information about cooking in the great outdoors (including camp oven info) and some recipes to go with it, head to Chapter 22.

FIGURE 2-6:
A Dutch oven for indoor use (left) and a camp oven, designed for cooking outdoors (right).

Photograph courtesy of Lodge Manufacturing Co.

PLAYING THE DUTCH OVEN NAME GAME

A cast-iron pot by any other name would cook as well. Basically, what it's called doesn't make a lick of difference. Lodge Manufacturing, a cast-iron manufacturer, for example, uses the term *Dutch oven* to refer to the flat-bottomed ovens and *outdoors camp oven* to refer to the oven with legs. Wagner, another manufacturer of cast-iron cookware (which went out of business in 1999), preferred the term *cowboy oven* for the outdoor ovens. Some people use the term *camp oven* to refer to Dutch ovens that you use outside and *Dutch oven* to refer to those that you use inside. What you need to know is that if you go looking for a camp oven, Dutch oven, cowboy oven, bean pot, or whatever it may be called in your neck of the woods, you may be at a linguistic disadvantage if the person you're talking to uses a different term. If that's the case, stick with *Dutch oven,* which seems to be the term that most people recognize and add any descriptors (with legs, that I can cook outdoors in, and so on) that you need to make yourself clear.

By the way, people can't even agree on why these devices are called *Dutch ovens* in the first place. Some claim the name was given to these pots because the sand-casting method was created in Holland (which may stun the Chinese who were making cast-iron products as early as 800 to 700 BC). Others claim that Dutch traders went around the United States selling wares and became famous for their cast-iron pots, which came to be referred to as *Dutch ovens.*

REMEMBER

Just because camp ovens are for outdoor use, don't assume that means that regular old Dutch ovens can't be used for outdoor cooking. They can. The outdoor ovens just have a few little amenities built right in to make outdoor cooking a little easier.

Size matters

Dutch and camp ovens come in all sorts of sizes. What size you get depends on how many people you're cooking for and what you're cooking. If you intend to cook breads and cakes, an oven with shallower sides works fine. If you cook mostly meats or stews and chilis, go for an oven with deeper sides.

Table 2-1 lists some common sizes of Dutch ovens and shows approximately how many people an oven of that size feeds. Most people do just fine with a Dutch oven in the 4- to 8-quart size range. (*Note:* A *deep* oven is one that simply has deeper sides than the regular ovens; for that reason, deep ovens can hold more food than regular ovens of the same size.)

TABLE 2-1

Dutch Oven Capacities

Size	Capacity in Quarts	Number of People Served
8 inch	2 quarts	1 to 2
10 inch	4 quarts	4 to 7
12 inch	6 quarts	12 to 14
12 inch (deep)	8 quarts	16 to 20
14 inch	10 quarts	16 to 20
14 inch (deep)	12 quarts	22 to 28

Mini cast-iron dishes

As a chef, one way to elevate a dish is by selecting the right vessel. Over the years, I've found that premium mini cast iron is a great way to add value to your visual presentation. Mini cast-iron dishes (see Figure 2-7) can range from skillets, Dutch ovens, woks, casserole dishes, and even mini pots with lids and are just a few small vessels you can find to create individual dishes. They're great for individual proteins, vegetables, side dishes, and desserts. If you love hosting dinner parties or are looking to take your presentation to the next level, these options might help you accomplish your goal.

FIGURE 2-7:
A 10-ounce mini cast-iron dish.

By Kori Price

Minis range in many different sizes, starting as small as 3.5 inches in diameter, holding about 3 to 4 ounces of food. Table 2-2 gives you an overview of the different minis available.

TABLE 2-2   ## Available Cast-Iron Minis

Type	Brand	Size			Prince Range
		Width (inches)	Height (inches)	Length (inches)	
Dutch oven	Lodge	5	2.37	6.68	$24 to $30
Skillet	Lodge	5–6.5 to 6.68	1.06 to 1.37	7.68 to 10.18	$19 to $25
Iron wok	Lodge	6.44 to 9.19	2.06 to 2.94	8 to 11.44	$17 to $24
Round server	Lodge	6.37	1.62	8.06	$25 to $30
Rectangular server	Lodge	4.5	1.95	7.72	$28 to $30
Oval server	Lodge	4.12 to 5.37	1.68 to 2.18	8 to 9.56	$25 to $30

TIP

Most of the minis also come with lids, which makes them great for outdoor events. When selecting the right mini, I recommend always going with a heat-treated pan. All the Lodge brand heat-treated pans are also preseasoned.

Here are some benefits to using minis:

» They showcase your creativity no matter your event theme, menu, and size. They're one of the few options that can cross between casual and high-end food.

» They maintain your dish's temperature, whether it's a hot dish or a cold dish. You can cook in minis and go from the oven to the table, plus they hold heat extremely well, so you don't have to worry about things cooling down quickly. On the other hand, if you're presenting a cold dish like individual salads, pop your cast-iron minis in the cooler to pre-chill before serving your amazing food.

» They're flexible to heat sources. You can use anything from a heat lamp or a preheated surface with minis. If you 're using induction, cast iron is a great option to use on a low setting especially if you're doing a buffet or a la cart station.

Specialty items and accessories

The skillets, pots, and griddles that comprise the basic collection of many cast-iron cooks are the workhorses of the cast-iron world. However, specialty pans are available, too. Some are primarily fun; others are primarily functional. Are any of them absolutely mandatory? No. Not unless you just gotta have it.

Bakeware

You can find cast-iron muffin pans, loaf pans, biscuit pans, sectioned cornbread skillets, cornstick pans in various shapes, and cake pans (regular round and square and Bundt shaped). Figure 2-8 shows a sampling of the types of bakeware available.

FIGURE 2-8: Cast-iron bakeware serves a variety of purposes: From left to right, a cornstick pan, a muffin pan, and a loaf pan.

Photograph courtesy of Lodge Manufacturing Co.

Fry kits

A fry kit (see Figure 2-9) isn't anything other than a deep-sided cast-iron pot with a wire basket for lifting the food from the hot oil. As its name implies, a fry kit is used for deep-frying foods. The slightly sloped sides are deep enough to hold the amount of oil necessary to submerge foods and cut down on splattering.

You can buy these items as a kit (you may get a thermometer and a recipe or two to get you started), or you can assemble your own, using any deep-sided cast iron pot — even a Dutch oven.

Serving ware

Serving ware includes items such as casserole dishes, serving platters/griddles (like those used in restaurants), and single-serving soup dishes. These items let you take food directly from the oven and place it on your table. (Of course, you can do that with all cast iron.)

FIGURE 2-9: A standard fry kit consists of a deep pan, a wire basket, and a thermometer (optional) for accuracy.

Photograph courtesy of Lodge Manufacturing Co.

Other implements

You can find many other cooking implements and wares made from cast iron — casserole dishes, roasters, fish pans, hibachi-like grills, and so on. A plethora of accessories designed especially for cast-iron cooks is also available: meat racks, grill presses, tripods, tote bags, and even dinner bells, just to name a few.

Getting Started — What Cast Iron You Need

One or two pans is really all you need to begin as a cast-iron cook. With a 10-inch skillet, you can perform just about any cooking task you want, and it's big enough to play around with breakfast, lunch, and dinner dishes.

TIP

If your family is a little larger (say six or more), a 10-inch skillet may not be big enough for main dishes, such as casseroles or roasted meats with vegetables. In that case, you may want to add a 12-inch skillet, a fryer (which is like a skillet but with deeper sides), or a Dutch oven to your collection. But keep the 10-inch skillet, too, for other dishes.

REMEMBER

What's *essential* depends on what you plan to cook. If you plan to spend every weekend outdoors cooking for friends and family, you're going to need a different pan than the person who only wants to make fried chicken the way their mother used to. Figure out what you want to do with your cast iron and then go from there.

Buying the Right Cast Iron

Nowadays you can find cast iron pretty much anywhere. If you're looking online, you can buy directly from the manufacturer as well as from retailers who carry cast-iron cookware. Retailers sell a ton of different cast-iron brands and varieties, but not all pans are made equal, so make sure you do your homework before making a quick purchase.

After you locate your cast-iron supplier, you need to do a little examination of the quality. Whether you're looking for cast iron that came straight from the foundry or that has spent a few years (or several decades) in someone else's kitchen, you need to pay attention to the pan quality you're buying.

If you're interested in used cast iron, you can find it at garage and rummage sales, farm auctions, or antique shops. If you're brave enough, you can even hit up an auntie or grandmother (but don't be surprised if they won't give it to you).

The following sections examine what you need to know in order to purchase the right cast iron for your kitchen.

Evaluating quality

Whether new or used, cast-iron pans are made from iron and steel formed in sand casts (or molds), hence the name *cast iron*. The process and materials give cast iron the texture it has. If you're used to shiny, smooth aluminum or stainless steel, you may not realize that new cast iron is supposed to feel rough and be a dull, gray color like, well, metal (unless you're lucky and find an old Griswold, which is known for its glass-like surface.)

The quality of the pan directly impacts how well it takes seasoning, how efficiently it heats, how long it lasts, and how safe it's to use. The material used, the mixture of the different metals (the *metallurgy*), and the quality of the mold determine the overall quality of the pan. When you shop for cast iron, look at the following:

>> **Surface texture:** The cast iron should be uniformly rough (like a cat's tongue) and even. It shouldn't be jagged, pitted, chipped, cracked, or obviously scratched. Nor should you find areas that look odd — that is, not like the rest of the surface. When you run your hand along the interior, you shouldn't feel waves or dips.

REMEMBER

Finer-grained cast iron is easier to cure or season. (See Chapter 3 for seasoning instructions.) Poorly made cast iron has a courser grain that's hard to season and that requires more attention and care after it's seasoned.

» **Width of sides:** To be an efficient and even conductor of heat (and thus avoid hot spots and warping), the thickness of the sides of the cast iron should be the same all the way around. Uneven sides also make the pan more prone to breaking. So if the sides seem thinner in some areas than in others, don't buy the pan unless you only want it for decoration in your kitchen.

» **Metallurgy:** The mixture of the metals matters. Much goes into the metallurgy of a cast-iron pan, and much of this, like the quality of the iron and steel used or the temperature at which it's heated, you can't judge just by looking. The metallurgy is as important to even heat conduction as is the mold tolerances that create a pan with uniform thicknesses. Either one can create hot spots or uneven heating — the bane of cooks everywhere. (See the nearby sidebar for more information.) Occasionally, however, you may notice that something is obviously wrong, like discolorations or blotchiness in the metal.

WARNING

Steer clear of cast iron that has these flaws. Cast iron that has discolorations or blotchiness can be brittle and easy to break. Also stay away from cast iron that has other odd spots — areas that just don't look like the rest of the pan. If the material wasn't heated at a high enough temperature, you can have uneven distribution of the various metals (more steel in one place or more iron in another, for example), and that creates hot spots.

» **Where it's made:** American manufacturers have to meet government-mandated safety requirements regarding the product itself (and the materials that go into it) and the manufacturing process. These safeguards protect both consumers and employees. Manufacturers in other countries may or may not have to abide by similar requirements.

REMEMBER

Although imported cast iron is often less expensive, make sure that your cast iron is made domestically, for both quality and safety reasons.

Buying used cast iron

The cost of used cast iron is generally quite a bit less than what you'd spend for new (which itself is relatively inexpensive). And, if the piece is still in cooking condition, the work (seasoning) has already been done for you.

MIXING UP THE METAL

Making a delicious cake requires that you mix certain ingredients in specific amounts into a batter and then cook the batter at a particular temperature. Making cast iron is essentially the same.

You gather your ingredients — pig iron, which is basically iron ore and steel. The steel has to be clean; it can't come from automotive parts (or worse, used automotive parts), and it shouldn't contain lead, cadmium (another metal), or any other substance that's toxic to humans.

You mix these metals (so much pig iron to so much steel). Instead of a blender, you use heat. When you heat up iron and steel at high temperatures (2,800 degrees), the substances mix automatically as their heated molecules perk up, begin to dance around, and then lose all control and start banging into each other. The temperature is important because, if the mixture isn't heated and poured at the proper temperature, the metal doesn't mix evenly, and you end up with more or less iron or steel in one spot or another.

Before the metal is poured into its mold, it should be tested with a *spectrometer* — a machine that can identify the amount and percentage of elements within a metal. Different spectrometers test for different elements. In a foundry that makes cast-iron cookware, the spectrometer should test to make sure that

- The percentage of iron to steel is what it should be. This test preserves the integrity and quality of the pan.

- That no problem metals (such as lead) are present. This test is performed for safety and health reasons.

Only when the mix is approved should the molds be poured.

TIP

Used cast iron — especially when it comes free from Grandma and includes a bunch of recipes to boot — is great. In fact, if you have a choice between a new cast-iron pan and an old one that's been well used and cared for, go for an old one.

You still need to evaluate the quality of the cast iron. When you buy used, pay attention to the following:

>> **How well it's been cared for:** Although you can refurbish many abused pieces of cast iron (Chapter 4 tells you how), some pieces aren't worth salvaging. Avoid pieces that are warped, cracked, pitted, or chipped. Although fine for hanging as a wall decoration, these pans aren't suitable for cooking anymore.

>> **How much work restoring the piece will take:** Some old cast iron is ready to use as soon as you get it, provided of course that you don't mind that the patina is the result of someone else's — a stranger's — cooking. (Absorbing the oil and fat of the foods that are cooked in the cast iron is the way that the cast iron is seasoned.) If you do mind, restoring the pan is fairly simple: You simply burn off the seasoning that's on it and reseason. (Go to Chapter 3 for instructions.) Some old pans, however, require much work because of rust, crusted on yuck, and other gunk that you have to remove. These pans can be reclaimed, but it'll take more work. Head to Chapter 4 for details on how to bring new life to an abused cast-iron pan.

>> **Whether the item has any paint spots on it.** Dishonest dealers often repair holes and cracks with *epoxy resin* (an adhesive that hobbyists use in abundance when they build model airplanes and cars) and then paint over the repair to hide it.

WARNING

Cast iron that looks like it has been used as a paint bucket isn't the issue; you can sand blast the paint off. The issue is black paint deliberately used on a black pan. Sure, black paint on a black pan may be as innocent as the bright yellow paint splashes and drips on another pan, but you can't be sure until you remove the black paint. If it's epoxy, you don't want to use the pan. Epoxy resin is a great adhesive: strong, durable, long-lasting . . . but it's also poisonous if swallowed, can damage skin on contact, can irritate eyes, and needs to be used in a well-ventilated area.

TIP

If you stumble across a cast-iron pan with the *Griswold* logo on it, and it's going for a couple of bucks, snatch it up. Griswold cast-iron cookware is a collector's item. Many pieces fetch upwards of several hundred dollars. For more info on collectible cast iron, check out the nearby sidebar.

COLLECTING CAST IRON

Cast-iron cookware is a collector's item. As you shop for used cast iron — particularly if you're browsing through an antique store — you may come across some pieces that are priced in the hundreds of dollars. If you're just looking for a biscuit pan, you probably don't want to spend what these people are asking. Still, in case you're interested, the cast iron from two companies (now out of business) are fetching a pretty penny:

- **Griswold Manufacturing Company of Erie, Pennsylvania:** Griswold was in business between 1865 and 1957. Family controlled until 1947, the company fell into decline during its last years; the Wagner Manufacturing Company of Sydney, Ohio, eventually bought the Griswold molds. Much sought after pieces of Griswold cast iron go for around $1,000; many sell for $400 to $600. The Griswold logo is on the bottom of its pans. Before you buy, though, keep in mind that some Griswold pans aren't valued as much as others. I'm referring to the pans made during the declining years and the ones that Wagner made and put the Griswold logo on. (Wagner also bought the Griswold logo in addition to the molds.)

- **Wagner Manufacturing Company of Sydney, Ohio:** Incorporated in 1891, Wagner Manufacturing was another family business; brothers Bernard, Milton, Louis, and William Wagner owned and controlled it. The company remained in business until 1999 and, until its closure, was the oldest continuously operating manufacturer of cookware in the United States. Many Wagner pieces sell for between $50 and $200.

If you're interested in collecting cast-iron pieces, several resources are at your disposal. First, head online and search for "heirloom cast iron" or "collectible cast iron." You'll generate a whole list of sites for cookware and other cast-iron collectibles, such as toys. Look around before buying anything.

Looking for (and avoiding) certain features

A pan may just be a pan, but many cast-iron pieces have little extras that make cooking in them, carrying them, and otherwise using them easier. So look for the following when you buy:

>> **Support handles:** Cast iron is just plain heavy. Add the weight of dinner to an already heavy skillet, and carrying the loaded cast iron to the table *without* a support handle opposite the usual handle requires a clear path, a mad dash, and a little luck.

- **Heat-resistant bails:** The *bail* is the arched metal handle that you often see on kettles. If you're using a Dutch oven in the oven or over a campfire, a heat-resistant bail comes in mighty handy.

- **Flanged lids:** You can use any cast-iron pan outdoors; the key is to have a *flanged lid* (a lid with a rim around it). The flange lets you put coals right on top of the lid without worrying that they'll roll off.

- **Lids that can serve double duty:** Some Dutch oven lids, when turned upside down, serve as griddles. If you have a choice between a regular lid and one of these, why not go with the lid that gives you added flexibility? ***Note:*** Cast-iron lids fit multiple, same-size pots and pans. If, for example, you have a 10-inch lid, you can use it on any 10-inch skillet, deep fryer, Dutch oven, and so on.

WARNING

Some cast-iron pans have wooden handles. Don't buy them. Sure, maybe they look pretty, and people may try to tell you that the handle stays cool, but that's only true if you use the pan on the stovetop. These handles reduce the functionality and life of your pan. You can't use the pans over the campfire, and the bolts that hold the handles on eventually loosen.

2

Treating Your Cast Iron with TLC

IN THIS PART . . .

Season and reseason your cast iron so you can maximize the flavor in each recipe you cook.

Discover the best ways to take care of your cast iron, including avoiding the dishwasher.

Store your cast-iron cookware in a moisture-free area and protect it so it's ready for the next time you use it.

Discover the different ways you can use cast-iron cookware, ranging from pan-frying to sautéing.

» **Seasoning a pan, step by step**

» **Recognizing what you need to start**

» **Maintaining a quality pan**

Chapter **3**

Seasoning Your Cast Iron

How well your pan is seasoned determines how well it cooks, how stick-free the surface is, and, frankly, how happy you'll be with the whole cast-iron cooking experience.

For most people, when they hear the word "seasoning," their mind automatically goes to dealing with dry herbs, exotic spices, and popular salt-blended mixtures. Fortunately seasoning isn't that difficult. Beyond seasoning the dish you're cooking, you need to start with your most important asset: your seasoned cast-iron pan. Any good protein requires you to season it before you cook and sometimes after, and the process is the same for cast iron. Because of the natural characteristics of cast iron — the rough, porous surface — you have to season new cookware before you use it, and you have to reseason old cast iron periodically.

The idea of seasoning cast iron often strikes terror in the hearts of otherwise brave kitchen dwellers. But I'm here to tell you that the seasoning process suffers from an undeserved, bad reputation: It's actually quite simple, and reseasoning is even easier. This chapter tells you everything that you need to know about how to season, reseason, and preserve the seasoning you have. If you have preseasoned cast iron, you can also find information on what you have to do to it before you cook.

Preseasoned cast iron — cast iron that's been seasoned at the foundry — is pretty much ready to use as soon as you take it from the box. Only slightly more expensive than cast iron that has a natural finish, the preseasoned variety is definitely worth the money. (Of course, if you don't want to buy new cast iron, another option is to get cast iron that's been preseasoned the old-fashioned way, through cooking. Buy it used — or talk a relative or old family friend into giving up their cast iron.)

Adding Some Seasoning to a New Pan

Seasoning your pan is just baking oil into cast iron, essentially giving your pan the power of Teflon without the chemicals. So what happens when you season your pan? How is this process possible?

Because of the materials that make up a cast-iron pan and the casting process, new cast iron is porous. It has a slightly rough texture and microscopic pores that you have to fill before you can use the pan. Seasoning, which is also called *curing*, is the process of filling these pores and smoothing the rough texture with oil, thus creating a smooth, nonstick surface. An added bonus is that this process also protects your pan from rust.

The pores in your pan work just like the pores in your body. Your body gets hot, your pores open up. Well, it's the same process for your cast iron. The metal gets hot and the pores expand, allowing the pan to absorb whatever it is that you put in it. The result in your cast iron's pores expanding is flavor! The more you cook in your pan, the more it becomes seasoned, imparting more flavor. That can also become a negative if say, you're cooking fish. You forget to clean your pan properly and move on to a cake . . . yep, you get my point — your birthday cake has a fishy taste (Chapter 4 discusses ways to clean your cast iron). Refer to the section "Seasoning your cast iron in two easy steps" later in this chapter for how to season your cast iron.

WARNING

If you try to cook in cast iron that hasn't been seasoned, you're going to end up with a burned, sticky mess. The pores in your hot pan (which expand slightly when you cook) will absorb whatever it is that you put in it. Hamburger? Eggs? You name it. It'll get cooked into the pores, and then your task to make the pan useable becomes a tad more time consuming. Head to Chapter 4 for information on how to restore an abused pan.

Here I examine supplies and different oils that can be used to season your cast iron. Depending on your lifestyle, dietary restrictions, or geographic location, your needs may be different. You can also find information about the different stages of seasoning your cast-iron pan.

Identifying what you need to season: Supplies and a little time

You don't need much to season a pan. Here's what you do need.

Oven

Any old oven will do — gas, electric, convection, or standard all work fine. Some people even cure their cast iron in an outdoor grill, which is fine as long as it has a lid and you can control the heat.

Oil or shortening

Chefs traditionally recommended using vegetable shortening or vegetable oil because it was readily available in most kitchens. However, nowadays depending on what part of the world you are in, affordability and availability can play a big part in the oil and fat you have to select from. In my experience, any oil with a high smoking point works great.

REMEMBER

The *smoking point* refers to the temperature that fat starts to smoke, which means it's burning. Different fats have different smoking points. Some can range from as low as 325 degrees and others closer to 500 degrees. A low smoking point means that the oil will burn fairly quickly. Table 3-1 lists the common oils used and their smoking points.

TABLE 3-1 **Common Oils Used for Seasoning and Their Smoking Points**

Oils	Smoking Point (Fahrenheit)	Smoking Point (Celsius)
Refined olive oils	465°	240°
Rice bran oil	450°	254°
Soybean oil	450°	232°
Peanut oil	450°	232°
Corn oil	450°	232°
Sunflower oil	450°	232°
Canola oil	400°	204°
Vegetable oil	400 to 450°	204 to 232°
Grapeseed oil	390°	199°
Vegetable shortening	360°	182°
Seasoning spray	470 to 560°	244 to 294°

Using oils that are shelf stable will help you protect your pan and the food you cook in it. *Remember*: Using the right oil to season a pan isn't just for the pan; it also protects the food you're cooking.

Shelf-stable oils have a longer shelf life and can be stored at room temperature without spoiling or becoming rancid. These oils are processed and refined to remove impurities and contaminants, extending their storage life.

Another benefit of shelf-stable oils is that they usually have a higher smoke point, which means they can withstand higher temperatures without burning or adding unwanted flavors to your dish. Remember, when seasoning your pan, apply only a thin layer of oil to your pan before baking it in a preheated oven. Head to Chapter 11 to discover more about the baking process.

WARNING

Some people say that you can season a pan with lard, bacon grease, butter (or margarine) or other animal products, but I don't recommend it. If you don't use your cast iron regularly, these seasonings can turn rancid.

Miscellaneous items

Here are a few other things you'll need to season your cast-iron pan:

>> **Towels for cleaning:** To make this process equitable, you can use anything from a clean old dishcloth to an old apron for the process, as long as it doesn't lint or tear. Over the years, I've found that using a soft and absorbent fabric like cotton or microfiber works best. The higher the percentage of cotton in the towel, the better it is for the job.

Good cleaning towels should be fairly large with secured edges (you don't want to use anything that might be fraying at the edges because they'll burn.) The best towels are thick and absorbent and easy to wash.

WARNING

I know a lot of people who use paper towels, but I don't recommend using them. Though quick to grab and easy to discard, certain brands tend to leave pieces behind in the pan, which can burn and get into your food.

Keep in mind that whatever you use will turn gray or black from being rubbed over the new pan.

REMEMBER

>> **Aluminum foil or baking sheet:** You use either one to catch any dripping oil. Aluminum foil can also be used to remove rust from your pan. Refer to Chapter 4 for more discussion.

Seasoning your cast iron in two easy steps

Regardless whether you're cooking meat, tofu, or even fish, if you want to enhance flavor, you need to season it. Your cast iron is no different. Follow these steps to find out how to season your cast iron like a pro.

Step 1: Preparing the new pan for seasoning

Cast-iron pans that aren't preseasoned come from the factory with a protective coating. Cast iron made in the United States uses a food-grade, FDA-approved wax. Imported cast iron uses a water-soluble shellac. Either way, you have to remove this preservative first before you can begin seasoning.

WARNING

In some rare occasions you may need to strip the protective coating off your cast iron, which means that you'll be starting with your seasoning. Without the coating, your pan may rust; then before you can season it, you have the hassle of removing the rust. If you find yourself in this situation, don't worry because there's a solution to your problem.

To get rid of the protective coating on new cast iron, follow these steps:

1. **Scrub the pan using the hottest water that you can stand, a mild dish detergent or soap, and a stiff-bristled (not wire) brush or a scouring pad (not steel wool).**

    Boil about 2 cups of water and pour it directly into the pan. Then add a small amount of dish detergent and scrub the pan. Be sure to scrub all surfaces of the pan: the bottom, the handle, inside, and out.

    Wear rubber gloves to protect your hands from the hot water.

TIP

    This is the only time when you'll ever use soap, a scouring pad, or a brush on your cast iron — unless, that is, you're reseasoning it because of some disaster, culinary or otherwise.

REMEMBER

2. **Dry the pan thoroughly.**

    Use a cloth that doesn't lint or tear. If the water is hot enough, most of it will evaporate by itself. You can also put the pan on a burner and let it warm until all the moisture is gone. I recommend using medium heat — if your stove has numbers, it'd be a 3 or 4. Depending on the size of your pan, this could take anywhere between 10 to 20 minutes. When the pan is clean and dry, you're ready to season.

Step 2: Seasoning your new cast iron

After your pan is clean, you're ready to season it. Follow these steps:

1. **Place aluminum foil on the bottom rack in your oven and preheat your oven to 450 degrees.**

Make sure that you cover the area underneath your cast iron. The foil catches any excess shortening that may drip off. If you prefer, you can use a baking sheet. Just place the cast iron directly on the baking sheet.

TIP

To save time, season multiple pieces at the same time. If your cast iron has a lid, season the lid when you season the pan. The only limit is the amount of cast iron that you can fit into your oven. The instructions are the same for seasoning multiple pieces.

2. **Set the cast-iron pan on a stovetop burner and add about a tablespoon of shortening or oil (refer to the list in the section "Oil or shortening" earlier in this chapter).**

TIP

Preheat your pan on high for about 60 seconds. Doing so takes the chill off the pan and allows it to preheat. Reduce the heat to medium. If you're working with a stove that has numbers, lower it to 3 or 4.

3. **Using a cloth that doesn't lint or tear, wipe the entire surface of the pan with the shortening or oil.**

Be sure to get all the surfaces: tops, bottoms, handles, and legs, too, that is, if you're seasoning an outdoor oven. You only need to cover the pan in a thin layer of oil, which is between 1 to 2 tablespoons. If your oil is pooling or dripping, you've used too much. Wipe away the excess.

4. **Place the cookware upside down in the oven.**

You place the pan upside down so that any excess shortening drips off instead of pooling inside the pan and carbonizing.

5. **Bake for 1 hour.**

As the cast iron cooks, you may notice a slight smell and perhaps some smoke. That's normal, and nothing to call the fire department about. The more shortening you use, the more pronounced the smoke and the smell will be. Fortunately, the smell and smoke dissipate pretty quickly. If you can't stand it, open a window to air out your kitchen a bit.

6. **When the hour's up, turn the oven off and leave the cookware in the oven until the oven cools down.**

Cast iron is still baking as the oven cools so you achieve a deeper cure.

7. **When the cast iron is cool, remove it from the oven.**

    Congratulations, this is a proud moment! Admire your handiwork. This will be the first of many times that you'll need to repeat this process, especially if you're planning on investing in more cast iron down the line.

REMEMBER

    Didn't get the shiny black surface that you were expecting? Don't worry. The black, shiny surface comes as you use your pan. What you've just done is the *initial* cure. Every time you cook with your cast iron, the cure will deepen, and in a few months' time, you'll have the deep black and satiny patina that you want.

8. **Put your cast iron away or start cooking!**

Protecting your seasoning

Keep the following tips in mind to protect and deepen the seasoning:

» **Use 1 to 2 tablespoons of healthy fat (refer to the section "Oil or shortening" earlier in this chapter) or a seasoning spray the first few times — say, six or seven — you cook in your cast iron.** Doing so helps deepens the seasoning of your pan faster, giving you the nonstick surface that you're aiming for.

» **Avoid cooking acidic foods (such as tomato-based dishes) and alkaline foods (such as beans) the first six or seven times.** The acid and alkali react with the iron, stripping the seasoning from the pan.

» **Use your cast iron frequently.** If you're new to cast-iron cooking, using it gives you practice, and every time you cook with your cast iron, you're essentially reseasoning it.

» **After you clean your cast iron, wipe a small amount of vegetable oil around the pan.** This puts back any seasoning that was lost during cleaning. Don't use soap — refer to Chapter 4 for more details.

Reseasoning a Pan

The best way to reseason a pan is to cook frequently in it. Every time you cook, the oils from the food are absorbed into the pan and deepen the seasoning. And when the meal is over and you're done cleaning the pan, wipe a little vegetable oil around its surface. Just doing these two things keep your pan nicely seasoned.

Occasionally, however, your seasoning may break down. If you don't use your pan for a long period of time, if you cook food with liquid (steaming vegetables or deglazing the pan with wine, for example,) or if you cook acidic foods, such as tomatoes, you may have to reseason your pan.

TIP

The following signs let you know that you need to reseason your cast iron:

>> Rust forms.

>> Foods begin to stick to the pan.

>> Your food tastes like metal — and you didn't intend for it to.

If you notice these signs, first get rid of any rust or whatever's burned on (see Chapter 4), and then follow the steps in the "Step 2: Seasoning your new cast iron" section earlier in this chapter.

Dealing With a Preseasoned Pan

Preseasoned cast iron, true to its name, has already been seasoned. You can skip the seasoning step entirely. All you need to do is clean it.

REMEMBER

Natural-finished cast iron comes from the foundry with a protective wax coating. (Refer to the section, "Step 1: Preparing the new pan for seasoning," earlier in this chapter for details.) Preseasoned cast iron doesn't have this coating because it doesn't need it. The *seasoning* is the protection.

Follow these instructions to get preseasoned cast iron ready to use:

1. **Using hot water and a stiff-bristled brush, wash the cast iron.**

WARNING

Don't use soap. You need to treat a preseasoned pan the way that you'd treat a seasoned pan, and soap is a no-no. If you use soap, you're just going to have to reseason it, and then what's the point of buying it preseasoned? (If you're concerned about bacteria, rinse the pan with boiling water. Of course, if the only way that you can feel comfortable using cast iron is to clean it in soapy water, go ahead, but remember that you need to reseason it more frequently.)

2. **Dry the pan completely.**

    After you wipe the water off, put the pan in a warm oven or on a warm burner to get rid of any remaining moisture.

3. **Wipe the cooking surface with a light coating of vegetable oil.**

    You can also use cooking spray if you prefer. Just spray it on the cooking surface and wipe away the excess. Now you're ready to cook.

Chapter **4**

Maintaining Your Cast Iron

ny good relationship takes work. Your relationship with your cast iron is no different. Fortunately, taking care of cast iron isn't that difficult. Yes, you do need to follow a few simple rules to keep your seasoning intact. (Head to Chapter 3 if you're not sure what seasoning is.) But it's nothing that requires a relationship coach.

This chapter tells you just what you need to know about cleaning and storing cast iron. And because even the best of cooks has a catastrophe every once in a while, this chapter also provides tips for how to get rid of stubborn stuck-on food that you burned into the pan's very core. This information is also helpful to anyone who's bought or been given an old piece of cast iron that needs a little extra attention before it's ready for seasoning. Finally, because cast iron is perfect campfire cookware, I explain how to transport your pots and pans safely from here to wherever there is.

REMEMBER

How your cast iron fares depends not only on how you clean and store it but how you use it, too. For information on cooking with cast iron, go to Chapter 5.

Cleaning 101 — What Not to Do

When you clean cast iron, your aim is two-fold: Clean off whatever remains of dinner and do so without destroying your pan's seasoning. (If your cleaning task is more dire than this and you want to get down to the bare metal so that you can start over, go to the section "Super-Cleaning for Old — or Abused — Cast Iron" later in this chapter.)

REMEMBER

When your task is just basic cleaning and you want to preserve your pan's seasoning, keep these rules in mind:

>> **Don't use soap.** Soap effectively cuts through oil and grease, and if you consider that *that's* what your seasoning is — oil and grease baked into your pan through possibly years of cooking — you can understand why soap is verboten.

   If you absolutely, positively can't give up the dish soap, be prepared to reseason your pan more frequently, possibly after every cleaning. See Chapter 3 for seasoning instructions.

>> **Don't use a wire brush or a steel-wool scouring pad.** These aren't necessary; other less abrasive ways are available for getting off stubborn bits of food. I explain more in the section "Getting stuck-on food off" later in this chapter.

   The reason you season the pan in the first place is to fill in the pores and valleys that are just part and parcel of cast iron's structure. By using a wire-bristled brush, you're just adding more little voids to fill.

>> **Don't let your cast iron soak or let water sit in it. For that matter, don't let it air-dry, either.** When you clean cast iron, your goal is to use as little water as possible in the shortest amount of time.

WARNING

>> **Never *ever* wash cast iron in an electric dishwasher.** Dishwasher detergent strips the seasoning you've lovingly applied, the rinse cycle throws water on the newly stripped pans, and then the pans are left to essentially drip dry during the dry cycle.

>> **Don't pour cold water into hot cast iron.** Doing so can cause your pan to break. When you clean your cast iron, you want to use hot water on a hot pan.

Now that I've told you all that you *don't* want to do, I'm ready to take a positive outlook on life. How about getting ready to clean your cast iron?

Cleaning Your Cast Iron — What to Do

Ready to clean your cast-iron skillet and pan? Never fear. These sections explain what you can do so that they're ready for the next time you use them.

Rub-a-dub-dub, removing the grub

Cleaning cast iron doesn't require anything more than hot water and elbow grease. To clean your cast iron after use, follow these steps:

1. **Remove any stuck-on bits of food.**

   In a well-seasoned pan, this task usually requires nothing more than scraping the sides and bottom with a spoon — the same task that you do to get the last bit out for leftovers. If your stuck-on bits are a bit more stuck on, hop to the next section for suggestions.

2. **Using hot water and a scrub (nonwire) brush, scrub the cooking surface.**

   Let the hot water flow over the pan as you scrub with a natural-bristled or stiff plastic brush. (You want the bristles to be about as stiff as the bristles on a medium or hard toothbrush.)

   If not using soap makes you worry about what sort of germs may be lingering, pour boiling water into and over the pan after you're done brushing it.

   TIP

3. **Immediately and thoroughly dry the cast iron with a towel.**

   Never *ever* let cast iron drip-dry. And don't leave it sitting on top of anything or touching anything — like the towel you dried it with — that has moisture. *Remember:* Any remaining moisture — whether it's on your pan or on the item that your pan is sitting on — will cause your cast iron to rust. And then you have to remove the rust and reseason it all over again.

   WARNING

   Put the cast iron on a burner or in a heated oven for a few minutes to make sure that all the moisture is gone.

4. **Coat the cast iron with a thin layer of vegetable oil while it's still warm and wipe it dry with a lint-free towel.**

   Doing so helps preserve the seasoning and replaces any that was removed during the cleaning.

5. **After you wash, dry, and re-oil your cast iron, put it away.**

   For storage instructions, see the section "Storing Your Cast Iron," later in this chapter.

Getting stuck-on food off

Sometimes high-tech approaches, such as picking at the food with your finger-nails or poking at it with a table knife, aren't enough to get the stuck-on bits off. In those cases, try these suggestions to remove the stragglers and then clean and dry the pan as usual:

>> Before you go at it again, heat the pan to a temperature that's still safe to touch. Doing this opens the pores and makes it easier to clean.

>> Instead of just water, try a mixture of vinegar and water. Keep in mind, however, that you'll probably have to reseason your pan. The acidity of the vinegar helps release stuck-on food, but it also may take off the season-ing, too.

>> Scrub the problem spots with table salt moistened with either oil or water.

>> Use really hot, almost boiling, water (be sure to use rubber gloves) and scrub the spot with crumpled up aluminum foil. Experienced foil users say that the foil breaks down before it can harm the pan's surface.

Skipping the cleaning altogether

TIP

When you use your cast iron to cook bakery-type foods — such as breads, biscuits, and cakes — you don't really have to clean it at all. Simply turn the bread or cake out of the pan to cool, wipe the surface with a clean paper towel, and then apply a light layer of vegetable oil. You're pan is good to go for your next round of cooking.

Super-Cleaning for Old — or Abused — Cast Iron

Many people get their cast iron from garage sales, farm auctions, antique stores, and so on. These items can have all manner of substances stuck or cooked on them — substances that you'll want to remove before you use the pan yourself. (The remnants of someone's 20-year-old cornbread just aren't that appetizing.) Figure 4-1 shows an abused pan that needs a little — or a lot — of care before it's in cooking trim again.

Photograph by Tracy Barr

FIGURE 4-1:
A mildly (believe it or not) abused cast-iron pan.

To super-clean a pan in order to get it ready for reseasoning, do the following:

1. **Remove the rust.**

   Most old pans (and some newer pans that haven't been cared for) have some rust on them that you have to get rid of before you can do anything else.

2. **Remove any gunk that seems to be permanently attached to the pan's surface.**

   This can be the old seasoning, bits of food from ages past, or any number of other pieces of gunk that you don't want.

REMEMBER

Keep reading to find out about cleaning methods that are more drastic. When you have a pan that needs serious cleaning, you're going to ruin the seasoning. Sometimes, such as when you need to remove rust, you may be focusing on one or two spots. At other times, your goal is to clean the whole darn pan, bringing it back to its natural, unseasoned state. In either case, you're going to end up reseasoning the whole enchilada. Head to Chapter 3 for details.

Removing rust

Several techniques exist for removing rust from a cast-iron pan. Which technique you use depends on how extensive the rust damage is and how many rusty pans you have.

If the rust is relatively minor, try the following:

>> **Sandpaper and elbow grease:** Be sure that your sandpaper has a medium to fine grit; otherwise, you may leave big scratches on the surface of the pan.

>> **Raw potato, cut in half, and scouring powder:** Use the potato as your scouring pad and scrub until the rust is gone.

>> **Steel wool:** Scour the rusty area until the rust is gone.

>> **Rust eraser:** These gadgets do exactly as their name implies. You can find them in hardware stores, woodworking shops, bike shops, and many other places that sell items that are susceptible to rust.

If the rust that you're dealing with is extensive or you don't have the heart to spend an afternoon (or longer) hand-sanding your cookware, you may want to give these suggestions a try:

>> **Use a drill or grinder and a wire brush:** This method can definitely get rid of the rust, but a wire brush whirling around at several hundred rpm (revolutions per minute) can change the look of your cast iron, possibly leaving it polished, which is a bad thing because a polished pan doesn't accept seasoning well — the seasoning wipes right off. If you use a drill or grinder be careful not to get carried away and start sanding valleys into your pan's surface.

>> **Take your pan to a local shop and have it sandblasted:** Again, this may be a viable option if you're facing a stack of pans to de-rust and are desperate. But keep in mind that this is the most drastic of the rust-removal methods and sandblasted pieces require *plenty* of reseasoning.

WARNING

Don't sandblast any piece whose markings (logos, distinctive characteristics, and so on) you want to preserve. This would include special family heirloom pieces, collector's pieces, and any other cast iron that you're particularly fond of for whatever reason. Sandblasting strips these markings right off — or ruins them. If the pan is worth a bit of money (as some collectible cast iron is) or it's special to you, hand-sanding it may be worth the time and trouble.

Removing old seasoning, leftover gunk, and mysterious chunks

When the rust is gone, you're ready to remove the old seasoning and whatever else may be lingering on your pans. Basically, you can turn the heat way up or go the chemical route:

>> Put the cast iron in a hot fire (outdoors obviously) until the fire dies down and the embers are cool. Everything that's on the pan — old, stuck-on food, burned lard, and all the old seasoning — should be gone.

>> Put the cast iron in your self-cleaning oven and turn that feature on. Essentially, it's like putting the cast iron in the hot outdoor fire: You're burning off the old crud at really high temperatures. When your self-cleaning oven unlocks itself, your pan should be free from its old seasoning.

>> Spray the pan with oven cleaner and put it in a plastic bag for a couple of days. When you remove the pan from the bag, scrub off the cleaner, and wash the pan in soap and water. Then rinse thoroughly. And then rinse it again to make sure that you've taken all the oven cleaner off.

WARNING

If you use this method, be sure to wear plastic gloves and be careful. The chemicals (notably lye) in oven cleaner are super caustic and can hurt you if you get them on your skin or in your eyes.

If anything that you don't want remains (such as paint), you're free to use pretty much whatever can remove it: putty knife, wire-bristled brush, nontoxic stain or paint remover, or trained elephants with sledge hammers.

After the old seasoning is burned off and you've removed anything else that was left, basically, you have a new cast-iron pan. Your next step is to scrub it in hot soapy water and reseason it. See Chapter 3 for details on seasoning a pan.

Storing Your Cast Iron

Cast iron is pretty easygoing. You can stack it in a cabinet or hang it from a hook or pan rack. If you take your only cast iron with you on camping trips, leave it in the box that it came in. Wherever you plan to keep (or arrange) your cast iron, follow these suggestions:

>> **Make sure that you store your cast iron in a cool, dry place.** Remember, moisture is the enemy.

>> **Store your cast iron with the lid off or ajar.** Cast-iron lids fit fairly tightly, and if any moisture is in the pan, a closed lid won't let it escape. The result is a rusty pan. This advice is especially important if you live in a humid environment.

TIP

If you want to leave the lid on, place a folded-up paper towel between the lid and the pan and place a crumbled-up paper towel inside the pan to absorb any moisture.

>> **If you hang your cast iron from the wall, be sure that the hook or nail is anchored in a stud and that it can bear the weight of your pan(s).** The same goes if you're hanging it from the ceiling. And never hang cast iron — even just decorative cast iron — over a doorway unless you're really, *really* sure it won't fall.

Hitting the Road with Your Cast Iron

Many people never take their cast iron anywhere other than potluck dinners, family reunions, or Thanksgiving get-togethers, and then they have a tendency to transport it on their lap, between their feet, or safely surrounded by towels in the trunk of their car. Not to protect the cast iron, mind you, but to protect whatever delectable dish is inside it.

Many other people, those who take their kitchens outdoors, consider their cast iron a transportable tool, something that they pack with the rest of their gear.

REMEMBER

If you're one of the latter group and plan to take your cast iron with you when you head out for an adventure in the great outdoors, the trick is to keep the pan from bouncing and banging around too much. Put it in the box it came in, wrap it in a towel or burlap sack, or wedge it securely against the skis or other paraphernalia. If you're feeling particularly protective, you, too, can cradle cast iron in your lap — but you don't need to. If cast iron could survive being carted thousands of miles west in covered wagons, it can probably survive your trip into the next county for a cook-off.

Chapter 5

Identifying the Best Cast-Iron Cooking Techniques

Making good food in cast iron isn't rocket science. Whether it's a skillet, pot, wok, or even a griddle, all you need is a well-seasoned pan (seasoning details and instructions are in Chapter 3) and a few simple cooking techniques. And because cast iron is such an efficient conductor of heat, knowing how to control the temperature and to take advantage of its heating properties is vital when you cook with cast iron. This chapter tells you everything that you need to know. Of course, having a few recipes doesn't hurt either. You can find these in Chapters 13 through 24.

Out of the Frying Pan and into the Fire: Heat and Temperature Control

Cast iron is a great heat conductor. It absorbs heat quickly, and it distributes it evenly. The advantages of this are

» **You can use less heat.** Often, when you cook with cast iron, you find yourself turning the heat down from its original setting, not up.

>> **Food cooks uniformly.** If you set something to simmer in a cast iron, for example, *all* the food in the pan simmers, not just the part that's directly over the burner.

>> **You're less likely to get hot spots that scorch or burn your food.** As a general rule, heavier pots and pans of any kind are less likely than lighter pots and pans of the same kind to have hot spots.

>> **Your food stays warm longer.** Even after you remove your cast iron from the heat source, the heavy metal of the pan keeps the food warm without cooking.

REMEMBER

If your cast iron is well seasoned and you can adequately control the cooking temperature, there really isn't anything you can't make in a cast-iron pan. Seasoning and temperature control, more than anything else, can determine whether you become a fan or a foe of cast iron. Remember, cast iron is different from other pans; learn the right temperature for your stove, and you're halfway there.

WARNING

Still, if you're not used to cooking with cast iron, the heating properties that make it such a good cookware may be exactly what trips you up. Keep reading to find out what you may struggle with until you're accustomed to your cast-iron pans.

Getting the temperature right

Because you use less heat, your temperature setting may need to be lower than what's specified in recipes not geared toward cast-iron cookware. Generally, you simply have to set the temperature as the recipe indicates and then adjust it downward as needed. If you notice, for example, that your stew's soft simmer is actually more of a pre-boil, simply turn the heat setting down until you get the result that you want. Eventually, you'll know what setting to use to get the appropriate cooking temperature.

TIP

Because cast iron absorbs and retains heat so well, you don't need to use temperatures as high as you may need for your other pans. Use the following general guidelines for the temperature settings for stovetop cooking. Keep in mind that these are simply guidelines; your stove and oven's heat settings may differ:

Cooking Method	Heat Setting
Braising	Medium-low to medium
Frying	Medium-high to brown, medium-low to medium to cook
Sautéing	Medium
Searing	Medium to medium-high
Simmering	Medium-low to medium
Warming	Low

As you cook a single dish, you can move your cast iron from one heat source to another. Many recipes in this book, for example, instruct you to begin the recipe on the stovetop and then place it in the oven to finish.

Getting the cooking time right

The actual cooking times on many recipes may be slightly less when you cook in cast iron. (*Note:* Because the recipes in this book are obviously based on cast-iron cooking, this generally isn't an issue that you need to worry about.)

A recipe's cooking time is an approximation — a pretty accurate approximation, true, but an approximation nonetheless. Just because most 3½-pound fryers are done roasting in a 325-degree oven in 1½ hours doesn't mean that yours will be. All sorts of factors can affect cooking times, such as the following:

>> The type of oven you have (convection or nonconvection)

>> The accuracy of your appliance's temperature gauge

>> The actual size (diameter, thickness, weight, and so forth) of what you're cooking

>> The altitude where you're cooking

>> The type of cookware you're using

IS IT DONE YET?

Because cooking times aren't exact, always check for doneness. The following signs indicate that your food is done:

- **Cakes and quick breads:** A toothpick or cake tester inserted in the center comes out clean. Another sign is that the sides of the cake or bread begin to pull away from the pan.

- **Yeast breads:** The top is light- to dark-golden brown, and the bread sounds hollow when you tap on the crust.

- **Poultry:** The legs feel loose (they begin to separate from the rest of the bird), and the juices run clear. The internal temperature is between 170 and 185 degrees.

- **Fresh pork:** Juices run clear, meat is white, or the internal temperature is 170.

- **Beef:** Internal temperature is between 140 degrees (rare) and 170 degrees (well done).

Warming up to the advantages of preheating

Cast iron works best when the heat source is the same size as the bottom of the pan, but burners on modern electric and gas ranges are usually smaller than that. To eliminate this problem, you simply have to preheat the pan when you're going to cook on top of the stove.

You can preheat your cast iron on the stovetop or in the oven. Follow these guidelines:

>> **On the stovetop:** Set your burner on low and let the cast iron warm slowly. After the entire pan is warm, turn the heat up to the temperature you want.

>> **In the oven:** Set your cast iron in a warm oven set to low (225 to 250 degrees). When it's heated, take your cast iron out of the oven, put it on the stovetop, and turn the burner to the appropriate temperature.

WARNING

Unlike a pan that's preheated on the stovetop, where the heat works its way from the burner surface outward, a pan that's preheated in the oven is surrounded by heat — which means that the handles get as hot as the pan's cooking surface. Remember to always use hot pads or oven mitts when you remove a preheated pan from the oven.

Unless the recipe indicates otherwise, you don't need to preheat your cast iron when roasting in the oven because the oven heats the cast iron evenly. If you do need to preheat the cast iron, simply put the cool cast iron in the cool oven and let it warm up as your oven does.

TIP

Many cast-iron recipes include preheating instructions. Non-cast-iron specific recipes may or may not include such instructions. If you're using a recipe that doesn't include preheating instructions for your cookware, use this rule as your guide: You almost always preheat your cast iron when you're making foods that you want to be crispy on the outside and tender or moist on the inside. These foods include the following:

>> **Cornbreads:** Good cornbread has a slightly crispy crust and is moist. Bad cornbread is gritty and dry. The difference between the two (aside from variations in recipes and the different types of cornmeal used) is often the preheating. Baking or frying your cornbread in a preheated pan is more likely to give you the consistency that you want. Head to Chapter 19 for cornbread recipes.

>> **Muffins and quick breads:** Often you preheat the pan to the same temperature as the oven. So if the recipe cooks at 350 degrees, you simply stick your

skillet or pan into the oven as it preheats and pull it out when it reaches that temperature. You can find muffin and quick bread recipes in Chapter 20.

» **Pancakes:** Preheating to the right temperature gives you pancakes that rise nicely, are light and fluffy on the inside, and have a slightly crispy edge. Your pan or griddle is hot enough if a bead of water skips across the surface. Head to Chapter 20 for pancake recipes.

» **Any seared dishes:** Searing browns the outside of your meat, poultry, or seafood, and holds the moisture inside. You can find recipes that require searing in Chapter 14, including Steak au Poivre and Cast-Iron Pot Roast.

Cooking by the campfire

When you cook outdoors over an open fire or hot coals, the rules for controlling your cooking temperatures are quite a bit different than those for indoor cooking. For outdoor cooking, you basically control your temperatures by the placement and number of coals. More coals closer to the pan mean higher temperatures; fewer coals farther from the pan mean lower temperatures.

REMEMBER

Getting and maintaining the right temperature when you cook outside is a little more complicated than simply counting coals. You also have to adjust for the weather: air temperature, humidity level, wind speed, and so on. Chapter 12 explains all about outdoor cast-iron cooking. Chapter 22 includes several easy and delicious recipes for the outdoor cook.

Working with new cast iron

Following these simple suggestions when your cast iron is new ensures that your initial journey into the world of cast-iron cooking will be successful:

» **Before you cook anything, season your cast iron.** Seasoning cast iron is simply baking oil or some other fat into the pores of the cast iron, thus creating a smooth, nonstick surface. Chapter 3 has seasoning instructions.

» **The first six or seven times that you cook in your cast iron, cook foods that are rich in natural fat or oils.** Cook bacon, hamburgers — not the lean kind — and sausage; fry chicken; or make fried potatoes. Doing so deepens the seasoning and enhances the pan's nonstick surface.

» **Wait until the pan is well seasoned before you cook some foods.** These foods include acidic foods (such as tomato-based dishes, or dishes that require citrus juice or mustard), alkaline foods (such as beans), or anything with a high-moisture content (such as soups or stews). Initially avoiding these types of foods preserves your new pan's seasoning.

If you can't wait until the seasoning builds and just have to cook your grandfather's favorite soup beans, go ahead and enjoy yourself. Just keep in mind that you may need to reseason your pan after you use it. See Chapter 3 for signs that your cast iron needs reseasoning and instructions. After your cast iron is broken in really well, you can cook just about anything in it.

Remembering other do's and don'ts

The following list offers a few random recommendations to keep in mind as you cook and serve in cast iron:

>> **Never put a cold pan on a hot burner, pour cold liquid into a hot pan, and so forth.** If you do, you run the risk of shocking your cast iron to the breaking point, literally. Let your pan heat up as the burner heats up, and if you have to add water to a hot pan, make sure that the water is warm or hot. (The same rule applies when you clean cast iron. Head to Chapter 4 for cleaning instructions.)

All metal cookware is susceptible to *thermal shock,* a drastic and quick change in temperature. Cast iron, being the most brittle of all metal cookware, is more likely to break; aluminum cookware is more likely to warp. Whether the result of thermal shock is a broken or warped pan, the outcome is the same: a pan that's no good for cooking anymore.

>> **Don't store food in cast iron.** The acid in the food breaks down the seasoning, and the food will take on a metallic taste. When you're done serving the food, transfer what's left to another container.

>> **Although you shouldn't use your cast iron to store your food, you can use it to serve food.** Follow these suggestions:

- Keep the food simmering until you're ready to sit down to eat.

- Be sure to put a hot pad or trivet under the pan. Cast iron stays hot for a long time, and it could burn or mar your tabletop.

- To keep food warm for second helpings, cover the pan while you eat.

- As soon as your meal is over, put the food in another container for storage and then wash up.

>> **Move your cast iron off an electric burner after you turn the burner off if you want the dish to stop cooking.** Unlike a gas flame, which goes out as soon as you turn the burner off, an electric burner takes a while to cool off.

Because cast iron retains heat in proportion to that emitted by the heat source, a dish left over a cooling burner will still cook. This may not present a problem when you're fixing a stew (and a little extra simmer time is not an issue), but it could be a problem if you're thickening a sauce and don't want it to caramelize. If you don't have an electric stove, don't worry. Nowadays, stove tops can range from induction to glass tops; if you use induction, that's fantastic. Cast iron works well on induction burners because they're a magnetic material, giving you the ultimate cooking experience.

On the other hand, be careful if you're using a glass-top stove. Glass-top is very temperamental, so you want to avoid leaving or dragging the pan across to the stovetop due to the weight of the pan. It could crack or scratch the surface of the stove.

» **Before you cook with cast-iron cake pans, cornstick pans, muffin pans, and other bakeware, oil them or spray them with nonstick cooking spray.** Even the fat-free kind can do the trick. Although these pans should be nonstick if they're properly seasoned, why take a chance if you're going for presentation in addition to taste?

Ending the Exile of Your Metal Utensils

Although cast iron requires some care, it isn't particularly fussy about the utensils you use. You can use wooden spoons, heatproof rubber spatulas, and metal utensils. That's right: Dust off your wire whisk and polish up that metal spoon. They're back in business.

In fact, if you find yourself facing a chunk of food that seems to have permanently attached itself to your cast-iron cookware, you can even scrape it with a (hopefully clean) putty knife to pick it off. If you're so inclined or desperate, remember that you may have to reseason the spot you scratched at.

REMEMBER

I don't recommend scrubbing your pan clean with a wire brush. First, it isn't necessary. You can usually get even the most stubborn stuck-on food off in less abrasive ways. (See Chapter 4 for ideas.) Second, although this type of brush won't hurt the iron, it will scrub off your seasoning, and then you'll have to start over again.

Starting with Safety First

You really don't need much to have a well-stocked cast-iron kitchen: one or two pans, a few good recipes (or the creativity to make your own), and the following:

>> **Hot pads — and good ones:** Cast iron gets hot, and it's unforgiving. All cast-iron cooks, sooner or later, grab a hot handle and then spend a few painful seconds trying to shake away the sting from their palms while cursing for being so careless. And you're not the only one to get burned.

Think about your tabletop, too. Hot pads are the answers. (Kitchen towels and tablecloths generally don't have enough heft.) You can even find hot pads made just for the skillet handle, which you can slide on and off.

>> **Stiff-bristled brush:** You need a stiff-bristled brush to clean your cast iron.

WARNING

Don't mistake a stiff-bristled brush for a wire brush. Wire brushes are too abrasive. They can scratch right through your seasoning; then you'll have to reseason your pan.

For the indoor cook, that's about it. Nothing fancy. And certainly not enough to break the bank.

If you're cooking outdoors, you'll probably want to add a number of other items to your laundry list to make the experience easier and safer. I discuss lid lifters, spyders, charcoal chimney starters, and a number of other outdoor accessories in Chapter 12.

Troubleshooting Cast Iron That Smokes

If your cast iron is smoking, look and adjust one of the following:

>> **Heat:** You're heating your pan at too high of a temperature. I recommend preheating your pan on high for about 30 seconds and then dropping the heat to medium to cook.

>> **The type of oil you're using:** When cooking with oil in cast iron, you always want to use an oil with a high smoking point, which means the pan can be heated to a higher temperature before it starts to burn and smoke. Chapter 3 lists oils and their smoking points.

>> **Food particles:** If food particles are left in the pan when preheating, they can burn, causing the cast iron to smoke. If you don't address the food particles, they can lead to burnt-tasting food.

3
Food Basics and Cast-Iron Cooking

Season, prepare, and carve red meat and poultry like a pro.

Select the perfect fish and understand how cast iron can enhance textures and flavors.

Cook with fresh vegetables and create sides, main dishes, and more in your cast iron.

Discover new tips and techniques from sautéing to pan-frying in your cast iron.

Create new memories and uncover new favorites with classic comfort food like cornbread, biscuits, and much more.

Finish your meal with a delectable dessert that will create a lasting impression.

Find out all you need to know about using cast iron when you're camping.

Chapter **6**

It's All about Red Meat

For many years people believed that red meat was an essential part of the daily diet. Even today, beef and pork are particularly popular, especially when it comes to American BBQ. But over the years, a lot of studies have shown that consuming too much red meat, especially processed, can have a negative long-term effect on your overall health. The good news: You can make healthier choices and pair your protein with a seafood or vegetable dish (see Chapters 8 and 9), while still enjoying your favorite red meat dish.

Cooking any protein comes down to two things: texture and flavor. This chapter provides pointers, tips, and tricks for choosing the right cut for the right dish. I also dive into the three Ts: tenderness, texture, and taste. After you drool all over the pages in this chapter, head to Chapter 14 to put your new skills to work with plenty of red-meat recipes you can prepare in your cast iron.

Getting the Lowdown on Beef

With protein, especially beef, the cut of meat makes all the difference in the amount of fat and how tender (or how tough) it is. Check out Figure 6-1, which provides you with a clear map of where the different cuts come from, which is the first step in understanding the right cut for you. The following sections explain how the different cuts have different tenderness and how you can use the USDA (United States Department of Agriculture) grading scale to evaluate meat.

FIGURE 6-1:
Cutting up, down
on the farm.

Illustration by Liz Kurtzman

Differentiating between tender and tough cuts

In general, if you start at the front of the cow and work your way back, the tenderness of the meat progresses from least to most tender and then back again.

To better understand tough versus tender, think in terms of which muscles get worked the most — front and rear legs or anything that moves a lot. Meat that comes from the shoulder is tougher than the meat that comes from the rib, which is tougher than the meat that comes from the loin, which is the most tender part of the cut of meat (not much movement happening here). Then the meat begins to get less tender as you move toward the rear legs. The meat from the belly of the cow (the brisket, plate, and flank portions) produces the toughest, fattiest cuts.

You aren't alone if your brain feels like the exploding head emoji. The best way to get the right information is by simply asking your local butcher, "Does this come off the front or the hind end?" Easy answer: The front is more tender.

REMEMBER

Butchers can carve a cow just about any way they want to. As a result, what a particular cut of meat may be called at your grocery store depends, in large part, on the butcher and the decisions they make when cutting the meat. If, for example, they see that the meat from the flank portion is lean, they may chop it into stew meat; if the meat can be removed whole, they may cube it (run it through a machine that scores the meat in order to break up the tough fibers) and call it a cube steak. If you don't have any idea what a particular piece of meat is or how best to cook it, simply ask. A knowledgeable butcher can be one of your best friends in the kitchen.

Relying on the beef's grading system

When you buy beef, use the USDA grading system to evaluate the quality of your beef. One of the factors that determines the grade is the amount of *marbling* (the distribution of fat and lean) the cut contains. More marbling generally means that the meat is more moist and tender than cuts with less marbling.

REMEMBER

Use the following information about the grades to help find the right cut:

>> **Prime:** Beef that falls into this grade has the most marbling. Beef in this category is also the most flavorful and the most tender. Not surprisingly, it costs more, too.

>> **Choice:** Meat of this grade is the biggest seller, simply because by applying a few tricks (which are explained in the following section) you can make it as flavorful and tender as prime cuts of meat but at a fraction of the cost.

>> **Select:** This is the leanest cut. It has the least marbling and isn't as flavorful or as tender as the other two grades. It's also the least expensive.

So how do you use this grading system? Good question. If you want to cook a steak, for example, choose Choice or Prime. If you're planning a dish that requires slow cooking the meat (braising it, for example), Select is the better choice. Slow-cooking methods tenderize the meat, so you don't need to spend the extra money for an already tender piece of beef that will become tough if cooked too long.

TIP

In the United States, some states operate without an inspection program. What this means is that all of the beef is sold at the same price and not separated into the three categories. If you know what you're looking for, you can get a great cut for a great price.

Cooking Beef

Cooking methods impact how flavorful and tender your beef is. Use the wrong cooking method, and what had been a nice tender cut of beef will be leathery tough. Use the right cooking method, and even a tough piece of meat will be tender.

Any cut of beef — even the toughest — can be a good cut. What makes a cut good depends on what you want and how you plan to cook it. If you want to grill a melt-in-your-mouth, juicy steak, for example, a good cut is a ribeye (which comes from the rib area) or a T-bone or porterhouse (from the short loin area). A bad cut is a flank steak or chuck steak. Similarly, using a porterhouse to make beef stew is just a waste of money. Stew meat works better.

The following sections focus just on what you need to know to cook beef, including how you can make a tougher piece more tender and what you can do to maximize the flavor of good cuts.

Focusing on the basics of preparing beef

When all else fails, just keep this simple rule in mind: Cook beef with liquid (braising and boiling) when dealing with tougher cuts. Hold the liquid (roasting, grilling, broiling, pan-frying, and so on) for tender cuts. The following list runs down the beef cuts used in this section, including the best cooking method:

>> **Pot roasts** come from the shoulder or chuck. There are two kinds of pot roasts: chuck roasts and arm roasts. You can use either in a recipe that calls for pot roast. Because pot roasts tend toward toughness, you cook them slowly in liquid. Refer to the Cast-Iron Pot Roast recipe in Chapter 14.

>> **Sirloin steak** comes from the sirloin. Although not as tender as meat from the short loin area, meat from the sirloin area is still really tender. Prepare sirloin as you would any other steak or you can cut it into cubes, as I do with the Campsite Beef Stroganoff in Chapter 22 and cook it in liquid.

>> **Flank steak,** a less-expensive alternative to sirloin in the Campsite Beef Stroganoff recipe in Chapter 22, comes from the flank area, on the underside of the cow. Flank steak is generally pretty tough, and many butchers either *score* it (make shallow cuts against the grain to break up the tough sinew) or run it through a *cuber* (a machine that scores the meat) to tenderize it.

>> **Brisket** comes from the cow's breast and, if not cooked properly, is notoriously tough. The only way to cook brisket so that it isn't tough is to slow cook it for a really long time. The Roasted Brisket recipe in Chapter 14 simmers and braises the brisket for hours. Cooked properly, you'd never suspect that the meat you started out with was less than melt-in-your-mouth tender.

>> **Round steak** comes from the hindquarter of the cow, the section behind the sirloin area. Round steak is a nice cut of meat, but you need to do a little work to make it tender. To broil or grill it as a steak, use a tenderizer. In the Chisholm Trail Swiss Steak recipe (see Chapter 14), you pound it with a meat mallet to tenderize and simmer it in liquid for a couple of hours.

>> The **tenderloin,** the most tender part of the whole beef, comes from the muscle on each side of the cow's spine, around the short loin area. This meat is naturally tender; filets sliced from here don't require Herculean efforts to soften them up. The simplest cooking methods (oven roasting or pan-searing) are best, as shown in the Steak au Poivre (Peppercorn-Crusted Steak) recipe in Chapter 14.

Making tougher cuts tender

Some cuts of meat are simply less tender than other cuts of meat. Chuck roasts, round steaks, briskets, and stew meat fall into this category, and they probably show up on your dinner table often. These cuts are common to many tables because they're affordable.

Keep in mind, however, that these meats can be as delicious, as mouth-watering, and, yes, *as tender,* as their more tender-from-the-get-go brethren, but you need to use the right cooking method. With tougher cuts, the best cooking method is a slow one over a low temperature that requires some liquid. Think braising or boiling.

In some places like New England, you can find corn beef, which is soaked in a brine solution consisting of only salt and water, in which the meat naturally turns a gray color. Other parts of the United States and the world use sodium nitrate in the brine, which allows the beef to maintain its pink color.

Getting the most from good cuts

Depending on the cooking method you choose (refer to Chapter 5), you can turn almost any cut of beef into a great culinary masterpiece. However, some cuts of meat like rib and loin areas are naturally tender and flavorful. When working with a higher quality piece of protein, the hard part is cooking it to the right temperature, which allows you to maximize its flavor and texture.

TIP

If you are going to invest in a good cut of meat, know that you're going to pay for it. Because you've spent more money on it, you want to be clear on the right cooking technique — and searing is a good method. Here are a few tips for locking in flavor when searing:

>> Before searing your protein, evenly season the beef with salt and pepper. Be sure to season both sides.

>> Preheat your cast iron over high heat for about 1 to 2 minutes. Then reduce the heat to medium-high so you can maintain control of the cast iron's heat. If

you see it smoking, it's too hot. If you put your beef in the pan and you don't hear it sizzling, it's too cold. Finding the right temperature is very important in the searing process.

>> When cooking, always put the *service side* down first, the side that you'll be looking at from the plate. Depending on your cut, make sure you get a good sear, deep golden brown on both sides.

>> Use tongs when turning the meat. You want to refrain from using anything like a fork that can prick the meat, which causes the juices to seep out, drying out the meat.

WARNING

Cooking slowly is a way to make dryer, tougher cuts moist. (See the section Focusing on the basics of preparing beef for details on the proper cooking methods for these cuts.) Slow cooking isn't the best cooking method for already tender meat; in fact, it's often a waste of time and money. First, the longer you cook already-tender meat, the drier it gets, and second, if you're going to take the time to tenderize a piece of meat, why not spend that time on a cheaper cut that could actually benefit from it?

Zeroing In on Pork

Dry rubs, wet rubs, fresh, smoked, pickled, stuffed into a sausage or my favorite, cut into beautiful thin strips and baked into crisp pieces of goodness, pork has definitely earned its place on the shelf in the meat market. One of the things that makes pork so popular is the protein's ability to take on flavor. The pig's diet (such as nuts, berries, and figs just to name a few) can have a tremendous impact on the meat's flavor.

PIGS USED TO BE FATTER — BELIEVE IT OR NOT

Pigs used to be valued for their fat almost as much as for their meat. Up until World War II, a pig with a hefty layer of exterior fat was prized for the amount of lard it would give. But then along came vegetable shortening and information about how bad animal fat was for you, and the fat that had once been so valuable became a liability. The result? Pigs that were genetically engineered to be leaner. An unfortunate (for taste at least) side effect of cutting down on the exterior fat was that the interior fat was reduced, too. With less marbling, pork is leaner, true, but it also tends to be dryer and tougher if you don't cook it carefully.

You can prepare pork in any number of ways as I discuss in the following sections. How you cook it depends on the cut and the preparation method. Smoked (or cured) pork, for example, requires different cooking techniques and times than does fresh pork.

Knowing where the meat comes from

As with beef and cows, where the pork comes from on the pig gives you some sort of indication about how tender or flavorful it is and which cooking method is best. Figure 6-2 shows where on the pig the various cuts come from, and the following sections explain the cuts you get from these areas.

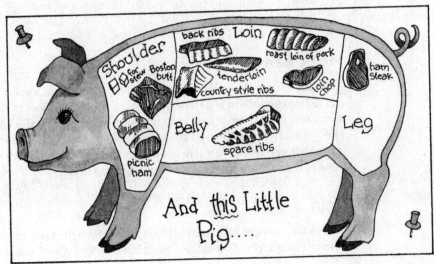

FIGURE 6-2:
Where pork cuts come from.

Boston butt

Contrary to what you may have assumed, the Boston butt doesn't come from Massachusetts or the neighborhood that a pig's tail occupies. No, this cut comes from the shoulder, hence the other common name for this cut — Boston shoulder. When cut into slices, the Boston butt yields pork steaks. You can cook pork steaks the same way that you cook a steak or the way you cook a pork chop. When it's not sliced, you cook it as a roast.

TIP

When you're figuring out how much to buy, remember that meat from the shoulder has quite a bit of fat, so think larger portions.

A PIG BY ANY OTHER NAME

Although most people use the terms *pig* and *hog* synonymously, a *pig* doesn't technically become a *hog* until it weighs more than 50 kilograms (a little over 110 pounds). Here's a breakdown to help:

- A *piglet* is a baby who becomes a *shoat* once it's weaned.
- A *gilt* is a female who turns into a *sow* after she matures.
- A *barrow*, alas, is a castrated male who will never become a *boar*.
- A *swine* can be any pig of any age or either gender.

Whatever this beast may be technically called, you probably simply call it dinner.

Picnic ham

The picnic ham, also called a *picnic shoulder*, isn't a ham at all. (Ham comes from the leg portion of the pig.) The picnic ham is a tough piece of meat. One popular way to prepare a picnic ham is to make barbecue (often called *pulled pork*). To do this, you slow cook the meat to make it tender, pull it apart, and mix and serve it with barbecue sauce. You also get ham hocks from here, which you can braise or cook in liquid. They're great for flavoring soup beans.

Loin

Just as on a piece of beef, the loin on a pig is where the most tender meat is. A pork loin is a long strip of meat that, when cut or sliced, yields these pieces:

>> **Roast loin of pork:** This piece of meat used to be called *backstrip tenderloin* because it's on top of the backbone and ribs. If you buy this piece whole, it's often rolled and tied into a roast. The roast loin of pork is also the *Canadian back* because, when smoked and sliced, it's Canadian bacon.

>> **Tenderloin:** The tenderloin, also called *catfish tenderloin* because it resembles a catfish, is under the backbone. It's the most tender piece in the whole pig.

>> **Baby back ribs:** After you remove the meat from the top of the backbone (the pork loin roast) and the meat underneath it (the tenderloin), you're left with the ribs.

>> **Loin chop:** If you leave the roast loin of pork and the tenderloin on the bone, and slice it, you get loin chops. Slices of meat from the tenderloin are boneless loin chops.

>> **Country style ribs:** This is simply yet another cut from the loin area of a pig.

If you're ready to challenge your skills, check out the Apricot-Ginger Glazed Pork Rib Roast with Fruit Stuffing recipe in Chapter 14. This dish not only tastes great but is an excellent way to showcase your skills.

REMEMBER

Which piece of meat you get depends on what the butcher cuts. Pork chops, for example, come from the loin area, too.

Belly

From the top part of the belly, you get bacon (unsmoked bacon is *fat back*, *salt pork*, or *fresh side*). After you remove the strip of bacon, you're left with a cut of pork ribs and breastbone, popularly known as spareribs.

Leg

The leg is also known as the ham. Hams come smoked and fresh, whole and half (or any other portion), with and without the bone.

A smoked ham can come either fully cooked or partially cooked. The distinction is important because you simply need to warm up a fully cooked smoked ham; an internal temperature of 140 degrees is fine. A smoked ham that hasn't been fully cooked (or a fresh ham, which hasn't been cooked or smoked at all) should be cooked long enough to attain an internal temperature of 160 degrees.

Other parts

Just about every single part of the pig is used as food. Some of the more popular remaining pieces include

>> **Pig's feet:** As the name implies, these cuts come from the hindfoot and forefoot of the pig. These can be pickled, braised, or cooked in liquid.

>> **Jowl:** The *jowl* is the pig's jaw. From here, you get jowl bacon (a less expensive cut of bacon).

Cooking pork

Like beef, you can cook pork either with liquid (braise or boil, for example) or without (roast, pan-fry, and broil). The cut of meat you have determines the cooking method.

REMEMBER

Because of the fear of *trichinosis* (a parasite that lives in pork that people can ingest and the basis for your grandmother's admonition, "You'll get worms!"), people for a long time considered pork done and the trichinosis dead when the meat had an internal temperature of 170 degrees. With the leaner cuts of today's pork, however, a 170-degree internal temperature means your meat is pretty dry and tough. Fortunately, trichinosis dies at around 140 degrees, so you can safely cook your pork without steaming every last bit of juice and flavor out of it. Today, many people cook pork until it has an internal temperature of between 145 and 160 degrees.

Carving Like a Pro

With so many ready-to-serve portions available at the grocery store, carving is practically a dying art. That's too bad, for the following reasons:

>> **You get more meat, especially with bone-in cuts.** Too many people ignore the bones or hack around them. The result is a lot of wasted meat. Knowing how to carve around a bone or remove it entirely yields more meat.

>> **How you carve has a direct impact on how chewy — or not — your meat is.** Even a tender cut of meat becomes chewy if carved incorrectly. All meat is essentially muscle, and muscle has grain. Cut *with* the grain, and your meat is chewy and stringing. Cut across the grain, as shown in the carving illustrations I include this section, and the meat practically falls apart in your mouth.

The following sections and illustrations show you how to carve some the cuts of meat prepared in this chapter.

Carving a brisket

Figure 6-3 provides step-by-step directions for carving brisket. Follow these guidelines, and you'll be on your way to the Meat Cutters Hall of Fame. The most important thing to remember about the brisket is to *cut across the grain*, rather than with it. Fortunately, the grain is very pronounced in a brisket.

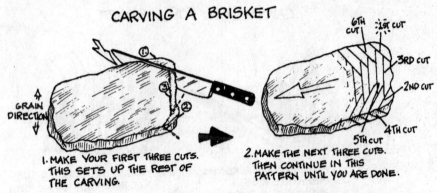

CARVING A BRISKET

6TH CUT   1ST CUT

3RD CUT

2ND CUT

4TH CUT

5TH CUT

GRAIN DIRECTION

1. MAKE YOUR FIRST THREE CUTS. THIS SETS UP THE REST OF THE CARVING.

2. MAKE THE NEXT THREE CUTS. THEN CONTINUE IN THIS PATTERN UNTIL YOU ARE DONE.

★ DON'T CARVE STRAIGHT DOWN. MAKE SURE YOU HAVE YOUR BLADE AT A SLIGHT ANGLE SO THAT YOU GO ACROSS THE GRAIN, NOT WITH IT!

FIGURE 6-3:
Beef Brisket 101.

Illustration by Liz Kurtzman

Carving a pot roast

When you carve a pot roast, you follow the same basic guidelines, regardless of the cut. Figure 6-4 shows a seven-bone pot roast (so called because the bone looks like the number 7).

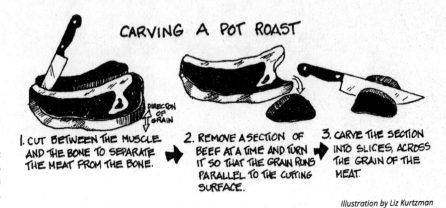

CARVING A POT ROAST

DIRECTION OF GRAIN

1. CUT BETWEEN THE MUSCLE AND THE BONE TO SEPARATE THE MEAT FROM THE BONE.

2. REMOVE A SECTION OF BEEF AT A TIME AND TURN IT SO THAT THE GRAIN RUNS PARALLEL TO THE CUTTING SURFACE.

3. CARVE THE SECTION INTO SLICES, ACROSS THE GRAIN OF THE MEAT.

FIGURE 6-4:
Follow this pattern for a perfect pot roast.

Illustration by Liz Kurtzman

Carving a pork roast

Several pieces of meat qualify as a pork roast. The steps in Figure 6-5 explain how to cut a loin roast. (*Note:* This piece of meat is also sometimes called a crown roast because you can tie the ribs together to make a crown, as I have you do in the Apricot-Ginger Glazed Pork Rib Roast with Fruit Stuffing recipe in Chapter 14.)

CARVING A PORK ROAST

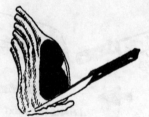

1. REMOVE THE BACKBONE FROM THE RIBS. WITHOUT THE BACKBONE OFF, YOU WON'T BE ABLE TO EASILY SEPARATE THE SLICES.

2. SITUATE THE ROAST SO THAT THE RIBS FACE YOU AND THEN CUT SLICES ON EACH SIDE OF THE RIB BONES.

☆ EVERY OTHER PIECE OF MEAT WILL HAVE A RIB BONE IN IT.

FIGURE 6-5: Boning up on pork rib roast.

Illustration by Liz Kurtzman

Chapter **7**

Tastes Fowl — Like Chicken (and Turkey)

M any birds qualify as *poultry,* domesticated birds that are kept for both their eggs and for their meat: chickens, turkeys, ducks, geese, guinea fowl, peafowl, pigeons, and others. Chicken, of course, is one of the favorite birds, hands (or wings) down. Turkey, that holiday staple, comes in second. Poultry is great tasting, but it also owes much of its increasing popularity to the fact that it's generally healthier than red meat.

But even before people were drawn to poultry as an alternative to fattier meats, it's always been a versatile staple of American diets: baked, roasted, fried, stir-fried, sautéed, broiled, barbecued, fricasseed, stewed, and more — and that's even before you get to the leftovers.

This chapter presents a range of concepts and guidelines to assist you in selecting, preparing, and caring for the perfect bird. I also share some important safety information. Whether you're cooking turkey, pheasant, Cornish hen, or chicken, this chapter helps you gain perspective for the recipes in Chapter 15 where you can put your newfound knowledge to the test.

Grasping Chicken Basics

When you go to the grocery store, you'll find plenty of chicken options. Basically, the difference is in the size and the amount of meat. Table 7-1 lists the types of chicken and the cooking methods.

TABLE 7-1   Types of Chicken and Cooking Methods

Bird	Weight	Cooking Methods
Game hens (Rock Cornish hens)	1½ pounds or less	Stuffed and roasted or split and broiled
Fryers (broiler-fryers)	1½ to 3 pounds	Broiled, fried, roasted, or stewed
Hens (stewing chickens)	2½ to 5 pounds	Stewed, fricasseed, or used in soup
Roasters	More than 4 pounds	Roasted
Capons (castrated roosters)	4½ to 7 pounds	Roasted

TIP

When you buy a chicken, plan on ½ pound of chicken per serving — less, if the chicken is boneless. If you're serving game hen, plan on ½ to 1 bird per person.

You can buy whole chickens, quartered chickens, or chickens that have been cut into individual pieces. You can also buy particular pieces: a package of drumsticks, for example, or thighs. Buying pieces is a good choice if you like (or your recipe calls for) particular pieces, or if you just don't want to take the time to cut up a whole chicken yourself. Buying whole chickens, on the other hand, is usually less expensive than buying pieces, and when they go on sale, they're cheaper yet.

TIP

If you run across a sale on whole chickens, buy a few. Leave some whole or quarter them for roasting; cut the others into individual pieces for other chicken dishes. (Figure 7-1 demonstrates one technique for cutting a whole chicken into parts.) Chickens store well in the freezer. Simply remove the giblets, wash the chicken and pat it dry, and then wrap it tightly in freezer wrap. It can stay in the freezer for up to 9 months at 0 degrees. You can freeze giblets for up to 3 months.

TIP

Don't throw the giblets away! They make great gravy, they're good fried, and you can cut them up and use them in any dish that calls for cut-up chicken.

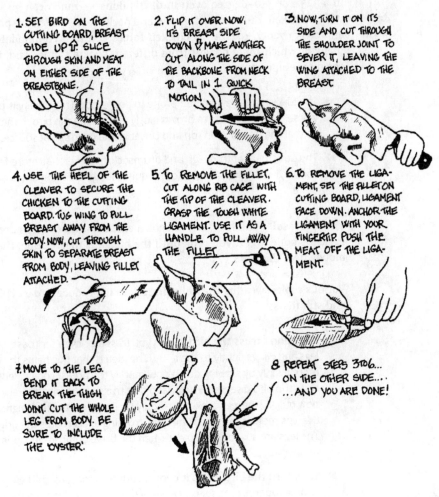

CUTTING A CHICKEN INTO PARTS

1. SET BIRD ON THE CUTTING BOARD, BREAST SIDE UP ↑. SLICE THROUGH SKIN AND MEAT ON EITHER SIDE OF THE BREASTBONE.

2. FLIP IT OVER. NOW, IT'S BREAST SIDE DOWN ↓ MAKE ANOTHER CUT ALONG THE SIDE OF THE BACKBONE FROM NECK TO TAIL IN 1 QUICK MOTION

3. NOW, TURN IT ON ITS SIDE AND CUT THROUGH THE SHOULDER JOINT TO SEVER IT, LEAVING THE WING ATTACHED TO THE BREAST

4. USE THE HEEL OF THE CLEAVER TO SECURE THE CHICKEN TO THE CUTTING BOARD. TUG WING TO PULL BREAST AWAY FROM THE BODY. NOW, CUT THROUGH SKIN TO SEPARATE BREAST FROM BODY, LEAVING FILLET ATTACHED.

5. TO REMOVE THE FILLET, CUT ALONG RIB CAGE WITH THE TIP OF THE CLEAVER. GRASP THE TOUGH WHITE LIGAMENT. USE IT AS A HANDLE TO PULL AWAY THE FILLET

6. TO REMOVE THE LIGAMENT, SET THE FILLET ON CUTTING BOARD, LIGAMENT FACE DOWN. ANCHOR THE LIGAMENT WITH YOUR FINGERTIP. PUSH THE MEAT OFF THE LIGAMENT.

7. MOVE TO THE LEG. BEND IT BACK TO BREAK THE THIGH JOINT. CUT THE WHOLE LEG FROM BODY. BE SURE TO INCLUDE THE 'OYSTER'.

8. REPEAT STEPS 3 TO 6... ON THE OTHER SIDE.... ...AND YOU ARE DONE!

FIGURE 7-1:
Making the cut.

Illustration by Liz Kurtzman

Understanding Roasting Guidelines

Cast iron is great for roasting because it holds and distributes heat evenly. Although you can buy cast-iron roasters, which have ridges cast into the bottom of the pan to hold your meat out of its juices, you don't need a roaster to roast in cast iron. Any skillet or Dutch oven big enough to hold your bird will do. To keep the cooking meat out of its juices, use a standard roasting V rack, just as you would in any pan, or a cast-iron trivet.

For as simple as roasting is — basically you just put the meat in a pan and stick it in a 325- or 350-degree oven until it's done — much can go wrong, especially with a chicken. Unlike roasting beef and pork roasts, which are pretty symmetrical and cook evenly, roasting a chicken forces you to accommodate all of its parts, many of which could benefit from different cooking times and, frankly, different cooking temperatures.

>> The breast meat is lean and prone to drying out. This liability is only made worse by the fact that to brown nicely you situate the bird in the roasting pan so that the breast is on top and closer to the oven's heat source.

>> The dark meat of the thigh and drumstick, however, has more fat and connective tissue and therefore requires longer cooking times before it's done.

The end result of all this? If you cook a chicken until the legs are nicely done, the breast is bone dry. If you cook until the breast is nicely done, the leg meat is still bloody near the bone.

Various cooks swear by the following tricks to produce a roast chicken that's done and still moist:

>> **They don't truss the bird.** When you *truss* a chicken for roasting, you bind its legs and wings tightly to the body. The idea is that this helps the chicken cook more evenly by slowing down how quickly the breast cooks. People who don't truss the bird disagree. They claim that trussing the bird actually slows down how quickly the *legs* cook, specifically the inner part of the thigh. And because the legs require *more* cooking time, trussing exacerbates the original problem: The legs are still too raw to eat when the breast reaches its optimum temperature.

>> **They turn the bird while it cooks.** Turning a roasting chicken or turkey is another option, precisely because of the problem of getting the parts of the bird to cook evenly. Basically, the goal is to move different parts of the bird close to the oven's heating element as a way to even out the meat's exposure to the highest heat. Some start the bird on its belly and then flip it to its back; others start the bird on one side, turn it to the other, and then finish it, breast up.

If you decide to turn your chicken during roasting, make sure that the bird is breast-side up for the last half of the cooking time.

Chicken can harbor *salmonella*, bacteria that causes food poisoning. The bacteria die when exposed to temperatures of 160 degrees and higher. Therefore, according to the U.S. Department of Agriculture, you need to cook chicken until it reaches an internal temperature of 165 degrees. This goes for individual pieces, whole, or cooked stuffed.

Southern Fried Chicken: The Ultimate in Comfort Food

People who make great fried chicken swear by their own unique recipes. If you don't yet have a tried, trusted, and true — not to mention knock-your-socks-off — recipe that you swear by, try experimenting with some of the following variations to see what suits your particular taste (or just check out the award-winning technique from the Southern Fried Chicken recipe in Chapter 15):

>> **Coating:** Apply different coatings and coating techniques. Try dipping the chicken in milk, then flour, then milk, and then the flour again. Some cast-iron cooks dip it in a milk-egg mixture and then dredge it in flour. Some don't use flour at all and cover it with cracker crumbs, potato flakes, or cornmeal.

After you coat your chicken, let it air-dry. Air-drying your chicken for 20 minutes to a half-hour after it's been coated lets the coating toughen and produces a crispier crust.

>> **Seasoning:** Use plain old salt and pepper or create special seasoning mixes. You may want to season the flour that you dredge the chicken through; you can also season the chicken itself. Some people swear that paprika enhances the flavor; others claim it's just there for color.

>> **Other prep:** Cook the chicken straight from the package (after washing and patting dry, of course); or let it soak in brine or buttermilk for a half-hour to make it juicier.

>> **Brining:** Another way to maximum your flavor and tenderness is by making a salt brine. This helps to break down the protein in the meat, allowing it to retain moisture during the cooking process. It's also a great way to infuse other flavors into the protein.

REMEMBER

The real secret to Southern Fried Chicken, however, isn't in the recipe; it's in the cooking. Properly pan-fried chicken is tender and moist (not greasy) on the inside and golden brown and crispy on the outside. Follow this advice:

>> **Keep your oil very hot.** To make sure that your chicken doesn't get greasy, you want the oil hot enough (375 degrees) that the water in the chicken stays above the boiling point during frying. The force of the steam leaving the chicken keeps the oil from being absorbed. The hot oil also makes the outside wonderfully crispy. Some tips for keeping the oil at the temperature you want are as follows:

- Use peanut oil, which has a hotter smoke point than vegetable oils or shortenings. If you're allergic to peanut oil, I suggest canola oil.

- Allow the chicken to come almost to room temperature before you cook it so that when you put it into the hot oil, it doesn't reduce the oil temperature as much as really cold chicken would.

- Don't overcrowd the chicken in the pan. Putting too many pieces in the pan causes the temperature to drop and takes it longer to heat up again.

- Use a deep-sided cast-iron skillet or Dutch oven and an iron cover. Cast iron is the cook's best friend when pan-frying. It absorbs heat evenly, eliminating hot spots, and its ability to retain heat keeps the temperature of the oil as even as possible.

>> **Brown the chicken quickly to seal in the juices.** After the initial browning, reduce the heat to allow the chicken to cook through without drying. Then return the heat to medium-high to re-crisp it before you remove it from the pan.

>> **Use tongs to turn and move the chicken.** Tongs won't pierce the chicken and let the juice escape.

>> **Drain fried chicken on a paper towel and then place it on a metal wire cooling rack in a warm oven.** This simple step keeps your cooked chicken crisp and warm. After all, what good's a crispier crust if it just gets soggy and cold while sitting in a puddle of oil?

Talking Turkey

Whereas chicken makes a popular weekday meal, turkey is usually reserved for the holidays. Part of the reason, surely, is tradition. How many preschool and kindergarten Thanksgiving celebrations *don't* include kids' handprints made into construction-paper turkeys? The other reason is the turkey's size. Even the size of a small turkey is enough to make most people think, at the very least, Sunday dinner.

Which is a shame, really. Like chicken, turkey is a healthy alternative to meats that have more fat. You can cook and use it in much the same way you do chicken. And the leftovers make great sandwiches, pies, chilis, and a bunch of other fun edibles. And who says that you have to buy a whole turkey? You can buy turkey breasts to roast. They're great for both traditional turkey recipes, like the delicious Chicken Marsala (yes, you can swap out the chicken for turkey), the classic Dutch Oven Turkey (both in Chapter 15), or those times when you just want a nice, warm turkey sandwich.

WARNING

Like chicken, turkeys can harbor salmonella. When you cook a stuffed turkey, it's not done until the internal thigh temperature is 165 degrees.

Carving Made Easy

Roasting whole chickens and turkeys is one of the easiest and most popular cooking methods for poultry. But when your beautifully roasted whole bird is done, your task is to get the meat off the bone.

You have a few options. You can pick up a knife and plunge right into the closest part. When the breast is gone (you'll probably target it first; most people who use this method do), use a table fork to pry and scrape whatever other meat you can see around the bird's legs and wings. Or you could dispense with the knife altogether and let people pull meat from the bone with their fingers. No kidding. I actually saw this done once at a Thanksgiving buffet.

Or you could carve the bird. With a sharp kitchen knife and a little know-how, you can get nice, even-size servings, more meat, and more control. And as an added bonus, you can ask the question "Light meat or dark?" without panicking that someone will actually state a preference.

Can you guess which method I recommend? Carving: It's simple, it's methodical, and it yields the most meat. Figure 7-2 provides easy, step-by-step instructions for carving poultry.

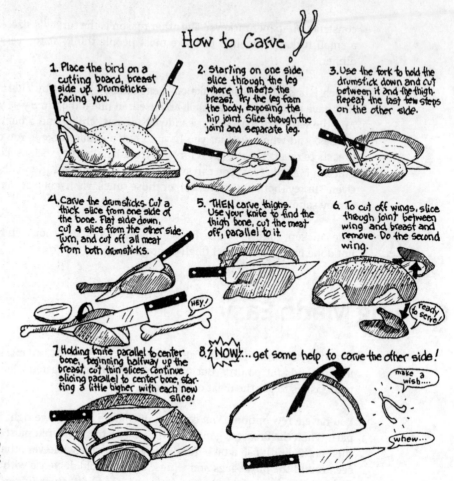

How to Carve

1. Place the bird on a cutting board, breast side up. Drumsticks facing you.

2. Starting on one side, slice through the leg where it meets the breast. Pry the leg from the body, exposing the hip joint. Slice through the joint and separate leg.

3. Use the fork to hold the drumstick down and cut between it and the thigh. Repeat the last few steps on the other side.

4. Carve the drumsticks. Cut a thick slice from one side of the bone. Flat side down, cut a slice from the other side. Turn, and cut off all meat from both drumsticks.

5. THEN carve thighs. Use your knife to find the thigh bone, cut the meat off, parallel to it.

6. To cut off wings, slice through joint between wing and breast and remove. Do the second wing.

HEY!

ready to serve!

7. Holding knife parallel to center bone, beginning halfway up the breast, cut thin slices. Continue slicing parallel to center bone, starting a little higher with each new slice!

8. NOW...get some help to carve the other side!

make a wish....

whew...

FIGURE 7-2:
Eight steps to the carving hall of fame.

Chapter **8**

Hitting the Water — Fish and Seafood

D epending on where you are in the world, you may be accustomed to either freshwater fish or saltwater fish. If you're lucky, you live in a place where you have access to both. Like with produce, fish and shellfish have seasons. Understanding the seasonality of fish in your area allows you to purchase and prepare fresher, higher quality seafood.

One of the beautiful things about cooking fish in cast iron is the enhanced texture. Cast iron's heating qualities allow you to achieve the best crispiness on the outside of the fish while skill keeping the inside tender and flavorful. Whether it's a pan-seared whole river fish or an ocean fish steak, your cast iron is unmatched in its ability to give you the best texture and flavor while cooking your favorite fish.

Here I discuss the basics of getting and cooking fish and seafood in cast iron. Chapter 16 has a wide selection of fish and seafood recipes.

Gone Fishin' — Getting the Freshest Fish Available

Sure, you can buy frozen fish — whole or in fillets. But the best-tasting fish is fresh fish, and the best way to get the freshest fish is to know your source. Nowadays supermarkets are plugged in to serving the local, regional, and national market. Some supermarket chains have corporate chefs whose job includes sourcing the best quality fish for their stores.

The better the quality of fish, the higher the cost. With higher quality fish, you also receive information about where and when the fish was caught. Some neighborhood fishmonger (for folks who are lucky enough to still have small fresh-fish shops) are still the best source for local and regional fish.

These sections identify what to look for when buying fish, important handling practices, and ways to cook fish.

Buying fresh fish — What to watch for

When you buy whole, fresh fish, look for the following:

» **Bright, clear, bulging eyes:** Sunken, cloudy eyes indicate that the fish is past its prime.

» **Firm flesh:** If you have the opportunity to touch it, the flesh should spring back slightly when you put a little pressure on it. If it feels mushy or soft, don't buy it.

» **Gills that have a reddish tint and bright-colored scales close to the skin:** The longer the fish sits in your grocer's case, the duller it becomes. The scales begin to loosen, too.

» **Smell:** Some people say fresh fish smells like the ocean; older fish smells like a tidal pool. I suppose that if you know the difference between an ocean smell and the smell of a tidal pool this description is probably all you need. However, if you're a landlubber, I suggest that you simply avoid fish that smells too fishy or that has an overpowering odor.

If you're buying fresh fillets, the same guidelines apply, with the obvious exceptions of the eyes and gills, which a fillet *shouldn't* have. But then, of course, you probably already know that.

When you buy frozen fish, make sure that it's frozen solid, that the flesh isn't discolored, and that the wrapping is tight, with little or no air between fish and wrapping.

How much fish you buy depends on whether the fish is boneless and whether you're cooking a *fish steak* (a thick, cross-section cut) or a *fish fillet* (the meat off of one side of the fish). If the fish is boneless, you need to buy less; if the bones are still in it, you need to buy more. In general, you also need more fish per serving for steaks and less for fillets. Table 8-1 gives you general serving guidelines; adjust them for the appetites at your table.

TABLE 8-1

Serving Sizes for Fish

Type of Fish	Amount Needed for a Serving
Whole fish	1 pound per serving
Whole fish (cleaned but not boned)	¾ pound per serving
Fish steaks	½ pound per serving
Fillets	¼ pound per serving

Being aware of handling precautions

Check out the following tips and recommendations for more on handling and preparing fish:

>> **Cutting:** Slightly frozen fish is easier to cut. If you want to cut a block of frozen fish, for example, do so before it's completely thawed. Your cuts will be cleaner, and the process won't be nearly as messy.

>> **Thawing:** Leave the fish in the refrigerator to thaw. *Don't* thaw fish at room temperature. If you have to speed up the thawing, place the fish in a water-proof bag and immerse it in cold water or hold it under running water.

Never refreeze thawed fish. Use it immediately after you thaw it. If something interrupts your cooking plans, you can store the thawed fish in the coldest part of your refrigerator for no more than a day.

>> **Turning:** Use a spatula to turn fish: Fish is too delicate to be turned with a meat fork. If you use a fork, you'll end up with a pile of fish pieces instead of a nice whole piece of meat. If you're grilling outdoors, use a basket made especially for grilling fish so that you don't have to touch the fish at all to turn it. You simply turn the basket.

Identifying basic cooking techniques

Fish can be steamed, poached, fried, boiled, broiled, and baked. Broiling and baking is best for fatty fish, such as mackerel, salmon, and trout. Lean fish, such as cod, flounder, haddock, tuna, and ocean perch, can be steamed and poached because they'll stay firm and moist. You can fry both fatty and lean fish.

REMEMBER

When you cook fish in cast iron, the best cooking methods are frying, broiling, pan-frying, and baking — basically, the cooking methods that don't require water. You want to avoid water-based cooking in cast iron.

The trick to cooking fish is knowing when it's done. Undercook it, and it'll feel chewy, and the flavor won't be developed. Overcook it, and you'll think you're eating chalk. Most fish is done when it flakes — that is, if the meat comes apart when you pick at it with a fork. Of course, how long it takes to reach the "flake stage" depends on the type of fish and the cooking method. In general, though, you can use these clues as guidelines to doneness:

>> Most fish, as it cooks, weeps a white liquid. So remember: No more crying; no more frying.

>> As it cooks, the color of the flesh doesn't usually change, but its opacity does. Uncooked white fish, for example, is less opaque than cooked white fish. If the flesh still seems shiny or translucent, it isn't done.

Warming Up to Salmon

Because of its huge health benefits, salmon has grown in popularity, and you can find fresh salmon (in fillet and steak form) in most grocery stores. Of course, you can still find canned salmon, too. Whether you buy a side of salmon, canned salmon, or salmon fillets depends on the recipe.

For instance, the Blackened Salmon recipe in Chapter 16, for example, calls for salmon fillets. But, because the only difference between a salmon fillet and a salmon steak is the cut (fillets come from the sides of the fish; steaks come from the cross sections), you can substitute one for the other in many recipes. Just remember to adjust the cooking time as necessary (particularly because salmon steaks can be cut to varying thicknesses).

Keep reading for an explanation of how to prepare salmon fillets and a side of salmon for cooking. For good measure, I even throw in some tips on preparing canned salmon, too, if you have a salmon-cake recipe you want to try or you just want to toss some salmon over a salad and call it dinner.

Preparing a side of salmon

At most supermarkets, you can buy a side of salmon, which is exactly what it sounds like: the meat stripped from one side of the fish. To prepare a side of salmon before cooking, follow these steps:

1. **Remove the pinbones.**

   To do this, gently run your fingers over the surface. You'll feel the *pinbones* (the small, sharp bones that are embedded in the flesh). Simply remove them with tweezers.

2. **Cut away the fatty portion of the belly (the whitish membrane).**

   Do this by holding a sharp knife at a slight downward angle and cutting just beneath this membrane. (**Note:** If you hold the knife at too steep an angle, you'll cut away the fish. It won't hurt anything, but it's a waste of perfectly good — and probably fairly expensive — salmon.)

Preparing canned salmon

Got a salmon cake recipe that you want to try with your cast iron? I don't blame you. Cast iron makes a great little salmon cake. It makes great tuna and crab cakes, too, for that matter. Just be sure to put a couple of tablespoons of oil in the bottom of the pan and let it warm up to cooking temperature before you add your cakes. Also remember to add oil between batches so that the cakes don't stick.

Of course, if you make salmon cakes, you need canned salmon. Check out how I prepare canned salmon:

1. **Dump the contents of the can into a strainer.**

2. **Sift through the contents with your fingers until you've removed all the small bones, pieces of cartilage, and skin.**

   You can leave the small bones if you want. They're edible (soft enough to be chewed) and a good source of calcium.

TIP

Honestly, this job is pretty ugly. If the task is too much for you, you can buy canned salmon that's packaged like tuna: just chunks of meat without all the yucky stuff. Or, in some recipes, such as many salmon cake recipes, you can substitute canned tuna for the canned salmon.

Preparing a salmon fillet

If your salmon fillet comes already skinned, you don't have to do anything to prepare it for cooking. You're ready to go. If it isn't skinned, however, you can remove the skin. To do so, simply run a sharp knife along the edge between the flesh and the skin and pull the skin away as you cut. Alternatively, leave the skin on the fish while cooking and then remove it afterward.

Pan-Frying Fish

You can pan-fry just about any fish: cod, trout, perch, catfish, and so on. The combination of flaky, tender flesh and golden-brown, crispy crust is a real treat, provided, of course, that the fish is fresh and the cook knows what they're doing. (For tips on buying fresh fish, head to the section "Gone Fishin' — Getting the Freshest Fish Available" earlier in this chapter.) Cast iron is ideal for pan-frying. The even heating and higher temperatures help you attain the nice crispy crust that makes pan-fried food worth the effort.

One of the favorite types of fillets to cook is trout. Here in Virginia the streams and lakes are full of fresh brook, rainbow, and steelhead trout, just to name a few. One of the things I love about my cast iron is the versatility it offers. Regardless whether you're camping or in the kitchen at home, your cast iron is always ready to take on a fresh catch. Check out Chapter 16 to see my favorite Pan-Seared Trout recipe.

These sections walk you through some basics to pan-frying fish, including breading your fish and tips and techniques.

Considering your breading options

TIP

If you ask me, a great piece of pan-fried fish starts with the best breading. When you're whipping up a breading, remember to try any of the breading combinations that follow when you pan-fry:

>> **Plain cornmeal:** Season both sides of the fish before you dredge it in the cornmeal. This simple coating is the lightest of the breading options in this list, but it's also most prone to falling away during frying. (**Note:** Flour alone usually isn't substantial enough to serve as breading; it gets absorbed right into the fish.)

>> **Egg and flour or cornmeal:** Dip your fish in egg that's been slightly beaten and diluted with water, shake off the excess, and then dredge in flour or cornmeal. Season the flour or cornmeal instead of the fillets because the egg bath rinses off your seasoning. This breading offers the lightness of the plain cornmeal breading, but the egg helps the cornmeal adhere during frying.

>> **Milk and flour or cornmeal:** Dip the fish in milk, shake off the excess, and then dredge in seasoned flour. With this breading, season the flour instead of the fillets. Like the egg and flour or cornmeal breading, this breading is also light.

>> **Flour, milk, and cornmeal:** This is called *bound breading*, or *three-stage breading*, because you dredge the fillet in flour, dip it in egg, and then dredge it in cornmeal, and it's the most substantial of the breading options. It also stays crisp the longest.

>> **Any other concoction or combination your heart desires:** Why not invent your own method? Use other liquids and experiment with other breadings — cracker crumbs, breadcrumbs, potato flakes — you name it.

So what seasonings do you use? Really anything that you want to use is fair game. Salt and pepper are obvious choices. Cayenne pepper is another popular option. You can also try any sort of seasoned pepper (such as lemon pepper) or seasoning mix (Cajun seasoning, for example). Just keep in mind that it's easy to overdo the seasoning and lose the flavor of the fish. So start light and increase the amount to suit your own tastes.

Preparing your pan-fried fish — Tips and techniques

Pan-frying differs from deep-frying in that when you deep-fry you submerge the food entirely in hot oil. When you pan-fry, you cook the food one side at a time in oil that only goes partially up the side of the food. For most fish fries, a half-inch of oil is sufficient for pan-frying. Some suggestions for pan-frying are as follows:

>> **Start at a high heat to brown the coating on each side and then reduce the heat slightly to finish.** Some people swear by higher heat and shorter cooking times; others swear by lower heat and longer cooking times. What matters is that you balance the two so that the breading doesn't burn before the fish gets done.

>> **Cut the fish into equal-size pieces.** Doing so helps even out the cooking time. Pieces that are around four to six ounces are easy to bread and fry.

>> **Keep the cooked fish warm while you cook the rest of the fish.** The best way to do this is to drain the fish on a paper towel and then transfer it to a wire rack in a warm oven.

>> **Serve the fish immediately.** Pan-fried fish (or pan-fried anything, for that matter) doesn't keep well. Have everyone at the table or within easy shouting distance when you're finishing up the last batch. Honestly, though, collecting people won't be much a problem: Most of the crowd will be hanging around hoping for a nibble anyway.

>> **When preparing saltwater fish, keep in mind that the keyword is *salt*.** Saltwater fish, thanks to the environment they swim in, their diet, and their active lifestyle in the vast ocean, tend to have a richer flavor and texture. On the other hand, if you're working with freshwater fish, you can expect milder flavors in comparison.

>> **Understand the difference between pan-frying, deep-frying, and pan-searing.** Some people interchangeably use pan-frying and pan-searing, but they mean two very different things. Here's a breakdown:

   • To pan-fry, you use enough oil to cover the item about halfway and then rely on the heat of the oil to cook the food.

RECOGNIZING HEALTH BENEFITS OF FISH

Fish and shellfish are near-perfect foods for the human body. Overall, they provide the benefit of protein without the saturated fat. Of course, different species have different nutritional composition. Freshwater fish are generally lower in fat than are marine fish, for example. But the fact is still the same: Fish is an important part of a healthy diet.

For a long time, scientists have known that fish or fish oil provides some protection against heart disease: Many have long touted the health benefits of omega-3 fats (found in fish), and studies have found that people whose diets include plenty of fish have lower levels of *leptin,* a fat-regulating hormone that, when elevated, is linked to obesity and cardiovascular disease.

Of course, people have been eating fish for thousands of years, and it probably hasn't been due to the health benefits. Even if you disregard the healthy reasons why fish should figure into your diet, you can still find a couple of reasons to eat more fish: It tastes good, and most fish dishes are easy to prepare. Try a few of the recipes in Chapter 16, and I think you'll agree.

- To deep fry, you completely submerge the food in the oil.

- To pan-sear, you rely on the pan's heat to cook the item. When you pan-sear something, you want to use about 1 to 2 tablespoons of oil that can hold a relatively high smoking point (say 375 to 410 degrees using a refined oil like a mild olive oil, avocado oil, or even peanut oil — all of which have smoking points higher than 400 degrees). Doing so allows you to achieve a good caramelization, which locks in flavor and texture.

Shellfish Galore — Shrimp, Scallops, Oysters, and More

Shellfish goes hand in hand with fish as part of a healthy diet. Keep reading to find out what to look for when you buy shellfish, how to store it safely, and how to prepare it so that it remains tender and flavorful.

In addition, because most shellfish requires some sort of preparation before you can use it in recipes (see Chapter 16), you'll want to find out how to clean, shuck, devein, and otherwise get your shellfish ready to cook.

If you've never cleaned shellfish in your life, you may be a bit grossed out at the process, but keep the following in mind: Getting shellfish that requires cleaning is one way to maintain freshness. This alone may outweigh any potential queasiness that you may suffer when you clean it yourself.

However, if that doesn't work for you, and you still can't stand the idea of cleaning shellfish yourself, you can usually buy it already prepared. This route may cost more, but if cleaning the food yourself makes it impossible for you to enjoy your meal, it's probably worth it.

The following sections take a closer look at popular types of shellfish and what you need to know about preparing them.

Getting a Grip on Shrimp

Shrimp is one of the most popular types of shellfish, and you can prepare it in your cast iron. Not all shrimp is the same though: You can't judge a book by its cover, and you can't judge a shrimp by its color. Raw shrimp can be white (more like gray, actually), brown, or pink. Check out the following types of available shrimp:

>> **White shrimp:** Coming from the Carolinas and the Gulf of Mexico, white shrimp grow to 8 inches long. Their flesh is sweet and firm.

>> **Brown shrimp:** These shrimp come from the Texas-Louisiana coast. They're usually firmer than white shrimp, so they're ideal for being battered and fried, and they have a stronger flavor, too. The boys reach around 7 inches, the girls around 9.

>> **Pink shrimp:** The color of these shrimp isn't always pink, and it's the color that often tells you where they hail from: Those from the Atlantic coast are usually brown; those from the northern Gulf coast are lemon-yellow; and those in the Florida Keys are pink. Pink shrimp are tender and sweet. They're also huge, reaching 11 inches long, which is great when the shrimp itself is the highlight of the presentation (think shrimp cocktail).

You may hear shrimp referred to as *green*, as in "How many green shrimp do you want?" or "We just got some green shrimp in today." This doesn't mean that the shrimp is actually the color green. Green shrimp is simply raw shrimp — pink, brown, or white — that's still in its shell.

Regardless of its original color, the shells of all shrimp turn red when cooked, and the meat turns white with reddish tinges.

Here I explain the best ways to purchase, store, and devein shrimp. Try out the Easy Shrimp Alfredo recipe and the Cajun Shrimp and Okra Gumbo recipes in Chapter 13, the Deep-Fried Shrimp and Oysters recipe in Chapter 16, the Sautéed Shrimp and Okra recipe in Chapter 17, and the Corn Maque Choux recipe in Chapter 18.

Buying shrimp

Shrimp comes in different sizes, from very small to very large: *Tiny, small, large, extra-large, jumbo, colossal,* and *super-duper jumbo colossal* are just a few of the adjectives indicating size. These terms are descriptive, sure, but they don't really tell you how big that *big* really is, and what one fishmonger may call *extra-large* may be another's *medium.*

Most grocery stores sell shrimp by the pound. You often see the count (how many shrimp you get per pound) accompanying the price. So, for example, shrimp with a 12 to 15 count means that a pound of that particular shrimp gives you between 12 and 15 pieces. The larger the shrimp, the fewer you get in a pound and the higher the cost (usually). Conversely, the smaller the shrimp, the more you get per pound and the lower the cost.

Storing shrimp

Ideally, you should buy shrimp fresh and use it the day that you purchase it. If you're going to eat it within the next day or two, you can store fresh shrimp in the refrigerator. Simply wrap the shrimp in ice and place it in a covered container. Then put the container in the coldest part of your refrigerator. As the ice melts, replace it and drain off the water.

If you have to store the shrimp longer than two days, place it in the freezer as soon as you bring it home. When you freeze fresh shrimp, leave the shell on, place the shrimp in a container that can hold water, such as a heavy-duty freezer bag, for example, or a covered Tupperware dish, fill it with water, and put it in the freezer. Freezing the shrimp in water maintains its freshness and flavor and keeps it from drying out. You can keep shrimp frozen this way in the freezer for up to seven months. If you're freezing shrimp in water, be sure that you divide your shrimp into useable portions.

Don't freeze thawed, shelled shrimp. The ice that surrounds it will destroy the shrimp's flesh, leaving it burned and shriveled.

WARNING

When you're ready to thaw your shrimp, place it in the refrigerator or hold it under cold running water. Never thaw shrimp at room temperature. Thawing at room temperature is a health hazard. During the time it takes the food to thaw, bacteria can grow and multiply in the warm environment. Never thaw shrimp in hot water either because the hot water temperature cooks the shrimp and makes it rubbery.

Deveining the shrimp

Most shrimp come with the head already removed, leaving just the legs, shell, and mud–vein for you to contend with. To clean and devein a shrimp at the same time (refer to Figure 8-1), follow these instructions:

1. **Using a sharp knife, make a shallow slit along the shrimp's back from the head to the tail.**

   TIP

   Buy easy-to-peel shrimp, which has already been slit.

2. **Pull the shell apart at the slit to loosen it; then pull off the shell by the legs.**

3. **Using your fingers or the tip of a knife and holding the shrimp under cold running water, pull the vein out.**

   The vein runs the length of the shrimp and is usually a mud-brown color, although sometimes it can be clear.

Cleaning and Deveining Shrimp

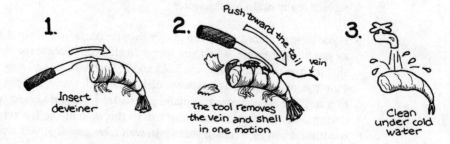

FIGURE 8-1:
How to clean and devein shrimp.

Illustration by Liz Kurtzman

Scallops: Sea or Bay, Sweet Anyway

When you go shopping for scallops, you'll find two main types:

>> **Sea scallops:** The larger of the two types of scallops, sea scallops are harvested in offshore ocean waters. They aren't as tender as bay scallops, but their meat is still sweet and moist. You get between 20 and 40 scallops in one pound.

>> **Bay scallops:** Coming from the bays and estuaries along the East Coast and into the Gulf of Mexico, bay scallops are the smaller of the two types of scallops; you usually get between 50 and 90 in a pound. The meat of bay scallops is sweeter and more succulent than the meat of sea scallops.

Buying and storing scallops

Scallops are usually sold *shucked* (removed from their shell). You can buy scallops fresh or frozen. When you buy fresh scallops, look for the following:

WARNING

>> **Color** that ranges from pale beige to creamy pink. Perfectly good scallops also have a slightly orange or pink hue due to the algae that the scallops ate.

Stark white scallops have been soaked in water to increase their weight. This doesn't hurt anything and won't ruin the taste of the scallop, and it's not done to hide any particular flaws, but it's not entirely honest. Fresh scallops are juicy enough. The increased weight from the water soak simply means that you're getting fewer scallops for your money.

>> **A sweet odor** is characteristic of fresh scallops.

>> **Fresh, moist sheens** also indicate freshness. Avoid scallops that look shriveled or dry.

When you buy scallops, refrigerate them immediately and use them within a day or two. If you're not planning to cook them within a day or two, store them in the freezer in their original container or in an airtight container. When you're ready to use them, place them in the refrigerator to thaw.

TIP

Scallops freeze well. If you run across a sale or if you buy too many, freeze the extra. Use frozen scallops within 3 months.

Removing tendons from scallops

Most scallops that you buy at grocery stores are ready to be cooked. You don't need to do anything but pop them into the fryer, skewer them on the kebob, or do whatever else your recipe calls for. Occasionally, however, the muscle that held the scallop to the shell may still be attached. This crescent-shaped muscle has a rough texture, and it toughens when cooked. To remove it, simply peel it away from the scallop.

Cooking scallops

Cooked properly, all scallops are sweet and tender yet firm. Scallops are key ingredients in soups, stews, and salads. And you can cook scallops using just about any technique you can think of — from sautéed to broiled to grilled to baked. Ruining scallops is actually pretty difficult as long as you keep these tips in mind:

TIP

>> Scallops benefit from brief cooking. If you overcook them, they turn tough. Be especially careful when you cook bay scallops, which are smaller than sea scallops and, therefore, easier to overcook.

>> Scallops are done as soon as they lose their translucence and turn opaque.

>> If you plan to put scallops in a sauce, cook the scallops and the sauce separately and combine them near the end of the cooking process. Cooking them separately ensures that your scallops won't be overcooked and that the sauce doesn't get runny when the water cooks out from the scallops.

Oysters Aren't Only for Rockefeller

Jonathan Swift's sentiment about oysters — "He was a bold man that first eat an oyster" — may be fitting, if your impression of oysters is formed by how they look and not by how they taste. Oysters, in fact, are one of the few dishes that are enjoyable both raw and cooked.

Three main types of oysters are sold in the United States:

>> **Atlantic oysters:** Also called Eastern oysters, these come from the eastern seaboard (places like Cape Cod and Chesapeake Bay). They range in size from two to five inches. Bluepoint oysters, considered best for eating and often served on the half shell, are Atlantic oysters.

>> **Pacific oysters:** Also called *Japanese oysters,* these come from the Pacific seaboard and can be up to a foot long. Because they're so big, Pacific oysters are generally cut to go in stews and soups.

>> **Olympia oysters:** These are small (usually no larger than 1½ inches) and come from Puget Sound, Washington. They're a favorite eaten on the half shell.

The following sections delve into what's important about oysters, including purchasing, storing, and shucking them. Refer to the Deep-Fried Shrimp and Oysters recipe in Chapter 16 if you're craving some oysters.

ARE YOU VULNERABLE TO VIBRIO VULNIFICUS?

Eating raw oysters does have some risk associated with it. The concern centers around *Vibrio vulnificus,* bacteria found in seafood, such as oysters, that can be passed on to people who eat raw or partially cooked seafood. Usually appearing within 16 hours of ingesting the bacteria, symptoms include nausea, chills, vomiting, diarrhea, confusion, weakness, and enlarged blood-filled or clear blisters, usually on the legs.

Although most people don't have to worry about developing the infection, for people with the following high-risk medical conditions, it can be serious and potentially fatal:

- Chronic kidney or stomach disease
- Diabetes
- Immune disorders, including HIV infection and AIDS
- Liver disease
- Lymphoma, leukemia, Hodgkin's disease

People undergoing radiation treatment or taking anti-cancer drugs or steriods (for conditions such as asthma, arthritis, and so on) should also avoid raw oysters. Pregnant women should avoid raw oysters, too. The reason isn't that pregnant women fall into the high-risk category — they're no more likely than others to contract the disease. But should a pregnant woman contract the disease, she can't take advantage of the standard treatment (tetracycline) that doctors administer to lighten the symptoms and shorten the duration of illness. Besides, when you're pregnant, you want to avoid any illness — especially a preventable one.

If you fall into one of the at-risk categories — or simply don't want to have to worry about this infection at all — all you have to do is make sure that the oysters you eat are fully cooked.

Buying oysters

You can buy oysters canned, packed (already *shucked*, or out of their shells), or live (still in their shells, which you can shuck yourself or have the grocer/fishmonger do for you). How you buy oysters depends on how you plan to prepare them.

If you're serving raw oysters, for example, buy them live and shuck them yourself. Live oysters are also better for presentation purposes: Raw oysters and some cooked oyster dishes (Oysters Rockefeller, for example) are usually presented on the half-shell — served with only the top shell removed — on a bed of crushed ice (raw) or a bed of rock salt.

TIP

When you buy live oysters, look for those whose shells are tightly closed. If the shell is open, the oyster has lost its grip, a sign that it's old, dying, or already dead.

For other recipes, however — like the ones in Chapter 16 — you can buy already shucked oysters. You can ask your fishmonger to shuck the live oysters to order (the best way to gauge freshness), or you can buy canned or packed.

>> **Canned:** Face it: Canned oysters aren't fresh. If you're making a recipe that includes the oysters primarily for flavor (oyster dressing, for example, or oyster stew), canned is okay — not great, mind you, but okay. Canned oysters have a stronger taste, and their texture can be rubbery or mushy. Freshly shucked oysters are preferable.

>> **Packed:** Packed oysters are shucked oysters that come in a plastic container. These are perishable, so you need to use them within a day or two of buying them. When you buy packed oysters, follow these guidelines:

- Make sure that the lid on the container is tightly sealed and that the package shows no signs of being bloated, which is an indication that the oysters are old. Oysters release gas as they age.

- Look for plump oysters that are uniform in size, have a good color (light beige or pale tan), a fresh smell, and a clear, not cloudy, *liquor* (the oyster juice).

- Buy the pack with the sell-by date that's the furthest into the future.

Storing oysters

Fresh oysters, packed or live, are best if you use them the day that you purchase them. If you're planning to use them within a day or two, store fresh, shucked oysters in their original container with their juice in the coldest part of your refrigerator. Cover live oysters larger shell down with a damp towel and refrigerate them for up to three days.

If you aren't going to cook your shucked oysters within a day or two, freeze them. You can freeze packed oysters in an airtight container, or you can leave them in their original container; just be sure to pour out a little of the juice so that the juice doesn't expand and cause the lid to pop. Oysters can remain in the freezer for up to 4 months. Thaw frozen oysters in the refrigerator hold or put the container under cold running water. Never refreeze thawed seafood.

TIP

Only freeze oysters that you're planning to cook. If you plan on eating raw oysters, you can forget about freezing them first.

Shucking oysters

To remove the shell of an oyster, hold the oyster cupped side down in a kitchen towel in the palm of your hand. Then follow these steps:

1. **Using the blade of a paring knife, find where the two halves separate.**

2. **Push the blade between the shells and wiggle it back and forth until you've pried the shell open wide enough to fit the top of your thumb inside.**

3. **Holding the oyster open with your thumb, cut the meat loose from the top shell (after you cut the muscle that holds the shell together, the shell pops open) and discard the top shell.**

4. **Detach the meat from the bottom shell.**

   If you're going to serve the oyster on the half-shell, save the bottom shell; otherwise, toss it.

TIP

The oyster liquor is full of flavor. Work over a bowl so that you can catch any that spills.

Tackling Soft-Shell Crabs

Next to shrimp, crabs are one of the most popular shellfish in the world. *Soft-shell crabs* are blue crabs that have been plucked from the ocean immediately after they shed their shell and before their new shell has a chance to harden. Unlike hard-shell crabs, whose meat must be removed, almost every single part of a soft-shell crab is edible. Crabs in general are noted for sweet, succulent meat, and soft-shell crabs are no exception.

Soft-shell crabs are always sold whole. They're in season from April to mid-September. When you buy soft-shell crabs, you buy them live. You can take them home and prepare them yourself for cooking, or you can ask your fishmonger to clean them for you. You may also be able to find them frozen. Try your own soft-shell crab dish with the Pan-Fried Soft-Shell Crab recipe in Chapter 16.

When you buy fresh soft-shell crabs, look for crabs that have soft, gray skin and whose odor is fresh but not overpowering. (A crab that has begun to spoil has a horrible smell.)

TIP

Most parts of a soft-shell crab are edible. You simply need to remove the mouth, the gills, and the triangular flap (called an *apron flap*) from the crab's belly. To remove these pieces, simply cut them off with a pair of kitchen shears. *Note:* You can remove the eyes if you want to, but you don't have to. The eyes are edible.

WARNING

Be aware, though, that cleaning soft-shell crabs yourself can be a horrible task. The crabs are alive when you start; they die during cleaning, specifically when you cut off the mouth (or face, if you're snipping the eyes off, too). And they may twitch a little as they die. If this tasks sounds like a bit too much for you, ask your fishmonger to clean the crabs for you.

Steaming Soft-Shell Clams

Soft-shell clams, also called *soft clams* or *long necks* (their entire body doesn't fit within the shell; the *snout,* or neck, hangs out), are a type of clam with thin shells that you can break with your fingers. You can buy soft-shell clams live in the shell or shucked. Check out the Steamed Clams with Lemon and Garlic recipe in Chapter 16.

TIP

When you buy soft-shell clams in the shell, make sure they're alive by lightly touching their necks. If they move, they're alive. When you buy shucked clams, look for plumpness and clear liquid.

Store all live clams in the shell in the refrigerator for up to two days; shucked clams can be stored in the fridge for up to four days.

REMEMBER

You can cook clams in a number of ways (steaming, baking, frying, and so on), but however you cook them, be sure not to overcook them. Like other types of shellfish, they get tough when they're overcooked.

You shuck clams in much the same way that you shuck oysters, with a variation or two:

1. **Steam the clams until they're open enough to allow you to insert the blade of a paring knife.**

2. **Pry the clam open with a paring knife and discard the top shell.**

   Be sure to hold the clam over a bowl to catch any juice that drips.

3. **Cut through the muscle that holds the meat to the bottom shell.**

   Unless you need the bottom shell, toss it, too.

The most popular East Coast soft-shell clam is the *steamer clam*, which as you can probably guess from its name, is great steamed; it's also good fried. The most famous West Coast soft-shell is the razor clam (it resembles an old-fashioned straight razor), which is also tasty steamed.

Hosting a Fish (and Shellfish) Fry — Cast-Iron Style

When you deep-fry fish and shellfish, you can't use the same guides to test doneness that you do when you steam or grill it. (These guidelines are explained in the section "Identifying basic cooking techniques" earlier in the chapter.) How do you know, for example, whether your fish is flaky, your scallops opaque, or your shrimp white when they're covered in breading or batter? Use the guide in Table 8-2.

To deep-fry fish or shellfish, you need a deep cast-iron pan. A Dutch oven or a fry kit is fine. (Head to Chapter 2 for descriptions of these items.) The key is the deep sides. You also want to have a thermometer so you can keep tabs on the temperature of your oil. Other items you may find helpful are a splatter screen and a wire basket.

TIP

When you deep-fry, keep these tips in mind:

>> You want the oil to be hot (between 350 and 375 degrees) so that the fish cooks quickly. The higher temperature also stops the batter or fish from absorbing too much oil.

TABLE 8-2

Timetable for Deep-Fried Fish and Shellfish at 375 Degrees

Breaded Fish and Shellfish	Cooking Time
Fish, 3-to-4-ounce piece	4 to 6 minutes
Clams	2 to 3 minutes
Oysters	2 to 3 minutes
Scallops	2 to 4 minutes
Shrimp	2 to 3 minutes
Battered Fish and Shellfish	*Cooking Time*
Fish, 3-to-4-ounce piece	5 to 7 minutes
Scallops	3 to 4 minutes
Shrimp	4 to 5 minutes

» To keep the temperature steady, don't overcrowd your pan. Also be sure to check the oil temperature between batches.

» When deep-frying, choose lean fish (cod, snapper, and catfish, for example). The hot oil seals the batter almost instantly, keeping the moisture and flavor inside. Don't use fatty fish (like salmon, tuna, or mackerel). The same process that keeps lean fish moist and flavorful makes fatty fish taste oily and fishy.

» If you don't have a deep-fry basket, use a slotted spoon or spatula to remove the fish from the oil.

» To keep your food warm between batches, drain the seafood on paper towels, and then place it in on a warmed wire baking rack in a 200-degree oven.

Soupy Sensations

In a nutshell, soup is a liquid food. It can be creamy or chunky, hot or cold, the main dish or its beginning course. You can make soup from any combination of meat, vegetables, fish, shellfish, and pasta; the common factor is that all soups are cooked in liquid.

Chapter 16 has some recipes on different varieties of soups, from the thick (gumbo) to the chunky (chowder). (You can also find the easy Cajun Shrimp and Okra Gumbo recipe in Chapter 13.) Cast iron is made for soups and stews. Chilis, chowders, and plenty of other soup dishes taste great and look especially appetizing when made and served in cast iron.

But keep in mind that liquid-based dishes (water- and tomato-based stocks and broths, in particular) can interact with the seasoning in your cast iron. Reserve these dishes for well-seasoned cast iron, which can tolerate the long cooking times that most soups, stews, and chilis require. If you're using a newly seasoned piece of cast iron, limit your soup repertoire to water- and milk-based soups (save the tomatoes for later) and be prepared to reseason the pan when you're done. In Chapter 3, I cover the signs that your pan requires reseasoning.

Firing up great gumbos

Gumbos are a Creole specialty. Thick like stew, gumbos traditionally include okra (of African origin, the word *gumbo* means *okra*), as well as other vegetables, such as tomato and onion, and meat, chicken, seafood, sausage, ham — or any combination of these ingredients.

Many people think of Creole cooking and Cajun cooking as essentially the same style: Both rely on green peppers, onions, and celery and use prodigious amounts of filé powder. Despite the similarities, however, they represent two different cooking styles:

>> **Creole:** French, Spanish, and African cuisines combined and more sophisticated than its Cajun counterpart, Creole cooking relies on butter and cream.

>> **Cajun:** This combination of French and southern cuisine is more down-home. Cajun cooking relies on a dark roux and plenty of animal fat — usually from pork.

You can thank the Creole cooks for gumbo; it was their creation. Cajun cooks get to take credit for jambalaya. But nowadays, you're just as likely to find a Creole jambalaya recipe as you are a Cajun gumbo.

Most gumbos begin with a dark *roux* — a flour-fat mixture used in both Creole and Cajun cooking to thicken soups and sauces. Different types of roux are distinguished by color:

>> **White roux:** This version is made with flour and butter and cooked just until it begins to turn beige. Folks use white roux to thicken white sauces and some soups.

>> **Blond roux:** Like white roux, blond roux is also made with butter, but it is cooked a little longer, until it begins to turn golden. Also, like white roux, it's used in white sauces and soups.

>> **Brown roux:** Also called *dark roux,* it can be made with butter, pork drippings, or beef fat. It's richer tasting and is cooked longer than white and blond roux; brown roux isn't ready until it turns a deep, rich brown. Brown roux is used in gumbo, as well as in dark soups and sauces.

TIP

Many gumbo (and jambalaya) recipes, including the one in Chapter 16, call for *andouille,* a heavily spiced smoked sausage. If you can't find andouille, you can substitute *kielbasa* (Polish sausage).

Talkin' chowdah

Chowders are thick, chunky soups. Traditionally, all chowders included seafood — the most famous being clam chowders — but now the term refers to any rich soup that has chunks of the main ingredient, such as corn chowder. The Seafood Chowder recipe in Chapter 16 holds true to the original chowders: Seafood is its main ingredient. In addition to clams, it includes mussels, oysters, and salmon.

Frying Frog Legs

Frogs certainly aren't new to the dinner table. The Medieval European courts served young frogs, eaten whole, as a delicacy. Nowadays, the legs are the only part of a frog that's eaten (by humans, that is), and people compare their taste, as you may expect, with that of the white meat of a chicken. Depending on what part of the world you are in, you may know frog legs as mountain chicken, which refers to the large drumstick size legs.

You can find fresh frog legs in the fish section in gourmet food markets, where they're usually sold in connected pairs. Look for legs that are plump and slightly pink. Fresh frog legs are available from spring through summer. You can buy frozen frog legs year-round. To store fresh frog legs, wrap them loosely and place in them in the refrigerator for up to two days. You can also freeze frog legs. Thaw them in the refrigerator overnight. I include the Pan-Fried Frog Legs recipe in Chapter 16.

IN THIS CHAPTER

» Making veggies shine as proteins

» Preparing a pot full of potatoes and beans

» Bursting with good nutrition: Squash

» Husking corn from the farmers' market

» Cooking okra, turnip greens, and green tomatoes

Chapter 9

Including Veggies in Your Meal

Vegetables can be so versatile and offer a wide range of possibilities in cooking. Pairing them with the reliability and adaptability of cast-iron cookware opens up even more options. Experimenting with different combinations of vegetables (and herbs) can lead to delicious and unique flavors. And with various cooking techniques like pan-frying, stir-frying, baking, braising, and caramelizing, you can unlock even more ways to prepare and enjoy vegetables in your cast-iron skillet. Get creative in the kitchen with your favorite veggies and explore the endless possibilities.

In this chapter, I explain how you can use cast iron, using simple cooking techniques and easy-to-find vegetables. But don't misinterpret *basic* as *plain*. Cast iron can help you make delicious veggie dishes. Chapters 17 and 18 cover a wide variety of veggie dishes.

Shining on Protein in Veggies

Many cultures think about vegetables as a side or an accompaniment to a meat protein. In fact, you're probably aware of the many health qualities of vegetables — the vitamins, minerals, and fiber they offer; however, many people rarely associate protein as an added benefit to eating your favorite veggies. The following vegetables are all great sources of protein:

>> **Lentils, peas, and beans:** Vegetarians have known this forever. All of these veggies offer nutrients similar to meat, poultry, and fish.

>> **Spinach:** Known as one of the most nutrient-rich vegetables on the planet, spinach is also a great source of protein. A cup of cooked spinach contains about 6g of protein.

>> **Edamame:** This veggie, immature soybeans still in the pods, packs a whopping 18g of protein per cup.

>> **Chickpeas:** Also known as garbanzo beans, this veggie can provide up to 14.5g of protein per cooked cup. Check out the Stewed Chickpeas recipe in Chapter 17.

>> **Broccoli:** This veggie is extremely versatile and can be eaten alone or added to a dish, bringing about 4g of protein to a dish per cooked stalk.

A few other veggies that have some protein include artichoke hearts, sweet corn, and asparagus (check out the Pan-Roasted Asparagus with Garlic and Parmesan recipe in Chapter 18).

Cast-Iron Favorites: Potatoes and Beans

When you think cast iron and vegetables, two standards stand out: fried potatoes and home-style green beans. Because no cast-iron cookbook would be complete without these two favorites, I discuss both.

This spud's for you

Potatoes can be mashed, fried, boiled, baked, scalloped, creamed — you name it, you can probably do it to a potato. Of all that you can do to a potato, one of the nicest is to cook it in cast iron. Potato dishes, in short, are easy to make and hard to mess up. Check out Chapter 18 for the Oven-Roasted New Potatoes recipe and Chapter 22 for the Herb-Roasted New Potatoes recipe.

Beans, beans, a wonderful fruit

Preparing traditional cast-iron bean dishes is a snap when you keep these secrets in mind:

>> **Cooking time:** The key words are *long* and *slow*. The best-tasting dishes often cook for an hour or more.

>> **Cooking liquid:** The beans pick up much of their flavor from the liquid they cook in and the ingredients you add to that liquid.

>> **Fresh or frozen beans:** Canned green beans won't hold up to long cooking times and will be mushy by the time that they're done. If you can't find fresh ones (or you don't like the quality you find), use frozen.

TIP

Preparing the beans that recipes referred to in this section for is simple. Just follow these instructions:

>> **Black beans:** Simply rinse and *sort,* that is, sift through the beans and discard out any bad beans or small stones. Yes, you may find small rocks in your beanbag. Chapter 22 has a yummy Slow-Simmered Black Beans recipe, great for when you're camping.

>> **Green beans:** Wash, *string* (remove the tough fiber that connects the halves of the bean pod), and break off the ends of the beans. Then cut or break them into the sizes called for in the recipes. Check out the Almondine Green Beans recipe in Chapter 17.

>> **October beans:** Simply shell and rinse.

>> **White beans:** Simply wash under fresh cold water and strain. Refer to Chapter 18 for the White Bean and Swiss Chard Soup recipe.

Featuring Squash

Squash has two main varieties with the most notable difference being the skin. Although squash is divided into the two following categories, these categories don't correlate to when the squash is grown:

>> **Summer squash:** Summer squash tends to have a thinner skin and can usually be eaten whole or with the skin on. These squash are eaten when the plant is still immature before the seeds and rind harden. You need to use your summer squash shortly after you purchase or pick it. Examples of summer squash include

- Crookneck

- Cymling also known as Pattypan or Patty pan

- Straight neck

- Zucchini

TIP

When you buy summer squash, pay attention to the skin and its weight. The skin should be shiny and smooth and the squash should feel heavy for its size.

» **Winter squash:** Winter squash tends to have a thicker skin, which in most cases isn't edible. These varieties are generally used when the plant is fully mature and the rind and seeds have hardened. Winter squash can be stored for several months. Examples of winter squash include

- Acorn: Chapter 18 has an Acorn Squash and Cranberries recipe.

- Banana

- Buttercup

- Butternut

TIP

When you buy winter squash, pay attention to

- **Color:** Should be a nice yellow-orange.

- **Rind:** Make sure it's thick and hard, with no soft spots.

- **Weight:** Go for heavy.

- **Size:** Be careful not to get one that's too small — a sign that it hasn't developed its full flavor. And avoid one that's too big, too. The flesh may be seedy and stringy.

The one squash that crosses over between the two seasons is delicata squash. Planted in spring and usually harvested in the fall, this beautiful squash tends to have a thinner skin and lends itself to either baking or pan searing. Check out the Rosemary Delicata Squash recipe in Chapter 18 and the Rosemary and Honey-Roasted Squash recipe in Chapter 17 for a great way to enhance its flavor.

Enjoying Corn On and Off the Cob

Although you can buy ears of corn in the produce section of any grocery, going out of your way to a farmers' market often yields the most flavorful ears. By mid to late summer, you can find all kinds of corn varieties at local produce stands. Most of what's available, though, are the sweet corns — the favorite of American consumers. Chapter 18 has a tasty Corn Maque Choux recipe.

TIP

When you shop for fresh ears of corn, don't pull back the husk to examine the kernels, as tempting as that may be. The husk protects the kernels and keeps them from drying out. In fact, some farmers make you buy any ear you even partially husk. Fortunately, you don't need to see the kernels to tell whether the ear is a good one. Using just a little pressure, run your fingers along the husk, feeling for the kernels underneath. A nice ear has smooth, plump, rounded kernels.

Appreciating the Diaspora of Southern Cuisine

Southern cuisine in the United States is so much more than food. It tells the story of a diaspora of people, places, and cultures that helped shape the perspective of American cuisine. With influences from Native Americans, West Africans, and Europeans, you can find everything from gumbo served with rice to southern stables like collard greens and fried green tomatoes. The following sections examine these veggies in closer detail.

Including okra in your dishes

Okra — known as ókùrù in Labo, a language spoken in Nigeria — is a staple in some of the most influential dishes in southern cuisine. Brought to North America by West African slaves, okra technically is a fruit, but you'd never add it to a fruit salad. Cooked as a vegetable, okra can be used as a thickener in soup or stews like Louisiana Seafood Gumbo in Chapter 16 and is also great sautéed like in the Cajun Shrimp and Okra Gumbo recipe in Chapter 13.

TIP

When you purchase okra at the store, look for tender, bright green pods that are about 4 inches long. To prepare okra, simply wash it, remove the ends, and cut it into lengths. The Sautéed Shrimp and Okra recipe in Chapter 17 highlights the okra.

Eating leaves

Turnip greens are the leafy tops of the turnip root and, in many areas, have surpassed the turnip itself for popularity and usefulness. The leaves are light green, thin, and covered in hair.

The most challenging part of cooking turnip greens is cleaning them. To clean turnip greens (or any other leafy green vegetables), follow these steps:

1. **Place the batches of greens in a sink of cold water and soak the greens for 20 minutes.**

   Don't pack the sink too full. Greens need room to float. As they rise to the top of the water, the dirt is left at the bottom of the sink.

2. **Remove the greens from the water, being careful not to stir the water, and repeat Step 1.**

3. **Rinse greens thoroughly in a colander under running water.**

4. **Remove thick veins and stems; break leaves into medium-size pieces.**

TIP

Don't want to go to the hassle of cleaning your own greens? Buy them precleaned from your grocery store. Many grocery stores carry ready-to-cook greens and collards.

When you're ready for a flavorful greens recipe, check out Southern-Style Turnip Greens in Chapter 18.

Frying green tomatoes

Native to South America and spreading around the world with the discovery of the New World, the tomato is an American classic. The Italians thought that tomatoes were an aphrodisiac when they first appeared in Italy, and the early American colonists thought tomatoes were poisonous. But the tomato is neither a love potion nor a death knell. It's another fruit that masquerades as a vegetable and comes in a number of varieties:

>> **Cherry tomatoes:** These bite-size red tomatoes are used in salads and as appetizers.

>> **Plum tomatoes:** Also known as *Italian tomatoes* or *Roma tomatoes,* they're egg-shaped and good for cooked dishes, such as sauces, stews, and chilis.

>> **Round tomatoes:** Also called *beefsteak* tomatoes, these are the workhorses of the tomato varieties. Good for slicing, dicing, quartering, or leaving whole, these tomatoes are in everything from sandwiches to salads to stews and sauces.

But a tomato doesn't have to be ripe to be delicious, as the Fried Green Tomatoes recipe in Chapter 18 proves.

Preparing Basic Veggie Crowd-Pleasers

You can add value to your veggies using cast iron in the following three ways:

>> **Griddle:** Use your favorite dressing or marinade on any vegetable and throw it on your cast-iron griddle. Its ability to hold high heat is a great way to add some char or as a chef would say, complexities to your favorite dish.

>> **Sauté:** Simply add 1 to 2 tablespoons of your favorite oil in your cast-iron skillet, preheat it for 1 to 2 minutes, and bam, add your vegetables. Cast iron is a great way to add a bit a caramelization to your seasonal vegetables.

>> **Braise:** Your Dutch oven is the perfect vessel for long cooking. Regardless whether it's braising your collard greens or creating your favorite soup, cast iron has the ability to regulate heat, which makes it the perfect vessel for indoor and outdoor cooking.

Chapter **10**

Tackling Everything Bread

Cornbread, biscuits, and pancakes are three foods that are ridiculously simple to make. They don't require you to assemble a long list of ingredients, spend much time preparing them, or master hard-to-learn cooking methods. In fact, from start to finish, you can get a version of them to the table in less than 30 minutes.

So why do cornbread and biscuits have a reputation for being hard to make? Because just as making good cornbread and biscuits is easy, making bad cornbread and biscuits is even easier — not inedible, mind you, but uninspired, flat, tough, gritty, dense, and dry. Making cornbread and biscuits isn't a mystery. In this chapter, I explain what you need to know about the ingredients and the mixing methods. (It matters, especially when you make biscuits.) Before you know it, your biscuits and cornbread will be the highlight of the meal.

REMEMBER

Anybody can make great cornbread, biscuits, pancakes, and muffins. All it takes is a little know-how and a cast-iron skillet.

The reason that cast iron is such a great cookware for breads is because it makes the crusts so much better than anything else you can find. Whether you're making yeast breads, quick breads, or pancakes, the same holds true: The even heat and dark color of cast iron produces a nicer, more consistent crust, one that's uniformly golden and tender.

Even with a well-seasoned cast-iron pan, you may have a problem with the batter or dough sticking. The solution is to simply make sure that you grease your pan with oil or shortening. Well-seasoned cast iron requires only a little greasing; newer cast iron needs a bit more. If you don't want to add calories and fat, you can use cooking spray. That's just one of many tips that awaits you as you make your way through the fabulous breads, muffins, and pancakes in this chapter. Check out Chapters 19 and 20 for recipes to make your own.

You're Cookin' Cornbreads Now

Good cornbread is moist on the inside and has a nice golden crust — not gritty, not dry. And it doesn't crumble like 2,000-year-old plaster. Cornbread is also versatile. You can serve it with soups and stews or anything else that has gravy that you want to sop up. You can crumble it for salads. You can use it in stuffing. You can even make a milkshake out of it. (No kidding! Check out Chapter 19.)

REMEMBER

The biggest factor affecting the taste and texture of your cornbread is the type of cornmeal you use. Cornmeal is divided by color and by the *milling* (grinding) method:

>> **Color:** Although the recipes in Chapter 19 specify a type of cornmeal, you can use whatever you have available. Just keep in mind that using a different meal than the one specified will influence the flavor of your bread. Here are your options:

- **Yellow:** This cornmeal, the favorite in the northern states, has a more potent corn flavor.

- **White:** Folks in the South favor white cornmeal, which has a milder corn flavor.

- **Blue:** The recipes in Chapter 19 don't call for the blue stuff. But if you're feeling creative, go for it.

>> **Grinding method:** Most of the cornmeal you buy from supermarkets is milled in either of two ways. The milling method is usually specified on the package; if it isn't specified, assume that it has been milled in the first of the following two methods:

- **Ground by steel rollers:** Many major supermarket brands are ground using steel rollers. The result is meal that's finer in texture. Cornmeal ground this way is almost always *degermed* — that is, it has had the *germ,* the outer coating of the kernel, removed. Its uniform color tells you that it's degermed cornmeal. You can store this cornmeal for up to a year in a cool, dry place, such as your kitchen cabinet or pantry.

- **Stone ground:** In this milling method, which is sometimes called *water ground,* the corn is ground with millstones. The result is a meal that's slightly coarser in texture than cornmeal ground by steel rollers. Cornmeal that's stone ground isn't completely *degermed,* which means that you can see flecks of different colors in the meal. You need to store stone-ground meal in an airtight container in your refrigerator or freezer because of its higher oil and moisture content. Simply bring it to room temperature before you use it.

REMEMBER

People, like cornmeal, fall into categories: those who have a favorite type of cornmeal and those who don't care and will use whatever's available. If you know that you like sweet cornbread, for example, or cornbread that has a crisper rather than moister texture, you can buy the cornmeal that produces the kind of cornbread you like. If you're not a cornbread aficionado and have a container of name-brand cornmeal that you want to use, use away. Remember, it's *all* good.

Ain't Nothin' Better than Biscuits

Biscuits are one of the simplest quick breads to make — if you know how. But many people don't know the tips and tricks, and that's probably why biscuits intimidate many cooks.

REMEMBER

Making a good biscuit requires a little know-how. A basic biscuit requires only four ingredients:

>> Flour

>> Fat (usually shortening)

>> Leavener

>> Liquid

So, as you can see, the ingredients aren't the key. When you make biscuits, the *process* — how you combine the ingredients — is more important than the ingredients themselves.

Keep reading to find out what it takes to make light, fluffy biscuits. You can find plenty of recipes in Chapter 19 that let you show off your new skill.

Cutting to the biscuit basics

You use a certain mixing technique when you make biscuits: First, cut the shortening or other fat into the dry ingredients using a pastry cutter or two knives, and then stir in the liquid. This simple technique doesn't seem fraught with peril but it is. Cutting in the shortening is the part that gives people the most trouble, whether they realize it or not.

TIP

When you cut *(rub)* in the shortening, you have to make sure that it's evenly distributed throughout the mixture *without* overmixing it. You can do this by hand or use two forks to avoid sticky fingers. The mixture should resemble coarse crumbs (or look like peas); if it has the consistency of paste, you've gone too far. These suggestions can help:

>> **Keep your shortening or butter cold.** Never make biscuits with butter that's warmed to room temperature. For that matter, refrigerate or freeze your shortening for a while to give it a nice chill before you begin. If your shortening or butter is too warm, you'll end up with a paste, which isn't good for fluffy biscuits.

>> **Cut the shortening in quickly** — as fast as you can without throwing dough all over your countertop. Use your fingertips (*not* your whole hand — it's too warm), two knives, a pastry blender, a food processor, or an electric blender on pulse. A *pastry blender* has about three to four thin blades attached to a handle. It's used to quickly cut shortening into flour. Depending on the type of recipe, especially for quick recipes, a food processor is absolute okay to use. Unlike a bread dough, biscuit dough is a lot more forgiving.

TIP

When you make biscuits, you also want to keep the following in mind:

>> **Don't overknead your dough.** Overkneading makes your biscuits tough.

>> **Don't roll out the dough too thin.** You don't want it any thinner that ½ inch. Better yet, don't roll the dough out at all. Instead shape it by hand.

>> **Don't leave out the salt,** which you may be tempted to do if you're watching your salt intake. The salt activates the leavening ingredients. Without it, your biscuits won't rise.

>> **For crisper sides, place biscuits so that they won't touch.** For softer sides, place biscuits so they're barely touching.

Whipping up traditional biscuits

Although you can use any type of flour when you make biscuits, the type does make a difference in the consistency of the biscuit. Consider the following:

>> **All-purpose:** Also known as *strong flour,* all-purpose flour makes the crust crisper and the crumb drier.

>> **Cake:** Also known as *soft flour,* cake flour gives your biscuits a tenderer, moister, more cake-like texture.

>> **Self-rising:** Known for its convenience, self-rising flour is easy to use and is a good option if you want consistent results.

>> **Spelt:** This is a popular alternative to traditional wheat flour that contains more protein and fiber than conventional wheat flour. Spelt is also lower in gluten, making it easier to digest.

>> **Whole-wheat:** This flour is famous for its distinct nutty flavor and it creates a dough that's denser and heartier. Packed with fiber and nutrients, it's the healthier option to choose.

>> **00 flour:** This flour is famous for its finely ground consistency, resulting in a biscuit dough that's typically more tender and lighter.

Breads at Home on the Range and in the History Books

Bread is, I believe someone once said, the staff of life. Well, staff of life or not, bread certainly has had a popular run over the years. It's been at the top of the charts since our prehistoric ancestors first realized that grain mixed with liquid wasn't just a mess but an edible concoction.

Early breads were simple breads with a simple purpose: to feed hungry people. Bread owes its historical popularity to other factors as well:

>> Bread is transportable and an ideal food for travelers. Think about it. You can't eat a salad while you're driving, but you can eat a bagel. Hardtack, for example — a dried, unleavened, and unsalted bread — has been a staple of sailors' diets since the 1800s.

>> Bread is easy to make. Believe it or not, you don't need a bread machine to turn out a nice loaf, and people 100 years ago made loaves daily, often on the open range or prairie.

>> Nothing beats bread for sopping up juices and gravy — absolutely mandatory for an era when the axiom "Waste not, want not" wasn't just a hen-pecking catchphrase but a guide for survival.

Chapter 19 has some recipes you can try. What they may lack in style they more than make up for as culinary Americana.

Baking Easy Yeast Breads

Few things beat a warm, fresh loaf of bread or rolls hot from the oven. But many cooks nowadays leave the actual bread- and roll-making to the pros. If they decide to do it themselves, they rely on a bread machine. And, really, who can blame them? Producing yeast breads that rise the way that they're supposed to, have golden crusts, and are light and airy inside is a feat many cooks struggle with. But I'm here to tell you that it is possible.

TIP

When you make yeast breads, keep these pointers in mind:

>> Use warm water to activate the yeast. Water that's too hot (warmer than 125 degrees) kills the yeast; water that's too cold (below 105 degrees) makes the yeast sluggish. A good temp is between 110 and 115 degrees.

>> Most recipes expect that you'll add some flour while you knead the dough, but many people keep adding flour until the dough is no longer sticky. The result is bread that's tough and dry. To avoid this problem, just cover your hands in a thin film of oil or shortening and keep kneading. As you do, the flour in the dough begins to absorb more of the liquid in the dough, and the dough grows less sticky.

Flipping Over Pancakes

The heat is what turns out perfect pancakes. A hot griddle and a hot muffin pan are musts. The heat helps with the rise and keeps the pancakes tender, but over-cooking makes them tough and rubbery. Chapter 20 has some pancake recipes you can add to your arsenal.

WHAT TO DO IF THE SYRUP RUNS DRY

If you discover that you don't have any syrup, don't panic. Don't make any sudden movements or rash decisions — such as throwing out those golden griddle cakes. Try one of these suggestions:

- Spread butter and jam or marmalade on top.
- Serve your pancakes with cut fresh fruit and whipped cream to please the kids.
- Serve them with a dollop of ricotta or small curd cottage cheese.
- Use the pancakes as bread and wrap sausage or bacon in them or make a scrambled egg taco.
- Make your own syrup: Heat up 1 cup corn syrup and 1 tablespoon butter until the butter melts. Then add ¼ teaspoon maple flavoring and just a touch of vanilla extract.

TIP

When you're making pancakes for a crowd and want to keep the pancakes warm until all are done, line the bottom of a baking sheet with a clean dish towel and preheat it in a 200-degree oven. As you remove pancakes from the griddle, put them on the lined baking sheet. (The dishtowel keeps the bottom pancakes from cooking on the baking sheet and getting hard.) If you have a convection setting on your oven, *don't* use it when you're keeping pancakes warm. The circulating air will just dry them out. And no one likes dry pancakes.

REMEMBER

When you make pancakes, don't turn them until they're ready — the top will be full of bubbles — and turn them only once. Also be sure to keep the griddle hot and well-greased through the entire cooking process.

Setting the Pace with Quick Breads and Muffins

Quick breads and muffins rely on chemical leaveners (baking soda and baking powder) rather than yeast for their rise. (See the section "Baking Easy Yeast Breads," earlier in this chapter.) Chapter 20 has several recipes. You can use several mixing methods when you make quick breads, but the two most common are

>> **Method 1:** Mix the dry ingredients separately from the wet ingredients and then combine them.

>> **Method 2:** Cream the sugar and eggs until they're light and fluffy, stir in the eggs and extracts, and then alternately add the wet and dry ingredients into the creamed sugar and eggs. The creaming method is a crucial step that allows you to create a light and fluffy texture by combining the fat and sugar.

TIP

Regardless of the mixing method you use, when you combine the wet and dry ingredients, don't overmix your batter. Doing so results in tough muffins and breads. Simply stir gently — don't beat. Mix the ingredients just enough to incorporate all the flour. (You don't want flour streaks.) But don't mix so much that the batter is smooth.

Chapter **11**

Making Delectable Desserts

When I was a kid, my favorite dessert was cheesecake. I was incentivized to eat whatever was on my plate so that I could indulge in about two to three slices of dessert. Dessert has the ability to change the perspective of any meal.

From pineapple upside cake to cobblers and pies, cast iron has the ability to regulate heat, making it the perfect vessel to create and re-create some of those memorable dishes from your childhood, or create new ones. This chapter includes general tips and suggestions for making cast-iron desserts. You can find an array of dessert recipes in Chapter 21.

Having Your Cake and Eating It Too

Most cakes include relatively few ingredients. You have your four basic ingredients — fat, flour, sugar, and eggs. Leavener, liquid, and flavoring are also commonly found in cake recipes. The basic procedure is pretty simple, too: Whip the ingredients into a batter, pour the batter into a pan, and bake.

Amazingly, these few ingredients, combined in different amounts and mixed in slightly different ways, create a bounty of different cakes. But you have to get the proportions right.

TIP

Following are some tips to ensure that your cakes come out right:

>> **Use the type of flour specified in the recipe.** Different flours have different protein levels, and this level directly affects how your cake rises. For general cake baking, use all-purpose flour.

>> **Use the finest grain sugar that you can find.** If a recipe calls for sugar and the granule is too large, it won't hold enough air when it's creamed or beaten into eggs. The sugar also may not dissolve completely as the cake cooks, leaving you with dark spots of crystallized sugar.

>> **Bring the eggs to room temperature.** Because cold eggs hold less air, your cake will be lighter when you use eggs at room temperature. Beating your eggs also incorporates more air, enhancing your cake's rise.

Don't let eggs stand at room temperature for longer than an hour. Researchers indicate that after that time, they become a health risk.

WARNING

>> **Let your butter warm to room temperature before you add it.** Butter that's too cold doesn't cream well; butter that's too warm breaks down during the creaming process, so don't let it get soft. Also, unless otherwise specified, use unsalted butter for a better tasting cake.

>> **Use pure vanilla extract.** For the sake of taste, don't use imitation.

>> **Roast nuts before you use them.** They're more flavorful that way.

CHEMICAL REACTIONS TAKE THE CAKE

When you bake a cake, a variety of chemical reactions occur:

- **Flour,** which gives the cake its substance, contains *gluten,* a protein that, when activated, makes the flour bind together and retain gas. This protein, combined with the protein from the egg, creates an elastic pocket that traps the gas released from the leaveners.

- **Leaveners** produce gas when they come in contact with liquid and when the heat from the oven activates them. Baking powder and baking soda are the most common ones used in cakes.

- **Sugar** adds sweetness, volume, and color.

- **Eggs** bind the other ingredients and add color, flavor, and moistness. Eggs act as a leavener, too: When you beat eggs, you create millions of tiny air pockets that, when heated, expand and make the cake rise.

- **Butter** adds richness and moistness.

- **Milk** adds moistness, flavor, and color to your cake. It also changes the protein in the flour to gluten and jump-starts the chemical reaction in the leaveners.

Together, all these ingredients give your cake its color, flavor, texture, moistness, and rise.

Perfectly Easy Pastries and Other Super Sweets

You can make traditional one-crust and two-crust pies in a cast-iron skillet. Just follow the directions for any pie recipe you have, but instead of using a pie plate, use a cast-iron skillet — a 9- or 10-inch skillet is a good substitute.

REMEMBER

Don't worry about your pie crust sticking to your skillet. The high-fat content of pastry combined with a seasoned cast-iron pan makes for a stick-free crust.

The trickiest part of making a good pie is making a good crust. Good pie crusts are flaky, tender, and golden. They literally melt in your mouth.

TIP

Following are a few guidelines for nailing your pie crust every time:

>> Cut the shortening or butter into the flour until the mixture resembles coarse, pea-size crumbs.

>> Add only the amount of liquid that the recipe specifies. Too much water or milk, as the case may be, makes the dough tough. If the dough is dry, add a little more shortening or butter instead.

>> Make sure that your water or liquid is ice cold. As the shortening or butter in the dough warms through handling, the dough becomes pasty — a bad thing for a tender crust. The cold liquid helps you avoid this problem.

>> Don't overflour your pastry board or countertop. If your dough is too soft to roll out easily, stick it in the refrigerator to firm it up a bit and then try again.

>> Don't overwork the dough. Mix the ingredients and roll the dough as expediently as you can. Too much handling makes the crust tough.

And don't limit yourself to pies (and cakes) when you want to make sweet temptations in cast iron. Cobblers and candies also fit the bill.

Creating Dutch Oven Desserts

Who doesn't like dessert? Dessert, after all, was the reason that the main dish was invented. And cast iron is desserts' best friend. Just because you're camping — or roughing it out in the wide-open spaces of your RV — doesn't mean that you can't enjoy a few civilized niceties, such as Easy Pineapple Upside Down Cake in Chapter 21. If you can find a way to keep ice cream or whipped cream cold while hiking the trail, these delectable desserts become decadent delights when served a la mode.

» Digging out a pit for your cast-iron coals

» Getting in touch with other camp-oven enthusiasts

» Going ape for campfire desserts

Chapter **12**

Cooking around the Campfire

Cast iron is a nearly perfect outdoor cookware. It travels well, cooks evenly, and cleans easily — just what you need when you're sometimes miles from home and without the luxuries that you take for granted, such as electric or gas ranges and running water. Anyone can cook in the great outdoors, preparing everything from simple one-dish entrees and desserts to complete multi-course meals. Doing so successfully isn't rocket science. It just takes a few hot coals, the right tools, and a few tricks up your sleeve. This chapter tells you what you need to know. Turn to Chapter 22 for some easy recipes for the beginning camp cook.

If you're just beginning as an outdoor cook, or you haven't had much success in the past and want to try again, this chapter is for you. It tells you about the tools you need (including pan types) and how to control your cooking temperatures. I also offer advice on outdoor-cooking techniques.

Outdoor cast-iron cooking is a big-time hobby for many people. Because you may become its next enthusiast, you can also find information in this chapter about how to locate others who share this interest.

Roundin' Up the Outdoor Hardware

Anyone can cook outdoors, using any kind of cast-iron cookware they have, but most people rely on one or two pieces: Dutch ovens (called *camp ovens*, when they're designed for outdoor use) and skillets with lids. With either of these pieces, you can cook any dish. (*Note:* All the recipes in Chapter 22 use a skillet or a Dutch oven.) But many outdoor cooks consider other items necessary, too.

Cookware — Anything you want

Although you can use any Dutch oven outside, cookware that has legs and a flanged lid, called a camp oven, makes outdoor cooking a little easier. The legs let you keep the Dutch oven itself off the coals (and thus avoid getting the cookware too hot), and the flanged lid lets you put coals on top without worrying about them rolling off onto the ground or, when you lift the lid, into your food. (See Chapter 2 for more on Dutch ovens and camp ovens.)

If you're shopping for a camp oven, look for one that has a reversible lid. These lids function as both a lid and, when flipped over, a griddle. The griddle side is usually slightly concave, which keeps anything you cook in it — pancakes, eggs, bacon, and so on — from spilling or dripping over into the coals.

Like Dutch ovens, you can also find skillets with flanged lids and legs that keep the bottoms of the pans off of the hot coals.

If you don't want to spring for skillets and ovens designed specifically for outdoor use, you can use a *spyder* (essentially a cast-iron trivet) to turn any stovetop cast-iron skillet or Dutch oven into an outdoor cooking machine. See the next section for more info on spyders.

Going for convenience and comfort

Although the following items aren't absolutely necessary when you cook outside, they can make your task a little easier and safer:

>> **Brush:** You use a brush to remove ashes and coals from on top of lids and around your pan. Any plain old ash brush will do.

>> **Oven gloves:** These gloves are essentially extra-long, extra-thick fire-resistant oven mitts that are sometimes made of leather.

>> **Long utensils:** You want utensils that are as long as possible and that you can still comfortably and safely wield. The longer the utensil, the farther from the

fire you are. You need the standards — spoon, spatula, meat fork, and anything else you need to stir, turn, or prod your food. But you may also want to invest in a pair of tongs or a poker that let you move charcoal coals around safely.

>> **Heavy-duty aluminum foil or metal trash can lid:** Using aluminum foil or an upside-down aluminum trash can lid (placed in such a way that it doesn't wobble) can help you control the temperature of the coals, especially if the ground is damp or cool. See the section "Adjusting for weather conditions" later in this chapter for more information.

>> **Lid hook:** Also called a *lid lifter,* this tool, shown in Figure 12-1, lets you remove the lid from your camp oven or skillet without spilling coals and ashes into your dish. Because they're generally long (around 18 inches), they also keep you away from the heat, and all the hair on your arms intact. Lid hooks come in a variety of lengths. Choose the longest one you can that still lets you comfortably lift the lid.

FIGURE 12-1:
Give that lid a lift.

Photograph courtesy of Lodge Manufacturing Co.

>> **Spyder:** Shown in Figure 12-2, a spyder (also known as a *trivet* or *lid stand*) is a three- or four-legged stand that can hold your pans over the fire as the food cooks, functioning as the "legs" for any flat-bottomed cast iron that you have, essentially turning it into outdoor cookware. Just place the spyder over the coals and your pan on top of the spyder. Instant legs! It can also serve as a place to set a hot lid when you're checking on the food. These come in varying heights.

FIGURE 12-2:
A spyder without
a web.

Photograph courtesy of Lodge Manufacturing Co.

TIP

If you use a spyder, you may want to have two or three of different heights so that you can adjust how close your pan is to the coals.

>> **Charcoal chimney starter:** A charcoal chimney starter (see Figure 12-3) is beneficial for starting hot coals. You're also going to need to replenish the hot coals that you use, especially for dishes that cook for a long time. This tool lets you keep extra coals ready and nearby as you cook.

FIGURE 12-3:
Start your
chimneys.

*Photograph courtesy of Lodge
Manufacturing Co.*

Controlling Temperature

In principal, outdoor cooking is just like indoor cooking: Using the right cookware and the right temperature, you can make any dish your heart — or your hungry brood — desires. The main difference between the two is *how* you control the temperature. Your stove has control dials; the rocks or grassy hill that you build your campfire on — even the fire pit in your own backyard — probably won't.

REMEMBER

When you're cooking outside, your heat source is either wood or charcoal. If you're using charcoal, you have three choices:

>> **Briquettes:** This type is most commonly used for outdoor cooking and is readily available at any supermarket, hardware, or discount department store. It takes a little longer to heat up but burns for about 45 minutes after it gets going.

>> **Hardwood lump:** This charcoal is made from leftover wood. The benefit of using this type is that it burns hotter, but that also means it burns faster.

>> **Quick-light:** This charcoal only takes a few minutes to light thanks to the chemicals added to the charcoal, but on the downside it only holds heat for about 20 to 30 minutes at a time.

The recipes in Chapter 22 use briquettes when cooking to give you a better burn and more time back during the cooking process.

REMEMBER

When you cook outside, you generally don't put your cookware over an open flame. With an open flame, the only way that you can control the cooking temperature is to lift and lower the pan, a task that, although possible, isn't easy either. (To make raising and lowering the vessel manageable, you need a tripod or cooking rig.)

The heat source isn't the only added variable when you move from the cozy confines of your kitchen to the great outdoors (or the great backyard). You also have to contend with air temperature, wind, humidity, and the other climactic conditions that Mother Nature doles out. Temperature control in outdoor cooking is as much an art as a science. You control cooking temps with the following:

>> Number of coals and their placement on the lid and under the pan

>> Location of the heat source

>> Adjustments for weather conditions

>> Your cooking techniques

I go into much greater detail about each of these variables in the following sections.

REMEMBER

The best way to figure out how to control your cooking temperatures is simply to practice and experiment. Before you know it, you'll be cooking up a storm, maybe even in a storm.

Knowing how many coals and where to place them

To control the temperature when you cook in a camp oven, the number of coals you use and where you put the coals are key factors. For some cooking techniques (boiling, frying, and sautéing, for example), you put all your coals under the pan. For these techniques, obviously, you don't need a lid. For other techniques (such as baking and simmering, for example), you arrange some coals on top (hence you need a lid) and some coals underneath, as shown in Figure 12-4. Simple enough.

Well, almost. Keep reading for explanations of the finer points.

FIGURE 12-4:
Pans designed for outdoor cooking have flanged lids and feet so that you can place coals on top and underneath.

Photograph courtesy of Lodge Manufacturing Co.

Counting coals

Many of the recipes in Chapter 22 and many recipes in other outdoor cast-iron cooking books tell you how many coals to place on the lid and how many to place underneath your camp oven or skillet to get the appropriate temperature.

The trick is figuring out how many coals you need when the recipe doesn't specify. Fortunately, cooking temperatures are about the same for indoor conventional ovens as they are for outdoor cooking. So if you'd roast a chicken indoors in a 325-degree oven, you'd use the same temperature when you roast a chicken outdoors. Table 12-1 shows you how many coals you need to attain certain temperatures. The next section tells you where to put these coals for different cooking techniques. With this information, you can convert indoor oven recipes (baking, roasting, and so on) for use outdoors.

TABLE 12-1 **Total Number of Coals to Reach Certain Temperatures**

Dutch Oven	325 degrees	350 degrees	375 degrees	400 degrees	425 degrees	450 degrees
8-inch	15	16	17	18	19	20
10-inch	19	21	23	25	27	29
12-inch	23	25	27	29	31	33
14-inch	30	32	34	36	38	40

TIP

To increase the temp, you simply add coals; to decrease the temp, you remove them. Although not precise, assume that every coal adds between 10 and 20 degrees of heat. When you just want to keep your food warm, remove all the coals except for a few under and over the dish.

REMEMBER

These guidelines are just that — guidelines. If no other factor impacts the actual heat of the coals, the conversions in Table 12-1 are pretty accurate. But add in the factors that often affect cooking temperatures outdoors (wind, air temp, and so on), and you're going to have to make adjustments. See the section "Adjusting for weather conditions" for information later in this chapter.

Understanding heat sources and cooking methods

You also need to figure out where the coals should go: on the lid, underneath, or both. How you divide the coals and where you place them depend on the cooking method.

CONVERTING OLD RECIPES

Many old recipes don't specify temperature settings. Instead, they offer vague descriptions — to the modern cook's thinking, anyway. If you find old recipes — a common occurrence when you go hunting specifically for cast-iron recipes — don't be surprised if the only temperature guide is "Cook (whatever) in a slow oven until done." Some equivalents are as follows:

Description	Temperature Equivalent
Slow	250 to 350 degrees
Moderate	350 to 400 degrees
Hot	400 to 450 degrees
Very hot	450 to 500 degrees

In a cast-iron skillet or Dutch oven, you can braise, bake, boil, simmer, sauté, deep-fry, and just about anything else. You can perform all these cooking techniques outside, too. You just need to know where most (or all) the heat should come from. If you're baking, for example, you need the heat to surround your pan; if you're frying, all the heat should come from underneath. Table 12-2 outlines where the heat source should be for the various cooking methods.

TABLE 12-2   **Location of Heat Source**

Cooking Method	Where the Heat Should Come From	Coal Distribution
Baking	More from the top than bottom	For every coal under the bottom, you need three on the lid.
Boiling	Bottom	All coals under the bottom.
Frying	Bottom	All coals under the bottom.
Roasting	Top and bottom equally	Same number of coals on the lid and under the bottom.
Sautéing	Bottom	All coals under the bottom.
Simmering	More from the bottom than top	For every coal on the lid, you need four under the bottom.
Stewing	More from the bottom than top	For every coal on the lid, you need four under the bottom.

Spacing out: Oooh, pretty patterns!

When you know how many coals you need and where they should go (refer to Tables 12-1 and 12-2), you need to arrange them properly. You can't just lump a bunch of coals under the pan and slap another bunch of coals on top. If you do, you create hot spots that can either burn your food or make it cook unevenly. Here's how to arrange the coals:

>> **For coals under the pan:** Space the coals evenly in a circular pattern, starting at least ½-inch within the outer edge of the pan's bottom.

>> **For coals on the lid:** Space the coals evenly in a checkerboard pattern.

Adjusting for weather conditions

You also have to take the weather into account. The air temperature, wind speed, humidity levels, ground temperature, and so on can affect the temperature of your coals. With this information, you can add or subtract coals as necessary to get the temperature that you want.

Your coals will burn hotter if

>> You have warm breezes or wind.

>> You're cooking in direct sunlight.

>> The air temperature is high.

Your coals will be cooler if

>> The humidity is high.

>> You're cooking in the shade.

>> You're cooking at high altitudes.

>> The ground temperature is cool or the ground is damp.

TIP

To take ground temperature out of the mix, consider not putting your coals directly on the ground. Instead, use heavy-duty aluminum foil, an old charcoal grill pan, or an overturned aluminum trash can lid as a base for your fire. If you find that you cook outdoors a lot, you may want to use a metal table specifically designed for outdoor cooking. The table has a lip around the edge that keeps your coals from falling off of it and a metal wall on three sides that keeps the wind away. Such a table accomplishes what the other bases do, plus because you're cooking on a table you don't bend over all the time.

What a hole in the ground! Outdoor cooking techniques

Cooking outdoors can be as authentic or as convenient as you want it to be. After all, technically speaking, you can place your cast-iron pot inside a covered barbecue grill, set the temperature to whatever you want and call yourself an outdoor cook. Most people, however, use one of the following techniques:

>> **Cooking a single dish over hot embers or coals.** This technique is the one that the recipes in Chapter 22 require. It's the easiest cooking technique for the beginning outdoor cook because you only have to manage a single dish at a time.

>> **Stacking pans over hot embers or coals to cook more than one dish at a time.** This technique (see Figure 12-5) lets you cook plenty of food without taking up any more ground space than single-dish cooking requires. You actually stack cast-iron pans on top of each other over a heat source. The food that requires the most heat goes on the bottom of the stack, and the food that requires the least goes on top. As you gain more experience with outdoor cast-iron cooking and want to broaden your repertoire, you may find yourself stacking pans.

FIGURE 12-5:
Stacked ovens let you cook more than one item at a time.

Photograph courtesy of Lodge Manufacturing Co.

This technique works best for foods that require an even distribution of heat rather than foods that require that the heat source come primarily from the top or the bottom of the pan. (Refer to the section "Understanding heat sources and cooking methods" earlier in this chapter for information.)

A challenge in stacked cooking is that, if you want to check or stir a dish that isn't on the top of the heap, you have to move all the pans above it. Of course, some would argue that this is part of the fun.

>> **Cooking in a pit:** If you're so inclined, you can actually bury your Dutch oven in a pit of coals. In this method, you build a fire in a hole that you've dug and lined with aluminum foil or stone and, when the coals are ready, place your covered cast-iron dish inside, cover it with dirt and more coals, and let it cook. This cooking technique is slow. Most dishes cooked in this method take 4 to 6 hours. It's best reserved for dishes that don't need to be tended and that (for obvious reasons) are covered.

More tips for the outdoor cook

Cooking outdoors isn't rocket science, but it does take a little special know-how. With the basic knowledge in this chapter and the following tips, chances are, your outdoor cooking experience will be a positive one:

>> When you figure outdoor cooking times, don't forget to figure in how long it takes to get your coals ready. For charcoal, start your coals 15 to 20 minutes before you need them.

>> If a dish takes a long time to cook, have hot coals available to replenish the ones you use up. (A charcoal chimney starter is good for this. See the section "Going for convenience and comfort" earlier in the chapter.) Add new coals when the old coals start to break up. When you add new coals, increase the amount proportionally on both the top and bottom. Don't add only to the top, for example, or you'll end up with uneven cooking.

>> To keep the cooking temperature even within the pan or Dutch oven, rotate the lid and the pan in opposite directions regularly. Every 10 to 15 minutes, give the lid a quarter turn in one direction and the pan or Dutch oven a quarter turn in the other direction.

>> If you have to move coals around (and chances are you will, either to replenish the coals you've used up or to increase or decrease the temperature by adding and removing coals), use long-handled tongs and wear thick oven mitts. After all, you're playing with fire, and what fun is cooking outdoors if you spend all your time indoors rubbing salve on your burns?

>> When you remove the lid to check on your dish or rotate the lid, be careful not to let ashes from the lid drop into your food. When the dish is done, go ahead and brush the ashes away entirely.

REMEMBER

When you're first starting out, start simple. Although you can cook anything in a Dutch oven, try your hand at easy dishes (stew, chili, cobbler, and roasted chicken, for example) first. The recipes in Chapter 22 are all great beginner recipes: easy to assemble, easy to make, and delicious.

Using a Dutch Oven to Cook Main Dishes

Dutch ovens are great for main dishes. The deep sides and tight-fitting lids are great for roasting, braising, and slow cooking — cooking techniques that let the flavors of the foods you cook blend together in delicious combinations. Some of the recipes in Chapter 22 let you try out these and other cooking techniques that you can easily adapt for other dishes. Keep the following few general recommendations in mind:

>> When you roast meat in a Dutch oven, use a trivet. Dutch ovens don't have the raised bottoms that many traditional roasting pans have. To keep your meat or poultry out of its own juices and dripping, you need to use a trivet or a roasting rack.

>> Brown your meat before you add the other ingredients, such as vegetables, sauces, and so on. If the recipe calls for you to cook your meat and vegetables at the same time, be sure to brown or sear the meat first. Doing so gives the meat a nice color and seals in the juices.

4

Time to Cook — Delicious Recipes Galore

Discover how to cook smarter and easy cast-iron recipes.

Make tasty red meat, chicken, and seafood entrees.

Introduce vegetables in your cast-iron cooking.

Focus on traditional cast-iron favorites, such as cornbreads, muffins, pancakes, and other breads.

Add some delectable desserts to your cast-iron cooking menu.

Prepare for your next camping and outdoors trip with some tasty recipes.

Get ready for the next big game with some tailgating recipes.

Add some international flair to your cast-iron cooking.

Chapter **13**

Cook Smarter, Not Harder — Easy Recipes

n the professional kitchen, chefs practice something called *mise en place*, which means everything in its place, or in other words, organizing yourself before you cook. Cooking smarter isn't about being the fastest person or having the best cooking techniques; it's about working effectively so you can efficiently complete your dish.

TIP

Even home cooks like you can practice *mise en place*. Try the following tips:

» Prep ahead and organize the items you need by putting them on a tray or bowl.

» Streamline your prep by chopping all the ingredients in advance and storing them in containers or plastic baggies. You can do this task the day before to save time when cooking.

» Before you start cooking, arrange your cooking station in a way that gives you easy access to all the necessary tools and ingredients, allowing for a good workflow.

>> Begin your week by planning your meals. In about an hour, you can select your favorite recipes and create a grocery list, ensuring you have all your *mise en place* needed for the week.

In this chapter, the recipes were thoughtfully curated with one goal in mind: to empower you on your culinary journey. Whether it's breakfast, lunch, or dinner, these recipes are intended to be simple, accessible, and above all, truly delectable.

Starting Your Day with Easy Breakfast Recipes

As a chef for many years, I'd skip breakfast and only have coffee. The repetition of that led to brain fog and a decrease in energy. By lunchtime, I was extremely hungry or, as my friend Tracy would say, "you become hangry" — a blend between hungry and angry. The meals in this section offer you substance and add value to your morning meal.

USING YOUR CAST IRON TO MAKE BREAKFAST STAPLES

By reading this book you want to be better at using cast iron. Good news: You can practice and make these simple breakfast staples; they don't require a lot from you:

- **Scrambled eggs:** A quick scrambled egg is all you have time for, and your cast iron is the perfect place to land your egg. Make sure your pan is properly seasoned before cooking. Head to Chapter 2 for a quick refresher on how to get the perfect patina.

  Preheat your pan over medium heat for about 3 minutes. If your pan is too cold, your eggs will stick. Before cooking your eggs, crack them into a bowl, season with salt and pepper, and either whisk or mix with a fork. This breaks up the eggs and makes the process easier.

- **Pancakes:** Nothing is better than a perfect pancake — golden-brown crispy edges and light and fluffy in the center. The real trick is even heat. Chapter 20 has pancake recipes.

- **French toast:** This is another great go-to for folks and perfect for camping.

- **Biscuits and gravy:** You can't lose with this classic. It takes a bit longer to make, but in the end it's so worth the time.

Easy Frittata

INGREDIENTS

6 eggs

¼ cup heavy cream

¼ teaspoon salt

⅛ teaspoon nutmeg

2 tablespoons olive oil

½ cup baby bella or button mushrooms, sliced

1 cup kale, chopped

½ cup gruyere cheese, grated

DIRECTIONS

1   Preheat your oven to 375 degrees. In a medium bowl add the eggs, heavy cream, salt, and nutmeg. Mix well.

2   Turn your stove to medium heat and preheat your 12-inch cast-iron skillet for about 2 to 3 minutes. Add the oil, mushrooms, and kale and cook for 5 minutes.

3   Turn the heat down to medium low and pour on your egg mixture. Finish with about ¼ cup cheese. Using a spoon or rubber spatula, stir to distribute the kale and mushroom evenly. Top with the remaining cheese.

4   Place your skillet in the oven and cook for 8 to 12 minutes or until the center is set and the edges are golden brown. Remove and serve warm.

TIP: To check for doneness make a slight cut in the center of your frittata. If the eggs are runny, give them another 3 to 5 minutes in the oven to fully cook the center.

PER SERVING: *Calories 380 (From Fat 291); Fat 32g (Saturated 12g); Cholesterol 470mg; Sodium 413mg; Carbohydrate 4g (Dietary Fiber 1g); Protein 19g.*

🍅 My Favorite Breakfast Potatoes

PREP TIME: 12 MIN	COOK TIME: 15 TO 20 MIN	YIELD: 3 SERVINGS

INGREDIENTS

2 tablespoons olive oil

1 pound pee wee potatoes, cut in half

1 cup onion, cut in half, sliced thin

Salt and pepper to taste

5 baby bella mushrooms or button mushrooms, quartered

2 red baby bell peppers, sliced thin

2 orange baby bell peppers, sliced thin

¼ cup banana peppers

2 tablespoons butter, sliced

½ red pepper flakes

½ teaspoon smoked paprika

DIRECTIONS

1 Preheat your oven to 400 degrees. Add the olive oil to the 10-inch cast-iron skillet and preheat it on the stove top over medium heat for 3 minutes.

2 Add the potatoes, mushrooms, and onions, season with salt and pepper, and sauté for 2 to 3 minutes. Place the skillet in the oven and cook for 10 to 15 minutes or until the potatoes are golden brown and fork tender.

3 Carefully remove the skillet from the oven and add the baby bell peppers and banana peppers. Place the skillet on the stovetop over medium heat to finish cooking, about 3 to 5 minutes.

4 Add the butter and adjust seasoning to taste. Finish with pepper flakes and paprika. Serve warm.

NOTE: Pee wee potatoes are also known as baby Dutch potatoes.

PER SERVING: *Calories 383 (From Fat 159); Fat 18g (Saturated 6g); Cholesterol 20mg; Sodium 83mg; Carbohydrate 51g (Dietary Fiber 9g); Protein 7g.*

Smoked Gouda and Virginia Ham Strata

PREP TIME: 10 MIN	COOK TIME: 45 TO 50 MIN	YIELD: 6 SERVINGS

INGREDIENTS

4 eggs

1½ cups half-and-half

¼ teaspoon salt

⅛ teaspoon nutmeg

⅛ teaspoon cayenne powder

2 tablespoons olive oil

3 cups old bread, medium diced

1 cup gouda cheese, shredded or small diced

¼ cup fresh Parmesan cheese

½ pound Virginia ham, small diced

DIRECTIONS

1 Preheat your oven to 350 degrees. Using a medium bowl, add the eggs, half-and-half, salt, nutmeg, and cayenne. Mix well with a whisk.

2 Coat the 12-inch cast-iron skillet with the olive oil. Starting with the bread, layer with the bread, ham, and then the gouda. Repeat the process until you've used all the ingredients. Slowly pour the egg mixture into your skillet. Make sure you evenly distribute the eggs. Top with Parmesan cheese.

3 Cook in the oven for 45 to 50 minutes, or until the center sets. When finished, remove from the oven and allow it to cool for 10 minutes; serve warm.

NOTE: What makes Virginia ham unique? Well traditionally it was the diet. Pigs were raised on a diet of peaches, nuts, grains, and Virginia peanuts. One of the most popular companies in Virginia is Smithfield. In 1926 the Virginia General Assembly defined Virginia ham as "cut from the carcasses of peanut-fed hog, raised in the peanut belt of the state of Virginia or North Carolina."

TIP: If the top of your strata hasn't achieved the beautiful golden color, fear not. Turn your oven on broil and place your strata under the broiler to finish the top. When using the broiler, the browning process happens very quickly, so don't walk away.

TIP: Soak the old bread overnight in the refrigerator and then cook it. This recipe is also good with sourdough loaf.

NOTE: Refer to the color insert for a photo of this recipe.

PER SERVING: *Calories 444 (From Fat 213); Fat 24g (Saturated 11g); Cholesterol 204mg; Sodium 664mg; Carbohydrate 31g (Dietary Fiber 1g); Protein 29g.*

Preparing Simple Lunch Dishes

If you're like me, lunch is a tricky meal period, especially during the week. You're probably so busy either working or running errands that the thought of making lunch is a daunting task.

In some countries, lunch is the most important part of the day. For example, some Spanish-speaking counties take a siesta, which means the whole country shuts down for a few hours to take a break. However, for many people, spending a few hours on lunch isn't realistic, but if you can make space for an hour, then the following cast-iron dishes are a perfect choice.

TIP

Take your time, review the ingredients, read the steps, and don't forget to taste your food. The more you taste, the better you'll understand the direction of the dish. Don't forget to smile; positive energy is contagious, especially when you're cooking.

MAKING SIMPLE LUNCH DISHES WITH YOUR CAST IRON

Here are three quick lunch favorites you can make using your cast iron:

- **Kale:** One tablespoon olive oil, 1 garlic clove, and ½ lemon is the perfect trio for kale. It's quick — less than 5 minutes to make — it's healthy, and it's freakin' delicious.

- **Blistered cherry tomatoes:** Take a bout ten cherry tomatoes and add 1 tablespoon olive oil, ½ shallot diced, 1 garlic clove, and a few pieces of torn basil. Heat your cast-iron skillet, add your ingredients, and then season with salt and pepper. They take about 5 minutes to cook and are a game changer.

- **Herb oil:** Add 2 cloves garlic, 1 sprig parsley, and 1 sprig thyme and/or 1 sprig rosemary. Preheat your oil in a cast-iron skillet and then add in your garlic and herbs. This oil is perfect for cast iron because not only does it heat evenly, but it also helps you keep your pan seasoned. I love using herb oil in everything. You can cook with it or drizzle it over a finished dish.

Couscous with Chicken

PREP TIME: 10 MIN | COOK TIME: 20 MIN | YIELD: 4 SERVINGS

INGREDIENTS

4 chicken thighs, bone in and skin on

Salt and pepper to taste

2 tablespoons olive oil

1 medium onion, thinly sliced

1 cup pearl couscous

1 tablespoon garlic, finely chopped

1½ cups chicken stock or broth

2 sprigs of thyme (optional)

DIRECTIONS

1 Preheat your oven to 400 degrees. Using a baking tray, evenly season with salt and pepper both sides of the chicken.

2 Preheat a 10-inch cast-iron skillet on the stove with olive oil for about 1 to 2 minutes over medium heat.

3 Add your chicken. Allow the chicken to render until the skin is crispy, about 8 to 10 minutes.

4 Flip the chicken and add the onions and pearl couscous. Allow them to cook until the onions begin to brown, about 5 to 8 minutes. Add the garlic and cook for 1 minute.

5 Add the chicken stock and thyme, cover with a lid, and place the pan in the oven. Cook for 10 to 15 minutes or until your chicken reaches an internal temperature of 165 degrees and the couscous is soft. Remove and allow the dish to rest for 10 minutes; serve warm.

VARY IT! Try adding different spices like cumin, smoked paprika, or even harissa to your chicken seasoning to add unique flavors to this dish. Experiment. The possibilities are endless as to what you can do with this dish.

TIP: Move your chicken to the side when adding your onions and couscous to give you space to work in your skillet.

PER SERVING: *Calories 401 (From Fat 152); Fat 17g (Saturated 4g); Cholesterol 51mg; Sodium 183mg; Carbohydrate 43g (Dietary Fiber 3g); Protein 18g.*

Easy Shrimp Alfredo

PREP TIME: 8 MIN	COOK TIME: 15 MIN	YIELD: 2 TO 3 SERVINGS

INGREDIENTS

½ pound shrimp, peeled and deveined

Salt and pepper to taste

2 tablespoons olive oil

2 tablespoons butter

1 tablespoon garlic, finely chopped

1 cup heavy cream

¼ cup Parmesan cheese, shredded

Pinch nutmeg (optional)

½ pound fettuccine noodles, cooked

1 lemon, zest and juice (you need about 1 tablespoon of the juice)

Red pepper flakes to taste

DIRECTIONS

1 Pat the shrimp dry with a clean paper towel or cloth. Place on a baking tray and season evenly with salt and pepper.

2 Using a 10-inch cast-iron skillet, preheat with olive oil for about 2 to 3 minutes over medium.

3 Add the shrimp to the skillet and cook until the color changes to pink. Remove the shrimp and place it on a clean baking tray or bowl to hold.

4 Add the butter to the skillet and allow it to melt. Add the garlic and cook, about 1 minute. Add the heavy cream, bring to a boil, and then reduce the heat to medium low to a simmer for 5 to 7 minutes or until the cream is slightly thick.

5 Whisk in the Parmesan cheese and nutmeg and taste with salt and pepper.

6 Add the pasta and shrimp to the sauce. Finish with lemon zest, juice, and red pepper flakes. Serve warm.

TIP: Reducing cream will naturally thicken it; keep your skillet at a low simmer.

PER SERVING: *Calories 819 (From Fat 458); Fat 51g (Saturated 26g); Cholesterol 251mg; Sodium 329mg; Carbohydrate 60g (Dietary Fiber 2g); Protein 30g.*

Berbere-Spiced Steak Bits with Chili Garlic Butter

PREP TIME: 20 MIN	COOK TIME: 10 MIN	YIELD: 4 SERVINGS

INGREDIENTS

2 tablespoons berbere

2 teaspoons salt

2 teaspoons brown sugar

½ teaspoon cayenne powder

1 onion, thinly sliced

¼ cup olive oil plus
2 tablespoons

1 pound sirloin steak,
large diced

2 tablespoons butter, soft

2 cloves garlic, finely minced

1 teaspoon chili flakes

¼ teaspoon smoked paprika

1 lemon, zest and juice

DIRECTIONS

1 Using a large zip-lock bag, add the berbere, 1 teaspoon salt, brown sugar, cayenne, onion, and ¼ cup of olive oil. Close the bag and shake to mix well. Add the steak to the bag and shake again. Allow the steak mixture to marinate for a minimum of 1 hour.

2 While the steak is marinating, use a small bowl and add your butter, garlic, chili flakes, smoked paprika, lemon (zest first and then the juice), and 1 teaspoon salt. Mix well and reserve for later.

3 Preheat a 10-inch cast-iron skillet over medium heat for about 1 to 2 minutes. Add 2 tablespoons olive oil.

4 Strain off your marinade from the steak and reserve. Add the steak to the skillet in single layers so the meat can properly sear. Cook the steak for about 2 to 3 minutes, flip, and cook for another 2 to 3 minutes. Add your marinade to the skillet and allow it to simmer for 3 to 5 minutes.

5 Turn off the heat. Add the chili butter and mix well. Serve warm.

TIP: Cook the steak in batches so the protein can properly sear.

NOTE: If you have the time, let the steak marinate overnight in the refrigerator — the longer, the better.

PER SERVING: *Calories 364 (From Fat 348); Fat 39g (Saturated 12g); Cholesterol 62mg; Sodium 1616mg; Carbohydrate 3g (Dietary Fiber 1g); Protein 24g.*

Focusing on Adventurous and Delicious Dinner Main Dishes

Many people find it incredibly challenging to decide what to prepare for dinner. With the added influence of food photos on social media, the pressure is on to deliver restaurant-quality meals every single night.

TIP

Not to worry. Here are a few smart tips to save you time:

>> **Remember mise en place.** As I discuss in this chapter's introduction, before you start cooking, prepare in advance your ingredients and equipment. Doing so allows you to focus with fewer distractions.

>> **Clean as you go.** Your kitchen workstation reflects what's happening in your head. Practice cleaning as you work. Keep a dish towel near and wipe messes into your hand or directly into the trash.

>> **Use a seasoned pan handle.** Working smart isn't just about how well you can cook, but it's also about the work that happens before you start cooking. That means ensuring your cast iron is seasoned and ready to cook. After each use, make sure you follow the steps in Chapter 3 to season your cast iron. Not only will seasoning your cast iron save you time, but it also will make your dish taste better.

Lemon Thyme Chicken Orzo

PREP TIME: 8 MIN   COOK TIME: 20 MIN   YIELD: 4 SERVINGS

INGREDIENTS

4 chicken thighs

Salt and pepper to taste

1 tablespoon olive oil

½ onion, sliced

2 garlic cloves, finely minced

1 cup orzo

3 sprigs thyme

1½ cups chicken stock

2 sprigs parsley, leaves only, chopped (optional)

2 tablespoons butter

1 lemon, sliced

DIRECTIONS

1 Place the chicken thighs on a baking tray and season both sides with salt and pepper.

2 Preheat a Dutch oven over medium heat for 3 minutes. Add the olive oil and chicken. Cook the chicken until the skin is golden brown, about 5 to 8 minutes. Flip the chicken, add the onions, and cook for about 3 minutes or until the onions are translucent.

3 Add the garlic and cook, about 1 minute. Add the orzo, thyme, and chicken stock. Cover and cook for about 10 to 12 minutes or until the orzo doubles in size and is tender to the tooth.

4 Remove from the heat, and add the parsley, butter, and lemon. Adjust seasoning and serve.

NOTE: The chicken should be cooked to an internal temperature of 165 degrees.

NOTE: See the color insert for a photo of this recipe.

PER SERVING: *Calories 397 (From Fat 177); Fat 20g (Saturated 7g); Cholesterol 66mg; Sodium 216mg; Carbohydrate 38g (Dietary Fiber 3g); Protein 18g.*

⏱ Curry Tofu with Mustard Greens

PREP TIME: 20 MIN | COOK TIME: 15 TO 20 MIN | YIELD: 6 SERVINGS

INGREDIENTS

2 tablespoons olive oil

1 onion, sliced

1 Yukon gold potato, peeled and medium diced

2 cups mustard greens, discard stems, chop leaves

1½ pieces of ginger, minced

2 cloves garlic, minced

2 Roma tomatoes, medium diced

2 tablespoons flour

2 tablespoons curry powder

1 teaspoon cayenne powder (optional)

Salt and pepper to taste

1 block extra-firm tofu, medium diced

2 cups vegetable stock

1 cup coconut milk

2 sprigs cilantro, leaves only, chopped (optional)

½ red bell pepper, sliced (optional)

1 lime cut into wedges

DIRECTIONS

1 Using a Dutch oven, preheat over medium heat for about 3 minutes. Add the olive oil, onion, potato, and mustard greens. Cook for about 5 to 8 minutes or until golden brown. Add the ginger and garlic and cook for another minute. Add the tomato, flour, curry powder, cayenne (optional), and salt and pepper to taste. Cook for about 3 minutes.

2 Add the tofu, vegetable stock, and coconut milk. Mix well. Bring to a simmer and cook for 8 to 12 minutes. Remove from heat and finish with lime. Add the cilantro and red pepper (optional).

VARY IT! Substitute the coconut milk for almond milk or add the red bell peppers for additional sweetness.

TIP: If you can't find extra firm tofu, you may need to press your tofu before cooking to remove excess moisture, allowing for a better sear.

PER SERVING: *Calories 271 (From Fat 154); Fat 17g (Saturated 8g); Cholesterol 2mg; Sodium 136mg; Carbohydrate 20g (Dietary Fiber 5g); Protein 12g.*

Cajun Shrimp and Okra Gumbo

PREP TIME: 20 MIN	COOK TIME: 1½ HRS	YIELD: 6 SERVINGS

INGREDIENTS

⅓ cup olive oil

3 pounds okra, cut into ½-inch round slices

2½ tablespoons Cajun seasoning

2 cups finely chopped onions

6 cups chicken stock

4 cups vegetable stock

2 cups peeled and chopped tomatoes

1 teaspoon minced garlic

1 stick unsalted butter

1 pound andouille, cut into ¼-inch slices

1 pound medium shrimp, peeled

¼ cup finely chopped green onion

6 cups hot, cooked rice (long grain)

DIRECTIONS

1 Heat the olive oil in a 7-quart cast-iron Dutch oven over high heat until smoking. Reduce the heat to medium-high, add ¾ of the okra, and cook about 3 minutes, stirring occasionally.

2 Stir in 1 tablespoon of the Cajun seasoning and continue cooking for about 10 minutes, stirring often. Stir in the onions and cook until soft, about 5 minutes, scraping the bottom of the pan often to keep it from scorching. Stir in 1 cup of either stock and cook 5 minutes, keeping the bottom of the pot scraped. Add the tomatoes and cook for 8 minutes. Stir and scrape often. Stir in another 2 cups of the stock, cooking for another 5 minutes. Continue to stir occasionally to avoid burning.

3 Turn the heat to high and stir in the remaining 1½ tablespoons of Cajun seasoning and the garlic. Add the butter; cook and stir until butter is melted, scraping the bottom of the pot well. Add the remaining stock and bring it to a boil, stirring occasionally.

4 Add the sausage and, after the pot returns to a boil, reduce the heat and simmer for 45 minutes. Add the remaining quarter of the okra and simmer for 10 minutes more. Add the shrimp and return to a boil. Remove from the heat. Stir in the green onions. Mound the hot rice in the center of a bowl and ladle about 1½ cups of the gumbo from out of the Dutch oven around the rice.

PER SERVING: Calories 892 (From Fat 460); Fat 51g (Saturated 22g); Cholesterol 219mg; Sodium 2,970mg; Carbohydrate 76g (Dietary Fiber 9g); Protein 35g.

Blackened Redfish

PREP TIME: 5 MIN	COOK TIME: 5 MIN	YIELD: 6 SERVINGS

INGREDIENTS

½ cup olive oil, mild

6 redfish fillets about
4 to 6 ounces each

½ cup butter, melted

2 tablespoons Cajun seasoning
to taste

½ cup all-purpose flour

DIRECTIONS

1 Using a medium bowl add the flour and Cajun seasoning. Preheat a 10-inch cast-iron skillet with the olive oil over medium heat, for about 2 to 3 minutes.

2 Coat each fillet well in the melted butter and then dust the Cajun seasoning and flour mixture generously over the entire fillet, patting it in.

3 Place 2 or 3 fillets in a hot skillet and carefully spoon the hot olive oil on top of each fillet, being careful not to cause a flame. Cook about 2 minutes until the cooking surface of the fillets is golden brown. Turn the fish over, carefully spoon the olive oil on the fillets, and cook until the fish is done, about 2 more minutes. After the fish is cooked, remove from the skillet and rest on a baking tray with a rack or on a plate with a few paper towels. Continue until all the fish is cooked and then serve.

TIP: When cooking fish, cook it to an internal temperature of 145 degrees.

PER SERVING: *Calories 466 (From Fat 322); Fat 36g (Saturated 13g); Cholesterol 100mg; Sodium 346mg; Carbohydrate 8g (Dietary Fiber 0g); Protein 28g.*

Chapter **14**

For Red Meat Lovers

Sweet peppercorn-crusted steak, roasted brisket, and Dutch oven roasted pork, are just a few of my favorite dishes here. This chapter takes you on a culture journey exploring dishes from the American South to Italy and France. Regardless whether it's a pan-seared steak, braised pork, or a hearty stew, this chapter can inspire you to cook in your favorite cast-iron dish and maybe invest in a few additional pieces.

I explore the power of braising in your Dutch oven and roasting in a cast-iron skillet. Each recipe offers the opportunity to explore a new cooking technique that enhances flavors and textures.

Preparing Beef Entrees

This section explores some of the best methods for cooking different cuts of beef. Here I explain using a quick sauté and your Dutch oven.

The following sections introduce beef recipes you can prepare for a special occasion or just an evening dinner with loved ones:

» **Cast-Iron Pot Roast:** Pot roast gets a bad rap as being tough, dry, and stringy. Not this recipe. Perfectly roasted and infused with herbs and the flavors of roasted vegetables, this dish will have your mouth watering for more.

» **Steak au Poivre (Peppercorn-Crusted Steak):** The cut that's famously used in this dish is filet mignon, one of the most tender (and most expensive) pieces of meat you can buy. This dish packs a ton of flavor, textures, and techniques.

» **Veal Scallopini with Mushroom Sauce:** Veal, known for its tenderness and subtle flavor, comes from a young calf. Paired with the earthiness of mushrooms, this dish is a culinary experience.

» **Chisholm Trail Swiss Steak:** Swiss steak is a round steak that has flour pounded into both sides and is then browned in fat and smothered with vegetables and seasonings. What makes this so amazing is the caramelization of the steak.

» **Roasted Brisket:** By slowly cooking the brisket, you're able to break down the textural barrier of shoe leather, creating something so tender that you can cut it with a spoon.

AUROCH ON THE LOOSE!

When you think of cows, *ferocious, wild,* or *awesome* probably doesn't spring to mind. But the *auroch,* the ancient wild ancestor from which domestic cattle come, was, it seems, a pretty impressive and intimidating animal. Aurochs were large, long-horned wild oxen that lived in German forests. They became extinct during the 17th century. The theory is that they died from embarrassment when they realized how wimpy their descendants turned out.

Cast-Iron Pot Roast

PREP TIME: 30 MIN | COOK TIME: 3 TO 3½ HRS | YIELD: 8 TO 10 SERVINGS

INGREDIENTS

5- to 6-pound shoulder roast or chuck roast

Salt and pepper to taste

1 to 2 tablespoons olive oil

2 medium onions, sliced

1 rib celery without top, cut into 2-inch pieces

4 carrots, peeled and cut into 2-inch pieces

2 bay leaves

2 sprigs thyme

2 quarts beef stock

5 to 6 medium Yukon gold potatoes, halved

2 tablespoons cornstarch

2 tablespoons water

DIRECTIONS

1 Rub the roast with salt and pepper. Heat the oil in a 5- or 7-quart cast-iron Dutch oven on medium high or high. Sear the roast on all sides until it's very brown.

2 Add the onions, celery, carrots, bay leaves, and thyme. Add enough beef stock to cover the roast. Reduce the heat to a simmer and cover. Allow the roast to braise for 2 to 2½ hours.

3 Remove the lid and taste. Adjust seasoning with salt and pepper. With the lid removed add the potatoes and cook for an additional 20 minutes.

4 Remove the skillet from the heat and allow it to rest for about 5 minutes.

5 To add more value to the broth, return it to the heat and bring to a boil. Using a small bowl mix the cornstarch and water. Whisk into the boiling liquid and allow it to slightly thicken. Remove from the heat and serve over the roast.

NOTE: If you'll be serving this dish on a platter, carefully remove the roast with either a large spatula or slotted spoon in Step 4.

VARY IT! Take the oven route. After searing the roast, add all remaining ingredients and place in a 350-degree oven and roast for 2 to 2½ hours, or until fork tender. Salt to taste during last 30 minutes. For additional flavor, add 1 cup red wine when adding liquid to almost cover in Step 2.

TIP: For tips on carving a pot roast, see Chapter 6.

PER SERVING: *Calories 493 (From Fat 158); Fat 18g (Saturated 6g); Cholesterol 136mg; Sodium 567mg; Carbohydrate 27g (Dietary Fiber 3g); Protein 54g.*

Steak au Poivre (Peppercorn–Crusted Steak)

PREP TIME: 15 MIN   COOK TIME: 20 TO 25 MIN   YIELD: 4 SERVINGS

INGREDIENTS

1 tablespoon fresh cracked black peppercorns, medium grind

1 tablespoon fresh cracked white peppercorns, medium grind (optional)

1 tablespoon fresh cracked green peppercorns, medium grind (optional)

1 teaspoon fresh cracked fennel seed (optional)

1 teaspoon kosher salt

2 New York strips or filet mignon

2 tablespoons olive oil

2 cloves garlic, skin on, crushed

1 shallot, halved and sliced

3 sprigs thyme

2 tablespoons butter

DIRECTIONS

1 Using a small bowl, blend the black, white, and green peppercorns with the fennel and salt.

2 Add the steaks to a baking tray and generously season both sides of the steaks with the peppercorn mix (don't be afraid to press the peppercorns into the steak).

3 Preheat your 10-inch cast-iron skillet with olive oil over medium heat for about 1 to 2 minutes.

4 Add your steaks to the skillet, allowing them to sear until they've reached a deep golden-brown caramelization, about 4 to 6 minutes. Flip the steaks over in the skillet and add the garlic, shallot, and thyme. Allow the vegetables to roast, infusing the flavors, about 2 to 3 minutes.

5 Add 1 tablespoon of butter at a time, allowing the butter to slightly melt. Spoon the butter on top of the steak for about 1 to 2 minutes. Repeat the process until all the butter has been added. Allow the steak to rest for about 5 minutes before serving.

Mushroom Cognac Cream Sauce

1 cup baby bella or cremini mushroom, chopped

1 shallot, chopped

1 garlic clove, chopped

2 tablespoons cognac or brandy

½ cup heavy cream

1 Using the same skillet that you cooked your steak in, preheat over medium heat for about 2 minutes. Add the mushrooms and cook for about 3 minutes. Add the shallot and cook for about 3 minutes. Then add the garlic and cook for another minute.

2 Remove the skillet from the heat and add the cognac. Allow the alcohol to cook off, about 1 minute. Return the skillet back to the heat and add the cream. Reduce the heat to medium low, allowing the sauce to simmer for about 5 minutes.

3 Adjust the seasoning with salt and pepper. Strain and serve with the steak.

TIP: To cook your filet without drying it out, sear the meat first to hold in the moisture and then finish it in the oven.

NOTE: If you prefer New York strips, use 5- to 6-ounce cuts. Go with 8 ounces for filet mignon.

NOTE: Most pepper grinders have an option to change the grind. The courser the grind, the more robust the flavor when eating.

NOTE: Don't let the word caramelization scare you. During this process the meat's natural sugars and amino acids respond to high heat. The result is a beautiful texture and flavor.

NOTE: The resting process is super important. When cooking any protein, give it a minimum of 5 minutes rest time before slicing. This gives the natural juices time to redistribute, helping you lock in flavor.

TIP: The time in this recipe produces a medium-rare steak. A medium steak has an internal temperature of between 140 and 148 degrees. If you want your steak cooked medium well, finish it in the oven at 400 degrees for an additional 3 to 5 minutes. Chapter 6 discusses cooking temperatures.

TIP: Pull your pan away from the heat when adding alcohol to avoid excess heat and flames in your face.

NOTE: Refer to the color insert for a photo of this dish.

PER SERVING: *Calories 553 (From Fat 441); Fat 49g (Saturated 22g); Cholesterol 132mg; Sodium 698mg; Carbohydrate 6g (Dietary Fiber 2g); Protein 23g.*

Veal Scallopini with Mushroom Sauce

PREP TIME: 5 MIN	COOK TIME: 30 MIN	YIELD: 4 SERVINGS

INGREDIENTS

1 to 1½ pound veal cutlets

Salt and pepper to taste

All-purpose flour for dredging

¼ cup olive oil

¼ cup butter

2 cups mushrooms, sliced

1 clove garlic, minced

½ teaspoon flour

½ cup sherry

2 sprigs thyme

1 cup beef broth

DIRECTIONS

1 Add the veal cutlets to a baking tray and season with the salt and pepper on both sides. Dredge in flour and be sure to shake off excess flour to prevent flour clumps.

2 Preheat a 10-inch cast-iron skillet over medium heat with the olive oil for about 2 minutes. Add the veal to the skillet and brown, about 7 to 10 minutes per side. Remove the veal from the skillet and set aside on a clean plate or tray.

3 Add the butter to the skillet and melt. Add the mushrooms and sauté for about 3 to 5 minutes. Add the garlic and the flour and cook for about 1 minute.

4 Add the sherry and thyme, allowing it to reduce by half. Add the beef broth and simmer for about 5 minutes or until slightly thick. Taste and adjust seasoning if needed. Serve the sauce over the veal.

PER SERVING: *Calories 409 (From Fat 246); Fat 27g (Saturated 10g); Cholesterol 119mg; Sodium 355mg; Carbohydrate 8g (Dietary Fiber 1g); Protein 27g.*

Chisholm Trail Swiss Steak

PREP TIME: 15 MIN | **COOK TIME: 1 TO 1½ HRS** | **YIELD: 8 TO 10 SERVINGS**

INGREDIENTS

3 pounds boneless round steak, cut into servings

¾ cup all-purpose flour

2 teaspoons salt

2 teaspoons pepper

3 tablespoons olive oil

1 cup chopped onions

½ cup chopped celery

½ cup chopped bell pepper

2 tablespoons garlic, diced

One 28-ounce can diced tomatoes

1 cup beef broth

1 tablespoon soy sauce

2 tablespoons all-purpose flour

DIRECTIONS

1 Using a meat mallet, pound the round steak between two pieces of wax paper until tender.

2 In a large bowl, combine the flour, salt, pepper, and garlic. Dredge the steak in the flour mixture and continue to pound the flour into the grain of the meat.

3 In a 13-inch cast-iron skillet, heat the oil over medium-high heat. Cook the steak until golden brown on both sides. Remove the steak from the skillet.

4 Add the onions, celery, bell pepper, and garlic. Cook until the vegetables are wilted, about 5 minutes. Return the meat to the skillet.

5 Add the tomatoes, broth, and soy sauce. Bring the mixture to a boil, reduce the heat, cover, and simmer for 1½ hours, or until the meat is tender. Remove the steak and vegetables from the Dutch oven to a serving platter.

6 In a measuring cup, combine ¼ cup of cold water with the 2 tablespoons of flour until the flour is thoroughly dissolved. Pour the flour/water mixture into the sauce and stir until thickened.

7 Adjust the seasonings if necessary. Pour the sauce over the meat and vegetables on the platter.

VARY IT! If you don't have a round steak on hand for this recipe, you can substitute an arm roast (from the chuck portion of the cow), but keep in mind that the arm may have a little more fat.

PER SERVING: Calories 302 (From Fat 105); Fat 12g (Saturated 3g); Cholesterol 77mg; Sodium 894mg; Carbohydrate 15g (Dietary Fiber 2g); Protein 33g.

Roasted Brisket

INGREDIENTS

4 pounds beef brisket

3 tablespoons olive oil

⅓ cup firmly packed light brown sugar

1 teaspoon garlic powder

1 teaspoon onion powder

½ teaspoon mustard powder

1 teaspoon chili powder

2 teaspoons salt

1 teaspoon pepper

1 teaspoon smoked paprika

½ teaspoon ground cayenne powder

DIRECTIONS

1 Preheat the oven to 300 degrees. Place the olive oil in bottom of 7-quart cast-iron Dutch oven and warm it in the preheating oven so that the oil coats the entire bottom surface of Dutch oven.

2 Make a dry rub by combining the brown sugar, garlic powder, onion powder, mustard powder, chili powder, salt, pepper, smoked paprika, and cayenne in a bowl. Mix well. Rub the dry rub into all sides of the brisket.

3 Place the brisket into the Dutch oven. Add 1½ cups water to the bottom of the Dutch oven, being careful not to disturb the dry rub. Bake the brisket, covered, at 300 degrees for 2 hours.

4 Increase the oven temperature to 350 degrees and continue cooking for another 1 to 1½ hours, checking the brisket every 15 to 20 minutes. Another ½ cup warm water can be added if necessary to prevent the brisket from burning.

5 Remove the brisket from the oven when it's very tender, but not falling apart. To serve, cut the brisket diagonally across the grain into ¼-inch slices and drizzle with pan juices.

VARY IT! Use beer or beef broth in place of the water for added flavor.

NOTE: A whole brisket, which comes from the front part of the cow's breast, is usually cut into two pieces: the flat cut and the point cut. The flat cut is leaner and, as a result, lacks some of the flavor that the fattier point cut has. Nevertheless, you can use either for any beef brisket recipe.

PER SERVING: *Calories 431 (From Fat 196); Fat 22g (Saturated 7g); Cholesterol 141mg; Sodium 763mg; Carbohydrate 9g (Dietary Fiber 0g); Protein 47g.*

Serving Pork Recipes

Fresh, cured, smoked, braised, grilled, or sautéed, the versatility of pork is absolutely amazing. Remember when selecting your pork to keep these three points in mind:

>> If you're unsure about the cut, ask. Every cut cooks differently.

>> When cooking pork, always focus on the internal temperature, not the cook time.

>> When cooking with high heat, rest the pork before slicing.

This section highlights the following pork recipes you can prepare:

>> **Apricot-Ginger Glazed Pork Rib Roast with Fruit Stuffing:** Pigs are amazing in that just about every part of them is used in some way as a food. This dish blends two great combinations — pork and apricot — and is great for a holiday or family gathering.

>> **Brunswick Stew:** Brunswick Stew gets its name from the region in Virginia from which it hails. This hearty version of the recipe calls for both chicken and pork.

>> **Dutch Oven Pork Roast:** A pork roast is any unsliced (and unsmoked) cut from the hog. You can use a fresh ham, a rib end roast, a loin end roast, a crown roast, a Boston shoulder, a fresh picnic — you name it. For this recipe, I recommend a loin end roast. If you prefer a boneless cut, use center cut pork roast.

>> **Pork and Sausage Jambalaya:** Jambalaya combines rice, tomatoes, onion, green pepper, and just about any combination of meat, poultry, and shellfish that you can think of. Although ham was the original main ingredient in jambalaya (*jambon* is the French word for ham), ham has given way to smoked sausage or other heavily spiced meat, such as andouille.

These recipes have two very important cooking methods: roasting and braising. These techniques require patience, but the results are absolutely worth it. The flavors that develop during these extended cooking periods have an incredible depth and complexity.

Apricot-Ginger Glazed Pork Rib Roast with Fruit Stuffing

PREP TIME: 20 MIN	COOK TIME: 2½ HRS	YIELD: 7 SERVINGS

INGREDIENTS

7-bone pork rib roast

2 tablespoons butter

1 cup chopped onion

1 cup chopped celery

1 box pork stuffing mix

½ cup dried apricot halves

⅓ cup dried cranberries

¼ cup chopped fresh parsley

1 teaspoon salt

½ teaspoon pepper

1 teaspoon dried thyme

One 9-ounce jar apricot preserves

1 tablespoon soy sauce

1 tablespoon lemon juice

½ teaspoon ground ginger

DIRECTIONS

1 Preheat your oven to 325 degrees. In a 7-quart cast-iron Dutch oven, melt the butter over medium-high heat. Cook the onion and celery until tender, stirring occasionally. Remove the cooked onions and celery and place in a large bowl. Add the stuffing mix, apricots, cranberries, and parsley to the onions and celery.

2 Rub all sides of the pork roast with salt, pepper, and thyme. With a heavy string, tie a loop around the end of the bones and pull until the roast fans out. Place the roast in the Dutch oven. Add ¾ cup water, cover, and place in the oven.

3 Meanwhile, in a small pan, make the glaze by combining the apricot preserves, soy sauce, lemon juice, and ginger and heating over low heat. Baste the pork roast with the glaze at 15-minute intervals for 1 hour.

4 Take the roast from the oven and remove the pan drippings into a small bowl, being careful not to disturb the roast. Skim the fat from drippings and discard it. Mix the pan drippings into the stuffing mixture, adding more water if too dry. Spoon the stuffing into the slits and around the roast.

5 Return the roast to the oven and cook, covered, for another 1½ hours or until a thermometer inserted into the thickest part of the meat registers 160 degrees. Let the roast stand 15 minutes before slicing. Heat the remaining glaze and serve over the meat.

NOTE: A 7-bone pork rib roast is simply a pork roast (from the loin) that has 7 bones attached.

TIP: For carving tips, see Chapter 6.

PER SERVING: *Calories 698 (From Fat 241); Fat 27g (Saturated 11g); Cholesterol 151mg; Sodium 1,024mg; Carbohydrate 50g (Dietary Fiber 3g); Protein 62g.*

Brunswick Stew

| PREP TIME: 10 MIN | COOK TIME: ABOUT 4 HRS | YIELD: 8 SERVINGS |

INGREDIENTS

3 pounds chicken pieces
(or whole chicken)

1 pound cubed pork (or ham)

1 teaspoon plus
1 tablespoon salt

2 medium onions, chopped

1 quart or more of chicken
stock (or bouillon)

2 pounds fresh tomatoes,
peeled, and seeded

2 jalapeño peppers, seeded
and diced

1 bay leaf

1 teaspoon thyme

1 teaspoon sugar

½ teaspoon pepper

2 tablespoons Worcestershire
sauce

1½ cups fresh or frozen baby
lima beans

4 medium potatoes, peeled
and cubed

3 cups fresh corn

2 tablespoons butter

DIRECTIONS

1 In 9-quart cast-iron Dutch oven, put the chicken and pork in enough water to cover. Add 1 teaspoon of salt and the onions. Bring to a boil, and then lower the heat and simmer until meat falls off the bone, 1½ to 2 hours.

2 Remove the chicken and bones from the Dutch oven. Cool the chicken enough to remove skin and bones. Shred the chicken and return it to the pan.

3 Add the remaining tablespoon of salt, the chicken stock, tomatoes, jalapeños, bay leaf, thyme, sugar, pepper, and Worcestershire sauce, and simmer for 1 to 1½ hours, stirring occasionally.

4 Add the lima beans, return to a slight boil, and simmer for 30 minutes. If necessary, add more chicken stock to keep the desired, thick consistency of stew.

5 Add the potatoes and corn, return to a slight boil, and simmer slowly another 45 minutes to 1 hour, or until the potatoes are tender. Adjust the seasoning if necessary. Remove the bay leaf and swirl in butter when ready to serve.

PER SERVING: *Calories 508 (From Fat 193); Fat 21g (Saturated 7g); Cholesterol 126mg; Sodium 1,905mg; Carbohydrate 43g (Dietary Fiber 6g); Protein 38g.*

Dutch Oven Pork Roast

PREP TIME: 10 MIN | COOK TIME: ABOUT 3 HRS | YIELD: 6 SERVINGS

INGREDIENTS

2 to 3 pounds pork roast

3 cloves garlic, sliced

½ teaspoon salt

½ teaspoon pepper

Salt and pepper

1 cup cider vinegar

1 cup water

3 bay leaves

2 sprigs thyme

1 spring rosemary

2 medium onions, chopped

3 carrots, cut into 2-inch pieces

3 celery ribs, cut into 2-inch pieces

DIRECTIONS

1 Preheat your oven to 325 degrees. With a small knife, pierce the top of the roast and force the garlic slices into the cuts. Rub the roast with the salt and pepper.

2 Pour the vinegar and water into a Dutch oven and then add the roast. Add the bay leaves, thyme, and rosemary around the pork in the liquid. Add the onions, carrots, and celery.

3 Bake the roast for 3 hours, or until an internal temperature of 150 to 155 degrees is reached. Baste the roast with the drippings frequently during cooking, about every 15 minutes.

4 Let the roast rest for 10 minutes before slicing.

TIP: You can sometimes find boneless loin roasts on sale in your grocer's case. It's a large piece of meat, enough to yield a nice combination of roasts and pork steaks. Your butcher will slice it for you for free.

PER SERVING: *Calories 382 (From Fat 133); Fat 15g (Saturated 5g); Cholesterol 122mg; Sodium 343mg; Carbohydrate 14g (Dietary Fiber 3g); Protein 45g.*

Pork and Sausage Jambalaya

PREP TIME: 20 MIN	COOK TIME: 2 HRS	YIELD: 6 SERVINGS

INGREDIENTS

1 pound applewood smoked bacon (thick cut), chopped

1 pound andouille sausage, cubed

2 cups mushrooms, sliced

2 cups onion, chopped

1 cup bell peppers, sliced

1 cup celery, sliced

1 clove garlic, minced

1 tablespoon Cajun seasoning

1 teaspoon gumbo filé

One 28-ounce can crushed tomatoes

2 bay leaves

2 sprigs of thyme

2 teaspoons Worcestershire sauce

1 tablespoon Tabasco sauce

Salt and pepper to taste

2 cups long grain rice

3 cups chicken stock

DIRECTIONS

1 Preheat a Dutch oven for about 2 minutes over medium heat. Add the bacon and sausage. Allow it to cook until golden brown on all sides, about 15 to 20 minutes.

2 Add the mushrooms and onions, allowing them to caramelize for about 15 to 20 minutes or until dark brown. Add the bell peppers, celery, garlic, Cajun seasoning, and gumbo filé and cook for about 5 minutes.

3 Add the tomatoes, bay leaves, and thyme. Allow the mixture to reduce by half, about 15 minutes.

4 Add the Worcestershire sauce and Tabasco sauce. Season with salt and pepper.

5 Add the rice and mix well. Add the stock and cover. Reduce the heat to a low simmer and allow the mixture to cook for about 20 minutes. Check for tenderness. If needed, cover and cook for an additional 5 minutes.

6 Turn off the heat and allow the jambalaya to rest for about 5 to 8 minutes before removing the lid and serving.

NOTE: If you can't find gumbo filé, you can replace it with cornstarch.

PER SERVING: *Calories 951 (From Fat 525); Fat 58g (Saturated 19g); Cholesterol 98mg; Sodium 2096mg; Carbohydrate 72g (Dietary Fiber 6g); Protein 34g.*

Chapter **15**

Poultry Entrée Recipes

For many home cooks, cooking chicken without drying it out is downright difficult. Here, I not only help you overcome this barrier but also include several recipes so you add new and interesting flavors paired with classic cooking techniques. When reflecting on classic fried recipes, most of them involve cast iron. Cast iron is renowned for its excellent heat retention and distribution properties, which help in achieving a delicious caramelization and crisping of foods.

TIP

Like with cooking any protein, pay attention to the internal temperature not the length of cooking time. To read more about cooking times and mastery of cooking techniques, go to Chapter 7 to deep dive in the world of chicken and poultry.

Here you can find a decent selection of recipes for cooking chicken and other poultry in your favorite cast iron.

Focusing on County Cookin'

When it comes to county cookin', you need to have these two dishes in your repertoire: potpie and fried chicken.

During my childhood in upstate New York, the winters were harsh and unforgiving. Chicken pot pie, with its enticing flavors and tender filling, serves as a bridge that connects the frigid evenings of New York's cold embrace to the comforting warmth it provides. Its remarkable ability to evoke vivid memories effortlessly transports me back to those wintry nights when the savory aroma mixed with the chill in the air, creating a cozy refuge.

And what can I say about fried chicken? These two culinary creations surpass the conventional boundaries of taste and texture, opening a gateway to a unique place where you can fully immerse yourself in the comforting embrace of genuine country cuisine:

>> **Chicken Potpie:** Many people think chicken potpie is difficult to make or it takes too long to cook. But if you use leftover chicken and an already-made pie crust, you have about 15 minutes in prep time before it goes into the oven.

>> **Southern Fried Chicken:** This recipe is simple, delicious, and easy to make. Just be sure to make enough for dinner and still have a few pieces leftover — as delicious as fried chicken is straight from the pan, it's even better cold the next day.

THE CENTURY OF THE CHICKEN

Most people today wouldn't think of a chicken as particularly pleasing to the eye. They certainly wouldn't think of the buggers as show animals. But before chickens became popular as food, they were quite the lookers, it seems:

- In Japan and other East Asian countries, chickens were used for decoration — live decoration, that is.

- As exotic animals in places such as India, chickens were part of royal menageries.

- During the 19th century, chickens were bred for show, with the emphasis on feather coloring and combs.

Chickens aren't just good-lookin', though. They were also hard workers and held down a couple other jobs. In particular, they were used for divination and religious rituals and entertainment — cock-fighting.

Chickens fascinated so many people that they even have their own century, The Century of the Chicken, which began in the early 19th century when Europe, and later the United States, was first introduced to new, ornamental (think pet) chickens from Asia. The introduction of these new birds fascinated the public, and huge numbers of people started breeding and raising the birds.

Chicken Potpie

PREP TIME: 15 MIN | **COOK TIME: 45 MIN** | **YIELD: 8 TO 10 SERVINGS**

INGREDIENTS

1 pound boneless, skinless chicken breast, medium diced

Salt and pepper

2 tablespoons butter

1 small onion, diced

2 cloves garlic, minced

¼ cup all-purpose flour

1 cup chicken stock

1 cup milk

1 cup mixed frozen vegetables

1 pack puff pastry

DIRECTIONS

1 Preheat your oven to 350 degrees. Season the chicken on both sides with salt and pepper.

2 Preheat a 10-inch cast-iron skillet over medium heat for about 2 minutes. Melt the butter and then add the chicken, cooking for about 8 to 10 minutes, or until golden brown.

3 Add the onion and garlic, allowing it to sweat for about 5 minutes.

4 Add the flour and cook for about 2 to 3 minutes. Whisk in the chicken stock and milk and bring the mixture to a simmer.

5 Add the vegetables and remove the skillet from the heat. Season with salt and pepper.

6 Place the puff pastry over the top of the skillet, pressing the edges down on the sides of the cast iron. After the entire pan is covered, use a knife to create a few score marks on the top of the crust.

7 Place the skillet in the oven and cook for about 30 minutes. Increase to 375 degrees and cook for an additional 15 minutes. Remove the skillet from the heat and rest for 5 minutes before serving.

NOTE: Refer to the color insert for a photo of this recipe.

PER SERVING: *Calories 311 (From Fat 152); Fat 17g (Saturated 4g); Cholesterol 46mg; Sodium 302mg; Carbohydrate 23g (Dietary Fiber 1g); Protein 17g.*

Southern Fried Chicken

PREP TIME: 30 MIN	COOK TIME: 35 MIN	YIELD: 4 SERVINGS (2 PIECES EACH)

INGREDIENTS

3 pounds chicken pieces

About 1 cup all-purpose flour for dredging

1 tablespoon seasoning salt

1 tablespoon paprika

1½ cups buttermilk

Salt and pepper

Peanut oil or shortening to fill skillet 1-inch deep

DIRECTIONS

1 Wash the chicken pieces and pat dry. Add the flour, seasoning salt, and paprika and mix well in a medium bowl.

2 Dip the chicken pieces in milk and then lay them on wax paper. Sprinkle both sides of the pieces with salt, pepper, and paprika and then dredge them in the flour mixture. Let the chicken stand for 20 minutes and dredge in flour again.

3 While the chicken is resting, heat the oil or shortening in a deep cast-iron skillet or Dutch oven on medium-high heat to 375 degrees. (The oil will be hot but not smoking.)

4 Add 4 to 5 pieces of chicken to the skillet, browning both sides. Turn and move the chicken as necessary to ensure even browning. (Use tongs so that you don't pierce the meat.)

5 Move the chicken to a platter to allow room for the next 4 or 5 pieces. Add the next 4 to 5 pieces of chicken and cook until all are brown.

6 When the second batch of chicken is about brown, return all the chicken to the skillet, reduce the heat to low or medium-low, and cover. At this point, stacking the chicken in the skillet may be necessary. Cook slowly and gently for about 20 minutes, or until fork tender. Check several times and turn or move the pieces as necessary to keep all the chicken browned evenly.

7 Remove the cover and return the heat to medium-high to re-crisp the chicken, about 5 minutes after the skillet is hot again. While re-crisping, watch the chicken carefully and turn the pieces so that all sides are crisp, taking care not to burn the bottom pieces of chicken.

8 Drain and move the chicken to a serving platter or place on a rack in the oven to keep warm.

NOTE: In Step 4, be careful not to add too much chicken at one time so that the oil temperature drops significantly.

TIP: Use an instant read thermometer to test the temperature in Step 3 and throughout cooking.

VARY IT! If you're allergic to peanut oil, you can substitute canola or vegetable oil.

PER SERVING: *Calories 670 (From Fat 361); Fat 40g (Saturated 11g); Cholesterol 163mg; Sodium 420mg; Carbohydrate 29g (Dietary Fiber 1g); Protein 45g.*

Cooking for the Uptown Crowd

Who says the only chicken dishes that you can cook in cast iron are the down-home favorites? Not me. You can cook *any* chicken recipe in a cast-iron pan, even more sophisticated ones, and this section includes dishes to prove it to you. For more recipes from around the world, go to Chapter 24. Here are the recipes in this section:

» **Smoky Coq au Vin:** Coq au Vin is a classic French dish that dates back centuries. It's a delicious and hearty chicken stew cooked in red wine, typically made with chicken, mushrooms, onions, bacon, and garlic. The name *Coq au Vin* translates to "rooster with wine," which reflects the traditional use of an older rooster in the recipe.

» **Classic Chicken Parmigiana:** The term *parmigiana* describes food that's dredged in a mixture of breadcrumbs, grated Parmesan cheese, and various seasonings, and then sautéed. For chicken parmigiana, for example, pieces of chicken (usually boneless breasts) are pounded thin, dipped in egg, and then dredged in the cornmeal-Parmesan mixture. You can prepare veal parmigiana, another common dish, in the same way. With cast iron, the breading is nice and crisp.

» **Chicken Marsala:** Marsala is a dark-colored, sweet wine made in Marsala, Sicily. (Of course, wines that look like the Sicilian Marsala but are made in other places are also called marsala.) In Chicken Marsala, this wine is a key ingredient in the sauce.

» **Chicken Picata:** Chicken Picata is simply chicken cooked in a sauce. You can find various picata recipes that differ in their specifics: for example, whether the chicken breast should be halved, sliced, or, as in this recipe, pounded thin, and whether wine or broth should be used. The basic cooking method, however, is the same: sautéing the chicken in butter or oil (usually olive oil), adding the other ingredients, and cooking until the liquid is reduced to a nice sauce. The result is a simple but elegant dish that you can serve alone or over pasta.

Smoky Coq Au Vin

PREP TIME: 10 MIN + 1 HR MARINADE	COOK TIME: 1½ HRS	YIELD: 4 SERVINGS

INGREDIENTS

2 cups red wine

1 cup sherry (optional)

4 chicken thighs, bone-in, skin on

4 sprigs thyme

2 shallots, sliced

Salt and pepper to taste

2 tablespoons olive oil

4 strips bacon, medium diced

1 large onion, thinly sliced

2 carrots, medium diced

2 garlic cloves, minced

1 cup baby bella mushrooms or button mushrooms, quartered

2 tablespoons tomato paste

2 tablespoons flour

1 quart chicken stock

1 smoked turkey neck (optional)

2 bay leaves

DIRECTIONS

1 In a medium bowl, mix together the red wine and sherry. Add the chicken, thyme, and shallots, allowing it to marinate for at least 1 hour — the longer, the better.

2 Remove the chicken from the marinade, allowing it to dry for about 5 minutes. Season well with salt and pepper. Reserve the marinade for later.

3 Preheat your oven to 375 degrees. Preheat the Dutch oven to medium heat with the olive oil for about 2 minutes. Add the chicken and sear for about 6 to 8 minutes on each side until brown. Remove the chicken and set it on a baking tray. Add the bacon and render until golden brown, about 8 minutes. Add the onion and carrots. Cook until caramelized, about 6 to 8 minutes. Add the garlic and cook for about a minute.

4 Add the mushrooms and cook for about 3 minutes or until they release liquid. Next, add the tomato paste and cook until it turns a rusty color, about 5 minutes. Add the flour, mix well, and cook for about 3 minutes.

5 Deglaze the Dutch oven with the wine marinade. Use a wooden spoon to scrape all of the stuff at the bottom of the pan and incorporate it into the sauce. Add the stock, smoked turkey neck, and bay leaves, mix well, and then add the chicken back to the Dutch oven. Season with salt and pepper. Cover, set in the oven, and cook for about 45 minutes or until the chicken falls off the bone. Remove from the oven, take out the thyme and bay leaves, and rest for about 5 minutes before serving.

PER SERVING: *Calories 453 (From Fat 247); Fat 27g (Saturated 7g); Cholesterol 88mg; Sodium 1871mg; Carbohydrate 24g (Dietary Fiber 2g); Protein 22g.*

Classic Chicken Parmigiana

PREP TIME: 12 MIN	COOK TIME: 10 MIN	YIELD: 4 SERVINGS

INGREDIENTS

4 skinless, boneless chicken breast halves

Salt and pepper

½ cup all-purpose flour for dredging

1 egg

¾ cup breadcrumbs, plain or seasoned

¼ cup freshly grated Parmesan cheese

4 tablespoons butter

1 tablespoon olive oil

DIRECTIONS

1 Wash the chicken breasts and pat dry. Pound the chicken breasts between two pieces of wax paper to ¼-inch thick. Season both sides of the chicken with salt and pepper.

2 Place the flour on a plate. Beat the egg in a large, shallow bowl. Combine the breadcrumbs and Parmesan cheese in another shallow bowl large enough for dredging.

3 Heat the butter and the oil over medium to medium-high heat in a 10-inch cast-iron skillet.

4 Dip the chicken in the flour to coat both sides, then dip it in the eggs, and then in the breadcrumb mixture.

5 Cook the chicken 5 to 7 minutes, turning once, until golden brown and cooked through. To serve, place the chicken on a bed of cooked pasta and pour over your favorite tomato sauce.

NOTE: Classic parmigiana recipes are served over *vermicelli* (thin spaghetti) and covered in a tomato sauce. So grab a box of pasta and your favorite tomato sauce for this one. For added authenticity, top it off with melted mozzarella cheese.

PER SERVING: *Calories 448 (From Fat 200); Fat 22g (Saturated 10g); Cholesterol 164mg; Sodium 480mg; Carbohydrate 27g (Dietary Fiber 1g); Protein 33g.*

Chicken Marsala

PREP TIME: 10 MIN | **COOK TIME: 10 MIN** | **YIELD: 4 SERVINGS**

INGREDIENTS

4 skinless, boneless chicken breast halves

4 tablespoons butter

½ teaspoon salt

Pepper

1 tablespoon fresh lemon juice

½ cup Marsala wine

½ cup chicken broth

½ pound mushrooms, sliced

Fresh parsley for garnish (optional)

DIRECTIONS

1 Pound the chicken pieces between two pieces of wax paper until ¼-inch thick.

2 Melt the butter in a 12-inch cast-iron skillet over medium heat. Cook the chicken for about 5 minutes on each side or until golden brown. Remove to a platter and keep warm.

3 Increase the heat to medium-high. Add the salt, pepper, lemon juice, wine, and chicken broth to the skillet and blend. Cook the wine mixture for a few minutes and then add the mushrooms and cook until tender.

4 Pour the sauce over the chicken and garnish with parsley, if desired.

PER SERVING: Calories 267 (From Fat 136); Fat 15g (Saturated 8g); Cholesterol 104mg; Sodium 483mg; Carbohydrate 3g (Dietary Fiber 1g); Protein 29g.

Chicken Picata

INGREDIENTS

4 or 5 skinless, boneless chicken breast halves

Salt and pepper

½ cup all-purpose flour

3 to 4 tablespoons butter

¼ cup white wine, or vermouth

⅓ cup chicken broth

Juice of ½ lemon

Lemon slices (optional)

Parsley sprigs (optional)

DIRECTIONS

1 Between two pieces of wax or parchment paper, pound the breasts until flat. Sprinkle with salt and pepper on both sides of the chicken. Dredge in the flour.

2 In a 12-inch cast-iron skillet on medium-high heat, sauté breasts in the butter. When both sides are brown, about 5 minutes, remove the breasts from the skillet, put them on a different plate, and keep warm.

3 Reduce the heat and add the wine and chicken stock to the skillet. Simmer for a few minutes and then add the lemon juice.

4 Place the chicken on serving plates and pour the pan juices over the chicken.

5 Garnish with lemon slice and parsley sprig, if desired.

VARY IT! Make Veal Picata simply by substituting veal for the chicken in the recipe.

PER SERVING: *Calories 280 (From Fat 109); Fat 12g (Saturated 6g); Cholesterol 97mg; Sodium 293mg; Carbohydrate 13g (Dietary Fiber 1g); Protein 29g.*

Tackling Other Poultry

For many people turkey is for only around the holidays because of its ability to pair well with almost anything and its size, which is perfect for family gatherings. But if you're single or tend to cook for one or two people, the Cornish hen may be a better option for you from both a time and yield perspective. Both birds can add value to any meal, and using the right pan can mean the difference between a beautiful texture and dried-out protein.

TECHNICAL STUFF

Did you know that the female turkey, once matured, is referred to as a hen? The hen is often considered superior in terms of meat quality because it's typically raised for an extended period, allowing the hen a longer growing time and the meat to mature, resulting in a deeper taste and richer flavor profile.

These recipes focus on the Dutch oven but can easily work with your favorite cast-iron skillet:

>> **Dutch Oven Turkey:** This succulent turkey recipe will tempt you to dive right in as soon as it's on the platter, but be patient. A turkey is easier to carve if you let it sit for 20 minutes first.

>> **Dutch Oven Cornish Hens:** Rock Cornish hens, also called *Cornish game hens,* are miniature chickens that weigh between 1½ to 2½ pounds. Because of the relatively small amount of meat to bone, one bird feeds one or two people, depending on the size of their appetites. Rock Cornish hens are often broiled or roasted; sometimes, they're stuffed.

>> **Pheasant Faisan:** Pheasant Faisan is a classic French dish that showcases the rich and delicate flavors of pheasant. Pheasant itself is a game bird with lean, firm, and flavorful meat, making it a popular choice for special occasions.

Dutch Oven Turkey

PREP TIME: 15 MIN	COOK TIME: 1½ HRS	YIELD: 6 TO 8 SERVINGS

INGREDIENTS

1 whole turkey breast (5 to 7 pounds) or whole chicken (giblets removed)

2 whole garlic bulbs, cut in halve across lengthwise

2 bay leaves

2 sprigs thyme

1 lemon, cut in half across lengthwise

1 tablespoon onion powder

1 teaspoon garlic powder

¼ teaspoon cayenne powder

1 teaspoon salt

½ teaspoon black pepper

1 onion, chopped

6 cloves garlic, sliced

¼ cup honey

½ cup orange juice

1 quart chicken stock

1 tablespoon cornstarch

10 cloves of garlic, thinly sliced

1 large onion, chopped

4 ounces butter, sliced

One 16-ounce jar honey

Two 14-ounce cans chicken broth

½ cup orange juice

3 tablespoons cornstarch

DIRECTIONS

1 Prepare the turkey by rinsing and patting dry. Place 2 whole garlic cloves, bay leaves, thyme, and lemon in the turkey cavity. Mix the onion powder, garlic powder, cayenne, salt, and pepper in a small bowl. Season the turkey both outside, under the skin, and inside. Set aside.

2 Preheat your oven to 350 degrees. Sauté the garlic slices and the onion in the butter in the Dutch oven over medium-high heat. Add the honey, orange juice, and 1 quart chicken stock, bring to a simmer. Whisk in the cornstarch. Cook for about 3 minutes and remove from heat.

3 Carefully place the turkey in a 7- or 9-quart Dutch oven and cover with a lid.

4 Bake for 1 hour to 1 hour and 20 minutes, depending on size of the bird, basting the bird every 15 minutes with pan juices. Add the chicken stock sparingly as needed to keep liquid at about the same level in the oven. When the turkey has reached 165 degrees on the meat thermometer in the thickest part of the breast, remove it from the oven. Remove to a platter and let rest 10 minutes before carving.

5 For delicious gravy, strain and defat the pan juices, reserving the solids. Return the juices to the Dutch oven. Dissolve the cornstarch into ½ cup of water and add to the pan juices. Simmer for about 3 minutes, scraping up any browned bits, until the mixture thickens. Add the reserved solids, if desired.

NOTE: In Step 3, if the turkey is touching the lid, spray some cooking spray on the underside of the lid to keep the turkey from sticking. Another option is to use foil to "tent" the Dutch oven and don't use the lid.

PER SERVING: *Calories 774 (From Fat 213); Fat 24g (Saturated 11g); Cholesterol 291mg; Sodium 709mg; Carbohydrate 78g (Dietary Fiber1 g); Protein 65g.*

Dutch Oven Cornish Hens

PREP TIME: 5 MIN	COOK TIME: 1 HR	YIELD: 8 SERVINGS

INGREDIENTS

4 Rock Cornish hens, halved

4 teaspoons salt

1 teaspoon pepper

6 tablespoons all-purpose flour

3 tablespoons butter

3 tablespoons vegetable oil

¼ teaspoon sage

¼ teaspoon dried thyme

¼ teaspoon marjoram

½ teaspoon chili powder

¾ teaspoon paprika

¼ cup sherry

½ cup chopped fresh parsley

DIRECTIONS

1 Preheat oven to 375 degrees. Season the hens with the salt and pepper and coat with the flour.

2 Melt the butter and heat the oil in a 5-quart cast-iron Dutch oven over medium-high heat. Add the sage, thyme, marjoram, chili powder, and paprika.

3 Brown each half hen on all sides, a few at a time, without crowding. As each half browns, about 12 minutes, remove it from the Dutch oven and keep warm.

4 When all halves are browned, return them to the Dutch oven, and bake uncovered for about 20 minutes, or until fork tender. Remove hens to a serving platter.

5 Place the Dutch oven on the stovetop over medium heat. Add the sherry to the pan juices, scraping the bottom to deglaze the pan. Stir and cook for 2 minutes.

6 Stir in the parsley and pour the sherry mixture over the hens.

NOTE: Wild rice is an excellent accompaniment to this recipe.

PER SERVING: *Calories 498 (From Fat 329); Fat 37g (Saturated 13g); Cholesterol 223mg; Sodium 1,266mg; Carbohydrate 5g (Dietary Fiber 1g); Protein 35g.*

Pheasant Faisan

PREP TIME: 5 MIN	COOK TIME: 30 MIN	YIELD: 4 SERVINGS

INGREDIENTS

2 pounds of pheasant, cleaned and cut into serving-size pieces

Salt and pepper

6 tablespoons cold butter

1 clove garlic, peeled and crushed

1 bay leaf

½ teaspoon dried thyme

¾ cup dry white wine

2 tablespoons fresh parsley, finely chopped for garnish (optional)

DIRECTIONS

1 Season the pheasant with salt and pepper.

2 Heat 3 tablespoons of the butter in a 10-inch cast-iron skillet over medium-high heat.

3 Add the pheasant pieces skin-side down and cook until golden brown, about 5 minutes. Turn the pieces and cook another 3 minutes. If necessary, brown the pheasant in batches.

4 Reduce the heat to medium and add the garlic, bay leaf, thyme, and wine. Cover and cook 20 minutes or until the pheasant is fork tender. Remove the pheasant to the serving platter.

5 Swirl the remaining cold butter into the pan sauce, scraping the bottom of the skillet to deglaze.

6 Remove the bay leaf and pour the sauce over the pheasant and garnish with the parsley, if desired.

NOTE: After an initial browning in butter, this recipe uses moist heat to cook the pheasant to doneness. This technique tenderizes the meat.

TIP: To save some time, have the butcher cut up your pheasant.

PER SERVING: *Calories 508 (From Fat 317); Fat 35g (Saturated 16g); Cholesterol 185mg; Sodium 226mg; Carbohydrate 1g (Dietary Fiber 0g); Protein 45g.*

Chapter **16**
Fish, Shellfish, and One Amphibian

I n the cooking world, a lot of people say the hardest thing to cook is seafood. Unlike chicken, beef, or pork that offers some forgiveness, most seafood is delicate and temperamental, meaning you can't just set it on the stove and forget it or you'll more than likely come back to something dry and unpalatable.

This chapter breaks down some barriers and empowers you to cook fish with grace in your favorite cast iron. Regardless whether you're cooking freshwater or saltwater fish or seafood, each recipe takes you one step closer to mastering your cast iron.

Fishing for Freshwater Fish Dishes

Unlike red meat, which doctors say you should eat in moderation due to its link with high cholesterol and pork with its link to saturated fatty acids, fish and seafood are usually lower in calories and saturated fat. They're also a great source of omega-3 fatty acids. Pair that with the iron benefits from cooking in cast iron and you have a winner!

Here are a couple of freshwater fish you can experiment with the following fresh-water fish recipes:

» **Pan-Fried Catfish:** Popularized in the Southern United States yet recognized internationally, catfish has a crispy exterior and tender, flaky flesh, which can be described as mild, slightly sweet, and earthy.

» **Pan-Seared Trout:** Pan-seared trout is loved for its tender, flaky texture and its ability to absorb and enhance the flavors of the seasonings and cooking fats, oh, and don't forget its delicate and mild flavor profile. It's well-known in regions with abundant freshwater sources, such as North America, Europe, and Asia.

I have to shout out here my current home state of Virginia where the combination of abundant water resources, recreational fishing opportunities, and a thriving culinary scene contribute to the popularity of fish on menus across the state.

Whether it's from a lake, river, or pond, freshwater fish often have a milder flavor than saltwater fish, allowing them to absorb other flavors and seasonings. Whether you prefer subtle flavors or bold seasonings, more than likely you can find a freshwater fish to accommodate your taste.

FISH, MERCURY, AND PREGNANCY

Nearly all fish contain at least trace amounts of mercury, more specifically *methylmercury,* a by-product of industrial pollution that accumulates in living organisms, such as fish, and is easily passed on to people.

Mercury is dangerous for pregnant women because it can harm the fetus. So does that mean you should swear off all fish if you're pregnant? No.

The U.S. Food and Drug Administration (FDA) recommends the following: If you're pregnant or may become pregnant, you should avoid eating shark, swordfish, king mackerel, and tilefish, which are known to contain higher levels of methylmercury.

Why avoid these fish and not salmon or cod, for example? Salmon and cod, as well as haddock, pollock, and sole, have shorter life spans. The longer that a fish lives, then the longer that it's exposed to mercury, and the more mercury it absorbs. For that reason, large predatory fish that live longer, such as shark or swordfish, accumulate the highest amounts of mercury and pose the largest threat to people who eat them regularly. Most shellfish contain relatively low levels of methylmercury.

If you're pregnant or trying to get pregnant and are concerned about this issue, talk to your doctor.

Pan-Fried Catfish

PREP TIME: 25 MIN | **COOK TIME: 5 MIN** | **YIELD: 4 SERVINGS**

INGREDIENTS

4 catfish fillets (about 1½ pounds)

1 cup buttermilk, or enough to cover the fillets

1 tablespoon Cajun seasoning

1 cup cornmeal

Salt and pepper

1 quart canola oil to fill skillet ¼-inch deep

DIRECTIONS

1 In a flat dish, soak the fish fillets in the buttermilk for about 20 minutes. Mix the Cajun seasoning with the cornmeal in a small bowl.

2 Lay the fish on wax paper. Discard the buttermilk. Season both sides of the fish with the salt and pepper. Dredge the fish in the cornmeal mixture.

3 Heat the oil in a 12-inch cast-iron skillet over slightly higher than medium-heat. Place the fillets in the skillet and brown on both sides, about 2 minutes on each side, turning carefully with a spatula.

4 After the fish browns, reduce the heat to medium or lower to finish cooking if your filets are thick.

TIP: When you prepare your catfish fillets, remove any skin and the dark fatty tissue that's directly underneath it. This tissue has a strong fishy taste.

PER SERVING: *Calories 427 (From Fat 196); Fat 22g (Saturated 4g); Cholesterol 78mg; Sodium 348mg; Carbohydrate 30g (Dietary Fiber 3g); Protein 31g.*

TARTAR SAUCE

You can easily whip up a batch of your own tartar sauce with this recipe. Mix all of the following ingredients together and refrigerate until you're ready to serve:

- 1 cup mayonnaise
- 1½ tablespoon finely chopped cornichons, plus 1 teaspoon cornichon juice
- 1 tablespoon finely chopped green onions — only the green part
- 1 tablespoon Dijon mustard
- ½ to 1 teaspoon minced garlic

Note: Cornichons are tart pickles make from tiny little gherkin cucumbers. If you can't find cornichons, you can substitute the same amount of any other pickle you like.

Pan-Seared Trout

PREP TIME: 5 MIN	COOK TIME: 8 MIN	YIELD: 2 SERVINGS

INGREDIENTS

2 trout fillets (4 to 6 ounces each)

Salt and pepper to taste

2 tablespoons olive oil

1 shallot, thinly sliced

2 garlic cloves, crushed

2 sprigs thyme

2 tablespoons butter

1 lemon, cut into wedges

DIRECTIONS

1 Place the trout fillets skin side up on a baking tray and score the skin of the fish twice with a sharp knife. Season both sides with salt and pepper.

2 Preheat a large cast-iron skillet with the olive oil over medium for about 2 minutes. Add the trout to the pan skin side down. Use your spatula to slightly press down on the trout for about 30 seconds to ensure it doesn't buckle.

3 Add the shallot, garlic, thyme, and 1 tablespoon of butter to the pan. Cook the trout skin side down for about 5 minutes or until golden brown. Use a spoon to baste the fish with the flavor-infused butter in the skillet while it's cooking. Flip the trout over, add another tablespoon of butter to the skillet, and cook for an additional 2 minutes.

4 Remove the trout and rest 5 minutes before serving. Discard the contents of the pan after the fish is removed. Serve with a lemon wedge.

NOTE: By adding the shallots, garlic, and thyme to your skillet, you're infusing flavors into the oil, which means those beautiful flavors will go into the fish.

NOTE: Often, when cooking a protein with skin, the hot heat causes the skin to retract, creating a buckle or fold in the meat. *Scoring* your protein refers to making shallow cuts or gashes on the protein's surface. The purpose of scoring is to enhance the cooking process and improve the overall texture, helping with even cooking. By scoring your fish, it helps release the tension and achieves more even cooking across the surface of your meat.

PER SERVING: *Calories 354 (From Fat 267); Fat 30g (Saturated 10g); Cholesterol 136mg; Sodium 156mg; Carbohydrate 0g (Dietary Fiber 0g); Protein 21g.*

Frying Some Saltwater Fish Dishes

Depending on where you grew up, your palate may have become accustomed to specific textures and flavor profiles. For instance, if you grew up near lakes and streams, you may have developed a taste for milder-flavored fish like trout. On the other hand, if you grew up near the ocean, your palate may be more attuned to bolder flavors, like salmon and other saltwater fish. A person's taste preferences are often influenced by the local culinary traditions and the types of fish readily available in their surroundings.

Take salmon for example. They spawn in freshwater where they fight their way downstream (and sometimes upstream) to return to the open sea. After that they face a whole new battle: different temperature, deeper water, bigger fish (that may eat them), and a much different diet. All of these help the salmon develop its beautiful texture and flavor.

The ocean acts the same way a marinade does to a protein — it naturally provides the fish with its unique briny flavor that brings out its amazing taste when the fish hits your cast iron. The caramelization gained from the cast iron's heat control is just one reason why cast iron is the best choice for the following classic saltwater recipes:

>> **Blackened Salmon:** If you're looking to take your salmon to the next level, blackening seasoning is the perfect way to kick it up a few notches. Aside from enhancing the flavor and texture, the spice creates a crust on the surface, which adds another layer of flavor.

>> **Blackened Tuna:** If you're a spiced and seared seafood fan, blackened tuna is the winning cast-iron dish for you. Originating in the culinary traditions of Louisiana, this dish offers a beautifully charred exterior with a tender and juicy interior.

>> **Cod Fish and Chips:** This classic British dish consists of battered and deep-fried cod fillets served with a side of thick-cut potato fries. The mild and flaky cod, crispy batter, savory potato, and tangy condiments create a well-rounded flavor profile.

Blackened Salmon

INGREDIENTS

2 salmon fillets, skin off
(4 to 6 ounces each)

2 tablespoons Blackening
Seasoning Mix

2 tablespoons olive oil

1 lemon, halved lengthwise,
sliced into thirds

DIRECTIONS

1 Add the salmon to a medium bowl or plate and generously season with blackening seasoning on both sides.

2 Preheat a 10-inch cast-ion skillet with olive oil over medium heat for about 3 minutes. Add the blackened salmon to the skillet, allowing it to cook for about 3 to 5 minutes, and then flip and repeat the process.

3 Remove the salmon from the skillet and allow it to rest for about 5 minutes. Serve with a lemon wedge.

NOTE: The fish should be cooked to an internal temperature of 145 degrees.

Blackening Seasoning Mix

2 tablespoons smoked paprika

1 teaspoon onion powder

1 teaspoon garlic powder

½ teaspoon black pepper

¼ teaspoon salt

¼ teaspoon cayenne powder

½ teaspoon dried thyme

½ teaspoon fennel seed, ground (optional)

1 In a small bowl add all ingredients and mix well. Store in an airtight container.

VARY IT: Substitute sweet paprika or Hungarian paprika to diversify your flavors.

TIP: Pair this recipe with Pan-Roasted Asparagus with Garlic and Parmesan in Chapter 18; refer to the color insert.

PER SERVING: *Calories 280 (From Fat 186); Fat 21g (Saturated 3g); Cholesterol 62mg; Sodium 341mg; Carbohydrate 0g (Dietary Fiber 0g); Protein 22g.*

Blackened Tuna

PREP TIME: 5 MIN | COOK TIME: 10 MIN | YIELD: 2 SERVINGS

INGREDIENTS

1 tablespoon smoked paprika

1 teaspoon salt

½ teaspoon garlic powder

½ teaspoon onion powder

¼ teaspoon ginger powder

¼ teaspoon cayenne powder

¼ teaspoon sugar

1 lemon, zest only

2 tuna steaks, sushi grade Ahi

2 tablespoons olive oil

1 shallot, sliced

2 garlic cloves, crushed

2 sprigs thyme

2 tablespoons butter

DIRECTIONS

1 In a bowl add the smoked paprika, salt, garlic powder, onion powder, ginger powder, cayenne, sugar, and lemon zest. Mix well.

2 Place the tuna on a baking tray and generously season with spice mixture on both sides. After it's completely coated, shake off any excess seasoning and reserve.

3 Preheat a large cast-iron skillet over medium-high heat with the olive oil for about 2 minutes. Add the tuna and allow it to sear for about 2 minutes. Around the tuna, add the shallot, garlic, thyme, and 1 tablespoon of butter. Use hot oil to baste the tuna while it's cooking for about 1 minute or until you have a beautiful sear.

4 Flip and repeat the process. Remove from the pan and allow the tuna to slightly cool for about 2 minutes before serving.

NOTE: Aim for an internal temperature of about 130 to 132 degrees for medium rare; look for a golden-brown crust.

NOTE: It's crucial not only to cook the tuna properly but also to purchase it from a reputable purveyor to ensure that the fish has been handled and stored following strict safety guidelines, minimizing the risk of foodborne illnesses.

PER SERVING: *Calories 349 (From Fat 235); Fat 26g (Saturated 9g); Cholesterol 82mg; Sodium 1288mg; Carbohydrate 1g (Dietary Fiber 0g); Protein 27g.*

Cod Fish and Chips

PREP TIME: 10 MIN	COOK TIME: 40 MIN	YIELD: 4 SERVINGS

INGREDIENTS

1½ cups flour

½ cup cornstarch

1 teaspoon baking powder

1 teaspoon salt

½ teaspoon smoked paprika

1½ cups soda water

½ teaspoon salt

¼ teaspoon garlic powder

¼ teaspoon onion powder

¼ teaspoon cayenne powder

1 quart peanut oil or canola oil

3 large russet potatoes cut into strips (rinsed and drained)

1 pound cod, cut into strips

DIRECTIONS

1 In a medium bowl, mix the flour, cornstarch, baking powder, salt, and paprika with a whisk. Add the club soda to make a batter.

2 Using another bowl mix the salt, garlic powder, onion powder, and cayenne, and reserve for the potato seasoning.

3 Add the peanut oil to your Dutch oven and preheat to about 350 degrees.

4 Add the potatoes to the bowl from Step 2, tossing together to ensure each potato is coated in seasoning. Carefully add half of the potatoes to the hot oil in the Dutch oven and cook until golden brown, about 10 to 15 minutes. Remove from oil with tongs or a slotted spoon if available. Place on either a plate with two to three paper towels or a baking tray with a rack to cool. Repeat the process until all are cooked. Allow the oil to reheat to 350 degrees.

5 Add the cod to the bowl from Step 1, carefully coating the fish with batter. Before cooking allow the fish to drip for about 3 to 5 seconds over the bowl to remove excess batter. Carefully add 3 to 4 strips of the cod to the hot oil in the Dutch oven and cook until golden brown, about 8 to 10 minutes. Remove from the oil with tongs or a slotted spoon if available. Place on either a plate with two to three paper towels or a clean baking tray with a rack to cool. Repeat the process until all are cooked and serve.

NOTE: Serve with malt vinegar and your favorite dipping sauce.

TIP: When you remove fried food, don't pile it on top of each other. Doing so causes the food to steam and you lose the beautiful crispy texture. Give the food enough space to spread out and stay crispy.

PER SERVING: *Calories 633 (From Fat 104); Fat 12g (Saturated 2g); Cholesterol 49mg; Sodium 968mg; Carbohydrate 100g (Dietary Fiber 5g); Protein 31g.*

Slaying Shellfish Dishes

One thing that most people don't consider when cooking shellfish is the value the shell adds to the dish. Here are three ways the shell can take your dish to the next level:

» The shells of mollusks like clams and mussels contain minerals called *carbonate,* which adds a slightly earthy flavor to the dish.

» Steaming or boiling shellfish traps their natural juices in the shell; they release when the shell is opened, allowing the flavors to intensify.

» Roasting the shells like lobsters and crabs after the meat is removed allows you to maximize flavor. You can use them in soups, stocks, and much more.

These recipes offer a wide range of ways you can add shellfish to your cast-iron cooking:

» **Seafood Chowder:** This is a popular dish in coastal regions around the world, which are known for their bountiful seafood, offering a comforting and rich dining experience. Seafood chowder is a hearty and flavorful soup that combines an assortment of seafood with vegetables, cream, and seasonings.

» **Louisiana Seafood Gumbo:** Gumbo is a popular and traditional Creole dish with both French and African influences. Thanks to its diverse combination of ingredients, gumbo is known for its rich and complex flavors.

» **Cioppino:** Cioppino is a delicious Italian-American seafood stew that originated in San Francisco. The name Cioppino is said to come from the Italian word *ciuppin,* which means *to chop* or *chopped up,* referring to the assortment of ingredients stirred together in the stew.

» **Lemon and Garlic Steamed Clams:** This classic seafood dish showcases the natural brininess of fresh clams. It's often served with the cooking liquid known as the *liquor.* The liquor is delicious and can be mopped up with crusty bread, enhancing the dish's overall taste.

» **Deep-Fried Shrimp and Oysters:** This recipe is a fried favorite but don't let that stop you from experimenting.

» **Pan-Fried Soft-Shell Crabs:** *Soft-shell crabs* are blue crabs that have been taken from the ocean as soon as they shed their shell, and they're delicious fried.

Seafood Chowder

INGREDIENTS

¼ cup unsalted butter

2 medium onions, diced

½ cup diced celery

1 cup diced carrots

1 cup diced potatoes

1 cup sliced mushrooms

1 cup white wine

4 cups clam juice

Juice reserved from oysters

1 sprig fresh thyme

2 tablespoons chopped fresh parsley

One can (6½ ounces) chopped clams

8 ounces shucked oysters, or one 8-ounce jar shucked oysters

8 ounces mussels in shell

8 ounces salmon fillets, de-boned and cut into 1-inch cubes

Salt and pepper

1 cup heavy cream

DIRECTIONS

1 In 7- to 9-quart cast-iron Dutch oven, melt the butter over medium-high heat. When the butter is bubbling, add the onions, celery, carrots, potatoes, and mushrooms. Sauté for 10 minutes.

2 Add the wine, clam juice, oyster juice (however much you have), thyme, and parsley. Bring the mixture to a rolling boil and reduce the heat and simmer for 15 minutes.

3 Add the clams, oysters, mussels, and salmon, stirring well. Cook for an additional 15 minutes or until the salmon begins to flake and the mussels open and rise to the surface. Season to taste using salt and pepper. Discard any muscles that don't open.

4 Add the heavy cream and continue to simmer for 5 minutes. Ladle the chowder into the soup bowls and serve hot.

TIP: When you buy mussels, make sure that the shell is tightly closed or snaps shut when you tap on it, indicating that the mussel is alive and kicking! Don't buy mussels with broken shells, mussels that feel heavy with sand, or that rattle when you shake them, because the mussel is dead.

TIP: When you cook fresh mussels, they'll open, giving your chowder a fresh-from-the-sea appearance.

PER SERVING: *Calories 319 (From Fat 182); Fat 20g (Saturated 11g); Cholesterol 138mg; Sodium 549mg; Carbohydrate 13g (Dietary Fiber 2g); Protein 21g.*

Louisiana Seafood Gumbo

INGREDIENTS

1 cup vegetable oil

1 cup all-purpose flour

2 cups onions, chopped

1 cup chopped celery

1 cup chopped bell pepper

¼ cup diced garlic

½ pound sliced andouille

1 pound claw crabmeat

3 quarts warm shellfish stock, chicken broth, or vegetable broth

2 cups sliced green onions

½ cup chopped parsley

Salt and pepper

Hot pepper sauce

1 pound large shrimp, peeled, and deveined

1 pound jumbo lump crabmeat

2 dozen shucked oysters, reserve liquid

12 cups hot, cooked rice

DIRECTIONS

1 In a 7-quart cast-iron Dutch oven, heat the oil over medium heat. After the oil is hot, add the flour, and using a wire whisk, stir constantly until you have a brown roux, about 7 minutes.

2 After the roux is brown, add the onions, celery, bell pepper, and garlic. Sauté until the vegetables are wilted, approximately 3 to 5 minutes. Add the andouille, blending well into the vegetable mixture. Sauté 2 to 3 minutes.

3 Add the claw crabmeat and stir into the roux. Then slowly add the shellfish stock, one ladle at a time, stirring constantly until all is incorporated. Bring to a low boil, reduce the heat to a simmer, and cook approximately 30 minutes. Add additional stock if necessary to retain the volume.

4 Add the green onions and the parsley. Season to taste using the salt, pepper, and hot pepper sauce. Fold the shrimp, lump crabmeat, oysters, and reserved oyster liquid into the soup. Return to a low boil and cook approximately 10 minutes. Adjust seasonings and serve over the cooked rice.

TIP: To make *brown roux*, you cook a mixture of flour and fat (in this recipe, vegetable oil) over low heat, watching it carefully as it darkens. It's ready when the mixture is a deep mahogany color.

NOTE: if you scorch the roux, you have to start all over again. Black specks are a clue that the roux has gone too far and needs to be thrown out.

PER SERVING: *Calories 709 (From Fat 273); Fat 30g (Saturated 5g); Cholesterol 183mg; Sodium 1,003mg; Carbohydrate 62g (Dietary Fiber 2g); Protein 43g.*

Cioppino

PREP TIME: 5 MIN | COOK TIME: 40 MIN | YIELD: 4 SERVINGS

INGREDIENTS

½ teaspoon turmeric

½ teaspoon saffron

2 tablespoons olive oil

1 medium onion, sliced

1 fennel, bottom only, halved lengthwise and thinly sliced

1 leek, white part only, halved lengthwise and thinly sliced

2 cloves garlic, minced

¼ teaspoon cayenne powder

½ teaspoon salt

2 sprigs thyme

2 bay leaves

1 cup white wine

1 cup tomato juice

1 Yukon gold potato, medium diced or cubed

2 cups seafood stock or vegetable broth

½ pound shrimp, peeled and deveined

½ pound washed mussels

½ pound washed clams

2 tablespoons basil, chiffonade

2 tablespoon parsley, chiffonade

2 tablespoons tarragon, chiffonade

1 lemon juice and zest

DIRECTIONS

1 Preheat the Dutch oven over medium heat for about 2 minutes. Add the turmeric and saffron, allowing to toast for about 3 minutes, slightly mixing with a wooden spoon.

2 Add the olive oil, onion, fennel, and leek. Cook for about 5 minutes or until soft.

3 Add the garlic and cook until fragrant, about 1 minute. Add the cayenne, salt, thyme, bay leaves, white wine, and tomato juice. Reduce by half, about 12 to 15 minutes. Add the potato and stock. Cook for about 10 to 12 minutes or until the potatoes are tender.

4 Reduce the heat to medium low. Add the shrimp, mussels, and clams. Cover with a lid and cook for about 5 to 7 minutes or until clams and mussels have opened and the shrimp is pink.

5 Remove from heat and add the basil, parsley, tarragon, and lemon zest and juice.

TIP: Serve with fresh baked bread.

PER SERVING: *Calories 321 (From Fat 85); Fat 9g (Saturated 1g); Cholesterol 105mg; Sodium 1043mg; Carbohydrate 27g (Dietary Fiber 3g); Protein 22g.*

Steamed Clams with Lemon and Garlic

PREP TIME: 15 MIN | **COOK TIME: 25 MIN** | **YIELD: 2 SERVINGS**

INGREDIENTS

1 quart water

2 teaspoons salt

1 pound clams

2 tablespoons olive oil

1 shallot, thinly sliced

4 cloves garlic, minced

1 cup white wine

1 cup seafood stock or vegetable stock

2 sprigs thyme

2 bay leaves

2 sprigs parsley, chopped

1 sprig tarragon, chopped (optional)

1 lemon zest and juice

DIRECTIONS

1 In a large bowl, add the water and salt and mix to dissolve. Add the clams and allow them to sit for about 15 minutes. Scrub, rinse, and drain; discard clams that are cracked or have broken shells.

2 Preheat your Dutch oven with olive oil over medium heat for about 2 minutes. Add the shallot and cook for 2 minutes.

3 Add the garlic and cook for an additional minute. Add the clams, white wine, stock, thyme, and bay leaves. Cover and cook for about 18 minutes, checking to see if the clams are open. Cover and cook for an additional 2 to 4 minutes or until the clams open. Discard any that don't open

4 Remove from the heat, and add parsley, tarragon, and lemon zest and juice, and serve.

PER SERVING: *Calories 254 (From Fat 125); Fat 14g (Saturated 2g); Cholesterol 12mg; Sodium 301mg; Carbohydrate 7g (Dietary Fiber 0g); Protein 5g.*

Deep-Fried Shrimp and Oysters

PREP TIME: 10 MIN	COOK TIME: 3 MIN PER BATCH	YIELD: 6 SERVINGS

INGREDIENTS

Peanut or vegetable oil for deep-frying

1 egg, beaten

1 cup milk

2 tablespoons Creole or spicy mustard

1 tablespoon yellow mustard

Salt and pepper

3 cups self-rising cornmeal

2 tablespoons garlic powder

2 dozen large shrimp

1 dozen shucked oysters

DIRECTIONS

1 Using a deep-sided cast-iron pan or deep-fryer, heat the oil to 375 degrees, about 10 minutes.

2 In a mixing bowl, combine the egg, milk, 1 cup of water, and mustards and season with salt and pepper. In a separate mixing bowl, combine the cornmeal and garlic and season with salt and pepper. Set aside.

3 Dip the seafood in the egg mixture and then into the cornmeal mixture. Place into the basket and carefully lower into the hot oil.

4 Cook until the seafood floats, approximately 3 minutes. Remove, drain, and keep warm. Continue until all the seafood is cooked. Serve hot.

NOTE: The cooking temperature for seafood and fish is always the same. Chapter 8 provides cooking times; mix and match the fish and seafood that you use with this recipe.

PER SERVING: *Calories 461 (From Fat 165); Fat 18g (Saturated 3g); Cholesterol 103mg; Sodium 1,242mg; Carbohydrate 58g (Dietary Fiber 5g); Protein 15g.*

Pan-Fried Soft-Shell Crabs

PREP TIME: 10 MIN	COOK TIME: 6 MIN EACH CRAB	YIELD: 4 SERVINGS

INGREDIENTS

Salt and pepper

8 medium soft-shell crabs, cleaned

½ cup all-purpose flour

½ cup cornmeal

4 tablespoons butter

Lemon wedges

DIRECTIONS

1 Salt and pepper the crabs. In a medium bowl, combine the flour and cornmeal. Dredge the crabs in the flour mixture; shake off the excess.

2 Heat your 12-inch cast-iron skillet over medium-high heat until hot. Drop the butter into the hot pan and swirl to keep the butter from burning as it melts. Place the crabs, shell side down, into the pan. Cover with a splatter screen and cook until the crab turns reddish brown, about 3 minutes. Turn the crabs over and cook until the other side is brown, about 3 minutes more. The crabs should be crispy and golden brown.

3 Drain crabs on paper towels and serve immediately with lemon wedges, or place in a warm oven.

VARY IT! Add some Cajun seasoning to the mix for more heat.

PER SERVING: *Calories 517 (From Fat 290); Fat 32g (Saturated 16g); Cholesterol 195mg; Sodium 600mg; Carbohydrate 26g (Dietary Fiber 2g); Protein 30g.*

STOCKING UP

Stock is the liquid you get when you cook vegetables, meat, chicken, or seafood, in addition to other seasoning ingredients, in water. Basically, stock is broth. It makes a nice base for soups. Whether you make beef, chicken, vegetable, or seafood stock, the steps are the same:

1. Add your ingredients to a *stockpot.* Cover with water. The ingredients include the following:

   - **Meat, seafood, or vegetables:** These ingredients provide the main flavor. Many cooks make beef or chicken stock from leftover bones. Roast a chicken, for example, and instead of tossing the bones, use them to make chicken stock. For vegetable or seafood stock, use fresh, whole veggies or fresh seafood — or the parts that you're not cooking. For example, when you clean fish for dinner, save the heads and bones for the stock.

   - **Other flavor-enhancing ingredients:** These ingredients often include celery, onion, carrots, and bay leaves.

2. Bring the stock to a boil; then reduce the heat to a slow simmer.

3. Let the stock simmer for several hours. During this time, skim off the foam and impurities that rise to the water's surface.

4. Strain the stock and toss out all solids (chicken, bones, vegetables, bay leaf, and any other ingredients, for example). You should have a clear liquid. Remove the fat from the stock. (You won't have to do this with vegetable stock.) Use or store the stock.

Making stock is becoming less common because it takes time. Plus chicken and beef broth are readily available canned. Still, if you're inclined to make your own stock, keep these tips in mind:

- Don't let the water boil. You want the liquid to be clear, and boiling gets everything stirred up; it also breaks the fat down into droplets that are too small to be caught by a strainer. The result? Greasy stock.

- Don't use vegetables with strong individual flavors: Put broccoli in a vegetable stock, for example, and it pretty much obliterates all the other flavors.

- Store stock in the freezer in portion-size containers. You can use ice-cube trays (one cube equals about 2 tablespoons) or 1- and 2-cup containers. Divided this way, you can take out just as much stock as you need.

Getting Amphibious — No Watercraft Required

Frog legs have an interesting history, dating back to the Egyptians who believed that consuming frog legs brought good luck and fertility. Ancient Greeks and Romans also considered them a gourmet food.

French chefs during the Renaissance period took frog legs to the next level by pairing them with refined cooking techniques, making frog legs legendary in the culinary word.

Today frog legs are still legendary around the world and considered a niche food. Their unique taste and texture continue to attract attention. I hope the recipe in this section inspires you be a bit more adventure with your cast iron.

Pan-Fried Frog Legs

PREP TIME: 2 HRS | **COOK TIME: 5 MIN** | **YIELD: 3 SERVINGS**

INGREDIENTS

12 small frog legs

1 egg

1 cup buttermilk

1 teaspoon salt

1 teaspoon pepper

½ to 1 teaspoon Cajun seasoning

Vegetable oil for deep-frying

½ cup self-rising flour

½ cup self-rising cornmeal mix

DIRECTIONS

1 Rinse the frog legs and pat dry.

2 In a large bowl, beat the egg, buttermilk, salt, pepper, and Cajun seasoning together. Add the frog legs and soak them for up to 2 hours.

3 Heat 5 inches of the oil in a deep-fryer to 375 degrees.

4 In a medium bowl, combine the flour and cornmeal. Dredge the frog legs in the flour mixture. Drop into the hot oil without crowding. Fry until golden brown, 4 to 5 minutes. Serve with tartar sauce.

TIP: Don't overcook your frog legs. Doing so makes them tough.

PER SERVING: *Calories 552 (From Fat 161); Fat 18g (Saturated 2g); Cholesterol 219mg; Sodium 1,652mg; Carbohydrate 38g (Dietary Fiber 2g); Protein 57g.*

Chapter **17**

Veggies Highlighted in Main and Side Dishes

Understanding the seasonality of vegetables empowers you to think differently about how to cook them. In springtime, when squash blossoms, baby beets, and spring onions emerge, and in the fall, as garlic, pumpkin, and sweet potato take center stage, you can find yourself filled with anticipation. These delightful seasonal ingredients can ignite your culinary imagination, prompting you to craft timeless dishes and forge lasting memories alongside those you choose to share these culinary adventures with.

This chapter dives into how you can use vegetables for various meals, including main dishes and sides. Vegetables know no bounds. With the perfect cast iron and cooking technique, the possibilities are limitless.

REMEMBER

Although not all the recipes in this chapter are vegetarian, they all do have vegetables as the star ingredients. To make these recipes pop with flavor, strive to use fresh, in-season vegetables.

Creating Vegetable-Centered Entrees

Often, people's perception of protein leads them to associate it exclusively with beef, chicken, pork, or fish. As vegetarians have known for decades, some vegetables, such as chickpeas and tofu, serve as excellent sources of protein. (You may find it surprising to discover that tofu, which is derived from soybeans, also falls under the vegetable category.) Although some of these entrée recipes aren't strictly vegetarian, they're all about the veggies (you can also try the Curry Tofu with Mustard Greens recipe in Chapter 13):

>> **Summer Squash Casserole:** Known for its creamy and comforting texture, this casserole is the perfect excuse to add squash and zucchini to a dish.

>> **Pan-Seared Tofu Steak with Peppers and Onions:** Tofu is one of the most versatile ingredients available. It takes on flavor well and also cooks really well with peppers. This dish provides a smooth and creamy texture that can complement the peppers and onions.

>> **Sautéed Shrimp and Okra:** Whether it's in the form of a shrimp cocktail, scampi, or even shrimp fried rice, this small marine crustacean never fails to entice taste buds. Its versatility allows it to shine in a multitude of dishes. This dish also has okra, also known as "lady's finger," which has gained recognition for its unique slimy texture. Interestingly, when cooked, okra has the ability to act as a natural thickener in stews and sauces.

🍅 Summer Squash Casserole

INGREDIENTS

4 tablespoons butter

1 medium onion, minced

2 cloves garlic, minced

4 tablespoons flour

4 cups milk

Salt and pepper to taste

¼ teaspoon nutmeg

2 sprigs thyme, leaves only, chopped

2 sprigs parsley, leaves only, chopped

1 lemon zest only

1 pound yellow squash, ¼-inch slices

1 pound zucchini, ¼-inch slices

1 cup Parmesan cheese

1 cup smoked gouda cheese, grated

DIRECTIONS

1 Preheat the oven to 350 degrees. Preheat a Dutch oven over medium heat with butter, for about 2 minutes, or until melted.

2 Add the onions, allowing to sweat for about 5 minutes or until soft. Add the garlic and cook for 1 minute. Add the flour, mix well, and cook for about 3 minutes. Whisk in the milk, adding slowly so that the mixture doesn't lump. Bring to a simmer.

3 Adjust the seasoning with salt, pepper, and nutmeg, allowing the mixture to cook for about 10 minutes or until slightly thickened. Remove from the heat and add the thyme, parsley, and lemon zest.

4 Using a 12-inch cast-iron skillet, add about ½ cup of sauce to the skillet. Layer the squash and zucchini, alternating with a slight overlap around the pan to create a spiral to the center of the skillet.

5 Cover with another ½ cup of sauce. Add the Parmesan cheese and gouda cheese, enough to cover (about ¼ cup). Repeat the process until you use either all the sauce or the vegetables. Cover, place in the oven, and bake for 45 minutes. Remove the lid and bake for an additional 15 minutes. Remove from the oven and allow to cool for 5 minutes before serving.

NOTE: A good indicator regarding the thickness of the sauce is if it can coat a spoon, then it's good.

PER SERVING: *Calories 361 (From Fat 200); Fat 22g (Saturated 14g); Cholesterol 69mg; Sodium 601mg; Carbohydrate 22g (Dietary Fiber 2g); Protein 20g.*

Pan-Seared Tofu Steak with Peppers and Onions

PREP TIME: 10 MIN	COOK TIME: 15 MIN	YIELD: 4 SERVINGS

INGREDIENTS

2 tablespoons olive oil

1 block extra firm tofu, halved, sliced lengthwise

Salt and pepper to taste

1 shallot, sliced

2 cloves garlic, crushed

2 to 3 sprigs of thyme

2 tablespoons vegan butter

1 bell pepper, sliced

1 small onion, sliced

Smoked paprika (optional)

DIRECTIONS

1 Preheat your 10-inch cast-iron skillet over medium with olive oil for about 2 minutes.

2 Place the tofu on a baking tray and season with salt and pepper. Add the tofu to the skillet, allowing it to cook for about 3 to 5 minutes on each side, or until golden brown.

3 After you flip the tofu, add the shallot, garlic, and thyme. Add 1 tablespoon of butter —use your spoon to baste the butter and shallot mixture over the top of the tofu steak. After the butter is completely melted, add in the second tablespoon and repeat the process.

4 Remove the thyme from the pan and add the pepper and onion. Allow them to sauté for about 3 minutes.

5 Remove the skillet from the heat and allow it to rest, about 3 minutes. Finish with sprinkled smoked paprika and serve.

NOTE: Check out the photo in the color insert.

PER SERVING: *Calories 196 (From Fat 137); Fat 15g (Saturated 6g); Cholesterol 0mg; Sodium 50mg; Carbohydrate 10g (Dietary Fiber 2g); Protein 8g.*

Sautéed Shrimp and Okra

PREP TIME: 15 MIN	COOK TIME: 25 MIN	YIELD: 4 SERVINGS

INGREDIENTS

2 tablespoons butter

2 tablespoons flour

1 cup onion, minced

1 cup celery, minced

1 jalapeño, minced (optional)

2 cloves garlic, minced

1 teaspoon ginger, minced

1 cup okra, fresh or frozen, sliced

2 Roma tomatoes, small diced

Salt and pepper to taste

1 cup vegetable stock

1 pound shrimp, peeled and deveined

Lemon, zest and juice

2 sprigs parsley, leaves only, minced

½ teaspoon cayenne powder (optional)

DIRECTIONS

1 Preheat a 10-inch cast-iron skillet over medium heat with butter for about 2 minutes, or until butter is melted.

2 Add the flour and cook for about 3 minutes until slightly brown. Add the onions, celery, and jalapeños, and sweat for about 5 minutes. Add the garlic and ginger, cooking for about 1 minute. Add the okra and tomatoes and cook for about 5 minutes. Season with salt and pepper. Add the stock, shrimp, lemon zest and juice, parsley, and cayenne.

3 Cook for about 3 to 5 minutes. Remove from the heat and rest for 5 minutes before serving.

NOTE: This dish is great over your favorite rice. Add some garlic and chili flakes to the rice to add more value to this dish. Refer to the color insert for a photo.

PER SERVING: Calories 232 (From Fat 72); Fat 8g (Saturated 4g); Cholesterol 188mg; Sodium 377mg; Carbohydrate 15g (Dietary Fiber 2g); Protein 25g.

Making Veggies the Star — Side Dishes

This section is completely devoid of cheese or bacon fat. These recipes resemble a pristine clear night sky, allowing the stars — your vegetables — to shine and showcase their inherent beauty. These recipes dive into the art of minimalist cooking, where you harness the power of simplicity to enhance the flavors of your vegetables. By carefully selecting complementary flavors, you create dishes that not only look stunning, but also tantalize your senses with their enticing aroma and extraordinary taste.

The following recipes are a great way to include more veggies in your diet. Add one or two to an entrée or make a meal out of a few:

» **Blistered Shishito Peppers:** Known for their mild yet slightly sweet flavor, these peppers make for a great summer snack. They're equally delicious when sautéed or grilled because they perfectly complement high-heat cooking.

» **Almondine Green Beans:** This dish features *haricots verts,* also known as french green beans. They have a distinct slim shape and a slightly higher price point. Combined with toasted almonds, they offer a nutty flavor and a delightful al dente texture.

» **Stewed Chickpeas:** Stewed chickpeas, or chickpea stew, are delectable and nourishing where chickpeas are simmered in a flavorful broth.

» **Three-Bean Succotash:** The Native American tribe known as the Narragansett would refer to this particular dish as "msickquatash," which translates to "boiled whole kernels of corn." Throughout the years, this recipe has undergone changes and now incorporates a diverse range of beans and vegetables.

» **Skillet Cabbage:** This dish is beloved in European and American cuisines and cherished for its versatility and simplicity. With its availability during the season, long shelf life, and flavorful characteristics, it serves as an ideal side dish or a flavorful complement to meat or plant-based protein in any main course.

» **Thyme-Scented Root Vegetables:** The process of roasting root vegetables results in a delicious caramelization, which gives them a unique, flavorful taste. This distinct flavor profile complements acidic and spicy elements, making it a versatile dish, which is good by itself or even better when paired with a sauce.

» **Rosemary and Honey-Roasted Squash:** I love this dish! The combination of sweet honey and aromatic rosemary takes the natural flavors of the squash to a whole new level. The honey adds a touch of sweetness that complements the savory notes of the rosemary perfectly. This dish is the perfect marriage of flavors and will not disappoint.

The Smoked Gouda and Virginia Ham Strata in Chapter 13 is a versatile dish that you can enjoy at special occasions throughout the year.

The flavors in the Lemon Thyme Chicken Orzo in Chapter 13 offer an herbaceous

Steak au Poivre, pictured above and below, in Chapter 14 is a classic French dish that consists of steak coated in coarsely ground peppercorns and then seared to perfection.

The Chicken Potpie recipe in Chapter 15 is perfect for those cold fall and winter evenings when you crave something warm and comforting, packed with delicious flavors.

Pan-Seared Tofu Steak with Peppers and Onions in Chapter 17 is a

Blistered Shishito Peppers in Chapter 17 are popular as an appetizer or side dish, especially during summertime when they're in season.

Pair the Pan-Roasted Asparagus with Garlic and Parmesan in Chapter 18 with the Blackened Salmon in Chapter 16 — a perfect combination!

The cooler weather enhances the sweetness and flavors of Thyme-Scented Root Vegetables in Chapter 17, making them a comforting addition to hearty dishes and roasts.

The freshness and vibrant flavors of Sautéed Shrimp and Okra in Chapter 17 are a perfect fit for picnics, barbecues, or outdoor gatherings.

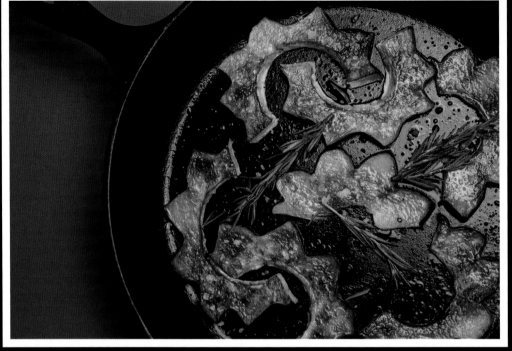

Delicata Squash's sweet, nutty flavor pairs beautifully with the aromatics of rosemary (see Chapter 18).

Particularly popular during the holidays, Buttermilk Drop Biscuits (refer to Chapter 19) are tender and fluffy.

The versatility of Spoon Bread (refer to Chapter 19) makes it a great choice for any time of the day.

The classic Easy Pineapple Upside Down Cake in Chapter 21 combines caramelized sugar and a sweet-tangy pineapple layer, all atop a moist and flavorful cake.

The Apple Crisp recipe in Chapter 22 makes for a great camping dessert.

Chicken Katsu with Tonkatsu Sauce in Chapter 24 is a beloved Japanese dish and widely

☙ Blistered Shishito Peppers

PREP TIME: 5 MIN	COOK TIME: 8 MIN	YIELD: 2 SERVINGS

INGREDIENTS

2 tablespoons olive oil

1 cup shishito peppers

Salt and pepper to taste

2 cloves garlic, sliced

1 tablespoon soy sauce

1 lemon, zest and juice

DIRECTIONS

1 Place your cast-iron skillet over medium heat, allowing your pan to preheat with olive oil for 2 to 3 minutes, until it smokes slightly.

2 Add the shishito peppers and season with salt and pepper. The peppers should start to blister right away. Shake the skillet so the peppers rotate (if you're uncomfortable with shaking the pan, use tongs or a spoon to move the peppers). Continue cooking for about 3 minutes.

3 While continuing to mix, add the garlic and cook for about 1 minute.

4 Turn off the heat, and then add the soy. Keep shaking or mixing to make sure all the peppers are coated. Remove the peppers from the skillet and plate. Finish with lemon zest and then juice.

TIP: If you add your peppers to the pan and they don't blister immediately, your pan might not be hot enough. One good way to test is by adding one to the pan, and if nothing happens, waiting a minute or so to allow the skillet to heat.

NOTE: This is one of my favorite things to cook. I love growing shishitos in the summertime; they're easy to grow and delicious to cook.

NOTE: Refer to the color insert for a photo.

PER SERVING: *Calories 141 (From Fat 124); Fat 14g (Saturated 2g); Cholesterol 0mg; Sodium 511mg; Carbohydrate 4g (Dietary Fiber 2g); Protein 2g.*

☙ Almondine Green Beans

PREP TIME: 8 MIN	COOK TIME: 8 MIN	YIELD: 2 SERVINGS

INGREDIENTS

1 tablespoon olive oil

½ pound haricot coverts, green beans, cleaned

1 shallot, sliced

2 cloves garlic, sliced

1 tablespoon butter

¼ cup almonds, sliced

Salt and pepper to taste

Red pepper flakes to taste

DIRECTIONS

1 Preheat a 10-inch cast iron skillet with the olive oil over medium heat for about 2 minutes.

2 Add the green beans and allow them to sauté slightly for about 3 minutes.

3 Add the shallots and cook for about 2 minutes. Add the garlic and cook for about 1 minute.

4 Move all the ingredients to one side of the skillet, creating a space. Add the butter, allowing it to melt slightly.

5 Add the almonds on top of the butter, allowing them to toast as the butter begins to brown slightly, about 2 minutes.

6 Add the salt, pepper, and red pepper flakes and mix well. Serve immediately.

NOTE: To add some dimension to this dish, finish it with lemon zest and juice.

PER SERVING: *Calories 231 (From Fat 174); Fat 19g (Saturated 5g); Cholesterol 15mg; Sodium 49mg; Carbohydrate 13g (Dietary Fiber 6g); Protein 5g.*

Stewed Chickpeas

PREP TIME: 10 MIN	COOK TIME: 60 MIN	YIELD: 4 SERVINGS

INGREDIENTS

1 teaspoon cumin, ground

½ teaspoon coriander, ground

½ teaspoon cinnamon, ground

¼ teaspoon nutmeg, ground

⅛ teaspoon cloves, ground

2 tablespoons olive oil

1 medium onion, thinly sliced

1 medium red bell pepper, thinly sliced

2 garlic cloves, minced

1 teaspoon ginger, minced

1 cup Roma tomato, diced

2 tablespoon flour

1 cup can chickpeas, drained and rinsed

1 quart vegetable broth

2 bay leaves

Salt and pepper to taste

4 tablespoons apple cider vinegar

DIRECTIONS

1 Using a Dutch oven, preheat over medium heat for about 2 minutes. In a small bowl, add the cumin, coriander, cinnamon, nutmeg, and cloves, mix well, and add to the Dutch oven. While shaking the pan back and forth over the heat to create movement of the spice, allow the spices to toast for about 2 to 3 minutes or until fragrant. Add the olive oil, onion, and bell pepper, mix well, and cook for about 5 minutes.

2 Add the garlic and ginger and cook for about another minute. Add the tomato and cook for about 5 minutes or until soft and then add the flour and cook for an additional 3 minutes.

3 Add the chickpeas and mix well. Add about 1 cup of vegetable broth and use a wooden spoon to deglaze the bottom of the pan; scrape well. Add the remaining stock and bay leaves, and bring to a simmer.

4 Taste and adjust the seasoning with salt and pepper. Cover and allow the chickpeas to braise for about 30 minutes; remove the lid and add the vinegar. Cook for an additional 15 minutes or until the chickpeas are tender. Remove from the heat and allow to cool for about 5 minutes.

VARY IT! You can use ½ cup dry chickpeas plus 1 quart of water (soak overnight) rather than canned chickpeas.

TIP: When braising, the best flavor develops over time, but if you're short on time, you can reduce the braising time to around 15 minutes because the beans are already soft.

PER SERVING: Calories 249 (From Fat 82); Fat 9g (Saturated 1g); Cholesterol 0mg; Sodium 741mg; Carbohydrate 35g (Dietary Fiber 7g); Protein 8g.

Three-Bean Succotash

PREP TIME: 10 MIN | COOK TIME: 70 MIN | YIELD: 6 SERVINGS

INGREDIENTS

4 strips bacon, medium diced

1 medium onion, thinly sliced

2 cloves garlic, minced

1 cup corn, can or shucked fresh

1 cup Roma tomato, small diced

2 tablespoons flour

1 teaspoon smoked paprika

¼ teaspoon cayenne powder

1 cup canned white beans, drained and rinsed

1 cup canned black-eyed peas, drained and rinsed

¼ cup lima beans, frozen

1 smoked turkey neck (optional)

2 bay leaves

3 sprigs thyme

2 quarts vegetable broth

Salt and pepper to taste

¼ cup heavy cream (optional)

DIRECTIONS

1 Preheat the oven to 375 degrees. Preheat the Dutch oven over medium for about 2 minutes.

2 Add the bacon, allowing it to render until golden brown, about 5 minutes. Then, add the onions and cook for about 5 minutes. Next, add the garlic, corn, and tomato and cook until fragrant. Add the flour, smoked paprika, and cayenne and cook for about 3 minutes.

3 Add the beans, smoked turkey, bay leaves, thyme, and stock, and bring to a simmer for about 15 minutes. Adjust seasoning with salt and pepper. Cover with a lid and place in oven, cooking for about 30 to 45 minutes allowing the flavor to develop. Remove and serve.

VARY IT: You can use ½ cup dry white beans plus 2 cups water soaked overnight in place of the canned white beans. The same goes for the black-eyed peas. When cooking dry beans, increase your stock by 1 to 2 cups and your cook time to around 45 minutes to 1 hour.

VARY IT: If you want to make this dish vegetarian, leave out the bacon and turkey. Try adding smoked tofu for additional great flavors.

PER SERVING: *Calories 279 (From Fat 108); Fat 12g (Saturated 4g); Cholesterol 17mg; Sodium 1042mg; Carbohydrate 35g (Dietary Fiber 6g); Protein 9g.*

☙ Skillet Cabbage

PREP TIME: 10 MIN | **COOK TIME: 15 TO 20 MIN** | **YIELD: 6 SERVINGS**

INGREDIENTS

3 tablespoons canola oil

2 large onions, sliced

1 green bell pepper, seeded and chopped

4 cups red or green cabbage, chopped

2 tomatoes, peeled and chopped

2 teaspoons sugar

Salt and pepper to taste

DIRECTIONS

1 Heat the oil in your cast-iron deep skillet on medium-high heat.

2 Sauté the onion and green bell pepper until the onions are translucent, about 10 minutes. Reduce the heat to medium.

3 Add the cabbage, tomatoes, and sugar. Stir and toss to combine.

4 Cook over medium heat for about 10 to 15 minutes, until the cabbage is tender but not mushy.

5 Add the salt and pepper to taste during last 2 minutes.

NOTE: Although you may be tempted to save time on this recipe by buying prechopped cabbage at the grocery store, try to resist the urge. Prepackaged cabbage is generally shredded rather than chopped and is best reserved for salads and slaws. In this recipe, the smaller shredded pieces will turn mushy during cooking.

PER SERVING: *Calories 121 (From Fat 67); Fat 7g (Saturated 1g); Cholesterol 0mg; Sodium 107mg; Carbohydrate 13g (Dietary Fiber 3g); Protein 2g.*

Thyme-Scented Root Vegetables

PREP TIME: 12 MIN | COOK TIME: 45 TO 50 MIN | YIELD: 4 SERVINGS

INGREDIENTS

4 tablespoons olive oil

2 sprigs thyme

2 cloves garlic, crushed

1 rutabaga, halved lengthwise, then cut into 1-inch pieces

2 parsnips, cut into 1-inch pieces

2 carrots, cut into 1-inch pieces

1 yellow beet, quartered or if you have a large beet, cut into 1-inch pieces

1 sweet potato, halved lengthwise, then cut into 1-inch pieces

Salt and pepper to taste

DIRECTIONS

1 Preheat your oven to 400 degrees. Preheat your cast-iron skillet over medium on the stove.

2 Using a medium bowl, add the olive oil, all the herbs, and all the vegetables. Season with salt and pepper and toss together.

3 Add half of the vegetables mix to the hot skillet on the stove (the vegetables should start to sear right away). Allow them to cook for about 2 to 3 minutes and then add in the other half of the vegetables. Mix well.

4 Place the skillet in the oven and allow the vegetables to roast for about 45 minutes, or until golden brown.

NOTE: When cooking your vegetables, make sure they're spread out evenly across your skillet to ensure they roast evenly.

NOTE: Check out the photo in the color insert.

PER SERVING: *Calories 237 (From Fat 126); Fat 14g (Saturated 2g); Cholesterol 0mg; Sodium 94mg; Carbohydrate 27g (Dietary Fiber 7g); Protein 3g.*

🍅 Rosemary and Honey-Roasted Squash

PREP TIME: 8 MIN	COOK TIME: 30 MIN	YIELD: 3 SERVINGS

INGREDIENTS

1 acorn squash, sliced about ¼-inch thick

2 cloves garlic, crushed

2 sprigs rosemary, broken into 1-inch pieces

2 tablespoons olive oil

Salt and pepper to taste

1 tablespoon butter

2 tablespoons honey

Salt to taste

⅛ teaspoon cayenne powder

DIRECTIONS

1 Preheat your oven to 375 degrees. Add a single layer of acorn squash into a 12-inch cast-iron skillet and top with crushed garlic and rosemary. Evenly distribute the olive oil on top. Finish with salt and pepper.

2 Place the skillet into the oven and allow the squash to roast for about 30 minutes, or until golden brown.

3 Remove the skillet from the oven and allow it to rest, for about 5 minutes. Remove and add the Hot Honey Sauce.

Hot Honey Sauce

¼ cup honey

2 tablespoons butter, melted

½ teaspoon cayenne powder

¼ teaspoon salt

1 teaspoon balsamic vinegar

While the vegetables are cooking, add the honey, butter, cayenne, salt, and balsamic vinegar together in a small bowl and mix well. After the vegetables cool for about 5 minutes, lightly drizzle the hot honey mixture and serve.

VARY IT: Try adding different herbs to this dish to create your own unique flavors. Other herbs like sage, thyme, and even chives add a ton of value to the olive oil while it's cooking, giving you a beautifully infused flavor.

PER SERVING: *Calories 369 (From Fat 186); Fat 21g (Saturated 9g); Cholesterol 31mg; Sodium 375mg; Carbohydrate 50g (Dietary Fiber 2g); Protein 1g.*

Chapter **18**

Seasonal Veggie Dishes

Nothing compares to cooking with in-season vegetables. Aside from optimum freshness and flavor, when you allow vegetables to develop in their natural cycle, they can ripen fully and reach their maximum taste potential, enabling you to guide flavors versus creating them.

Each season brings a different selection of vegetables, encouraging you to explore new flavors, experiment with different recipes, and enjoy a more diverse range of meals. In the Northern Hemisphere (including the continental United States) certain vegetables have become synonymous with specific seasons. Asparagus is commonly associated with spring, tomatoes are often enjoyed during the summer, and carrots are frequently enjoyed in winter. Although vegetables may be associated with a certain season, their availability and growing practices can vary depending on location and farming techniques.

Availability may vary depending on the specific state and region. Local farmers' markets or supermarkets are good sources for finding the most accurate and up-to-date information about seasonal vegetables in your area. Aside from the amazing flavors, eating vegetables in season means they're usually harvested at their peak ripeness, equating to freshness and plenty of nutrients.

The side dish recipes in this chapter can inspire you to think differently about how you incorporate vegetables into a meal.

Highlighting Spring Vegetables

After a long winter of cabbages and root vegetables, spring vegetables offer a refreshing change. With the warm weather comes vegetables like asparagus, peas, artichokes, and spinach, just to name a few, all of which are bursting with flavor and amazing textures. Try these spring-focused recipes:

>> **Fried Green Tomatoes:** Originally popularized in the American South, green tomatoes, which are unripe tomatoes, offer a firm texture with a tangy and slightly sour flavor. Coating them with breadcrumbs and frying them accentuates these three qualities, creating a textural flavorful culinary masterpiece.

>> **Pan-Roasted Asparagus with Garlic and Parmesan:** Asparagus is one of the most versatile vegetables. It has a distinct flavor with slightly earthy and grassy notes along with a unique texture that pairs well with bold flavors like garlic and Parmesan cheese.

>> **Cumin and Hot Honey-Glazed Carrots:** Sometimes all you need is three things to balance the harmonic flavors of the season: The cumin offers a warm and earthy flavor. The heat from the hot honey adds a punch with a hint of floral sweetness. The caramelized carrots offer a deep sweetness with a slight crisp texture.

Fried Green Tomatoes

PREP TIME: 30 MIN	COOK TIME: ABOUT 6 MIN PER BATCH	YIELD: 6 SERVINGS

INGREDIENTS

4 firm medium green tomatoes

½ teaspoon salt

½ teaspoon garlic salt

¼ teaspoon pepper

½ to 1 cup all-purpose flour

1 stick butter

1 quart vegetable oil

DIRECTIONS

1 Wash and core the tomatoes but don't peel. Slice into ½-inch slices. Lay the slices on wax paper or parchment paper. Sprinkle the salt, garlic salt, and pepper on both sides of the tomato slices. Set aside for 15 to 30 minutes. Dredge the tomato slices in flour and place the slices on a baking sheet.

2 Put the butter in a 12-inch cast-iron skillet and place the skillet on a burner set to medium high. Melt butter and, if needed, add enough vegetable oil to fill the skillet to about ¼ inch deep.

3 When the butter is hot (a pinch of flour sizzles but doesn't burn), add a layer of the tomato slices. Place the slices in the skillet so that they don't touch. Fry each side until light golden brown, about 2 to 3 minutes per side, turning carefully with a spatula or tongs.

4 Remove to the paper towels to drain. Use a slotted spoon and skim the oil to keep it clean between batches. Add more butter and oil if necessary and repeat the frying process for the remainder of the tomatoes.

VARY IT! Use cornmeal to coat the tomatoes instead of flour. Or use a coating of half cornmeal and half flour. If you add cornmeal to the recipe, forgo the butter and simply use vegetable oil for frying.

PER SERVING: *Calories 202 (From Fat 139); Fat 15g (Saturated 10g); Cholesterol 41mg; Sodium 287mg; Carbohydrate 12g (Dietary Fiber 1g); Protein 2g.*

🍅 Pan-Roasted Asparagus with Garlic and Parmesan

PREP TIME: 5 MIN	COOK TIME: 10 MIN	YIELD: 2 SERVINGS

INGREDIENTS

2 tablespoons olive oil

6 medium asparagus spears, bottoms cut about one inch

2 cloves garlic, sliced thin

1 teaspoon fennel seed powder (optional)

Salt and pepper to taste

1 lemon, zest and juice

1 tablespoon Parmesan cheese

DIRECTIONS

1 Preheat the cast-iron skillet with olive oil over medium heat, about 3 minutes.

2 Add asparagus and allow to sauté for about 5 minutes; make sure you rotate the asparagus to ensure they cook evenly (with either tongs or a spatula).

3 After the asparagus starts to develop color, add the garlic and fennel seed and season with salt and pepper. Cook for 1 more minute and remove from the heat.

4 Finish the dish with lemon zest and lemon juice. Sprinkle on Parmesan cheese and serve warm.

NOTE: To take this dish up a notch, season the asparagus with the Blackening Seasoning Mix in Chapter 16 in the Blackened Salmon recipe. Refer to a photo in the color insert.

TIP: When cooking this dish, don't overcrowd your pan. Putting too much into your pan will cause you to change the cooking technique from a sauté to a sweat, thus creating a different texture and flavor.

PER SERVING: *Calories 140 (From Fat 128); Fat 14g (Saturated 2g); Cholesterol 2mg; Sodium 39mg; Carbohydrate 2g (Dietary Fiber 1g); Protein 2g.*

Cumin and Hot Honey–Glazed Carrots

PREP TIME: 5 MIN	COOK TIME: 15 MIN	YIELD: 2 SERVINGS

INGREDIENTS

2 tablespoons olive oil

1 cup baby carrots

Salt and pepper to taste

¼ teaspoon cayenne powder

¼ teaspoon cumin

2 teaspoons brown sugar

2 tablespoons honey

½ cup vegetable stock

2 tablespoons butter

1 lemon, zest and juice

1 tablespoons chives, thinly shaved (optional)

DIRECTIONS

1 Preheat a large cast-iron skillet with olive oil over medium heat for about 2 minutes. Add carrots and cook until they start to brown, about 8 to 10 minutes. Season with salt and pepper to taste

2 Add in cayenne, cumin, brown sugar, and honey and mix well. Add in the stock and allow it to reduce for about 5 minutes or until a glaze starts to form. Finish with butter, lemon zest, and half of the lemon for juice. Mix well to incorporate. Fold in chives and serve.

TIP: In Step 1, make sure you periodically shake the skillet to get a good roast on the carrots. By doing this you're not only cooking them but you're also creating the first layer of flavor.

NOTE: Be careful when you add the brown sugar not to burn it. If you allow it to cook longer than 2 minutes, you run the risk of burning the sugar.

NOTE: Fresh herbs really amp up the flavor in this dish.

PER SERVING: Calories 335 (From Fat 227); Fat 25g (Saturated 9g); Cholesterol 31mg; Sodium 266mg; Carbohydrate 30g (Dietary Fiber 2g); Protein 1g.

Focusing on Summer In-Season Veggies

If you ever want to know what makes summer season so exciting for foodies, just go to your local farmers' market and allow all of the beautiful produce to inspire you. The warm sunny weather allows vegetables to flourish and develop vibrant colors and delicious flavors throughout the summer months.

The recipes in the following section highlight a few summer dishes that taste great and are nutritious (you can also fine other great veggie–focused side dishes in Chapter 17):

» **Patty Pan Squash and Vidalia Onion:** The name patty pan comes from the shape, which resembles a small, flattened pan or saucer. This vegetable also comes in a variety of colors: yellow, green, and white. This squash is very versatile and can be used with different cooking techniques like stir-frying, grilling, sautéing, and roasting. Combined with the mild, yet sweet flavor of the Vidalia onion, together they're the perfect pair.

» **Rosemary Delicata Squash:** The combination of the delicate texture and mild sweetness of the squash with the aromatic and earthy flavors of rosemary creates a beautiful balance of tastes, resulting in a truly satisfying dish.

» **Eggplant Parmesan:** This is a great vegetarin and non-vegetarian option for folks who are looking to switch it up. The crispy breaded eggplant offers a great crunch, and the tomato sauce adds a tangy sweetness. Add the cheese (for my vegan friends, feel free to substitute your favorite vegan cheese) and there you have it! A tasty and satisfying dish great for any occasion.

Patty Pan Squash and Vidalia Onion

PREP TIME: 10 MIN	COOK TIME: 30 TO 45 MIN	YIELD: 8 SERVINGS

INGREDIENTS

3 tablespoons butter

1 large Vidalia onion, sliced

6 Patty Pan squash, sliced

1 teaspoon sugar

¼ teaspoon pepper

DIRECTIONS

1 Place the butter in a 12-inch cast-iron skillet and set your burner to medium high.

2 When the butter is bubbling, add the onion and sauté until almost brown. Add the squash, sugar, and pepper and toss with a spatula to combine. Reduce the heat to medium and continue cooking for about 15 minutes uncovered, turning once with the spatula. Cover and steam until the squash is tender, about 15 to 20 minutes. Reduce the heat if necessary.

3 Adjust the seasoning with the pepper and sugar to taste during the last 5 minutes of cooking.

NOTE: Grown in Georgia and available in early summer, Vidalia onions are famous for their sweet flavor.

VARY IT! If you can't find Vidalia onions for this recipe, you can substitute any other sweet onion.

PER SERVING: Calories 177 (From Fat 42); Fat 5g (Saturated 3g); Cholesterol 12mg; Sodium 11mg; Carbohydrate 36g (Dietary Fiber 5g); Protein 3g.

SQUASH STEALS THE SHOW

Offering as many flavors as colors and shapes and loaded with nutrients, squash is a cook's and a nutritionist's delight. As a group, squash stands out in terms of vitamins and minerals. Even cooked squash is hard to beat for sheer good-for-you-ness. It provides vitamins A and C, potassium, and dietary fiber. Studies also show that it contains compounds, such as flavonoids, that fight cancer.

Rosemary Delicata Squash

INGREDIENTS

2 tablespoons olive oil

1 delicate squash

¼ teaspoon cayenne powder

Salt and pepper to taste

2 tablespoons honey

2 sprigs rosemary, broken into pieces

DIRECTIONS

1 Preheat your oven to 375 degrees. Cut the squash in half and remove the seeds. Continue cutting it into about ¼ inch think half-moons. Place the squash on a baking tray, evenly coat with olive oil, and season with cayenne, salt, and pepper on both sides. Place the squash on a cast-iron griddle in a single layer.

2 Drizzle with honey and evenly spread the rosemary on top. Place in the oven and bake for 25 minutes or until golden brown. Remove and allow to cool for about 5 minutes before serving.

NOTE: Refer to the color insert for a photo of this recipe.

PER SERVING: *Calories 269 (From Fat 123); Fat 14g (Saturated 2g); Cholesterol 0mg; Sodium 8mg; Carbohydrate 40g (Dietary Fiber 3g); Protein 2g.*

🍅 Eggplant Parmesan

PREP TIME: 35 MIN	COOK TIME: 6 MIN PER BATCH	YIELD: 6 SERVINGS

INGREDIENTS

2 eggplants

Salt and pepper

1 egg, slightly beaten

½ cup milk

1 cup of all-purpose flour, or more

Vegetable oil to fill skillet ½-inch deep

DIRECTIONS

1 To prepare the eggplant, peel and slice it into ½-inch-thick rounds. Place the eggplant slices in a very large bowl with very cold salted water. Cover with a plate to keep the eggplant submerged in the water. Let it stand for about 30 minutes. Discard the water and drain the eggplant in a colander. Lay the eggplant slices on wax paper and sprinkle them with the salt and pepper.

2 In a shallow, wide-mouthed bowl, combine the egg and milk. Put the flour on another piece of wax paper.

3 Prepare a baking sheet covered with wax paper. Dip the eggplant slices into the milk mixture; then dredge them in flour. Lay the eggplant slices on the baking sheet.

4 Pour the vegetable oil in your 12-inch skillet; set it on a burner to medium-high heat. If a pinch of flour sizzles but doesn't burn, the oil is hot. Place the eggplant slices in the skillet so that they don't touch. Cook the eggplant slices until they're golden brown on both sides, about 3 minutes per side.

5 In between batches, clean the oil by skimming with a slotted spoon or skimmer. Adjust the heat if necessary to keep the oil from becoming too hot or cool.

TIP: When you buy eggplant, look for ones that are smooth and firm and have an even, dark-purple color. One medium eggplant (approximately 1½ pounds) is enough to feed four people.

PER SERVING: Calories 264 (From Fat 144); Fat 16g (Saturated 2g); Cholesterol 38mg; Sodium 123mg; Carbohydrate 26g (Dietary Fiber 4g); Protein 5g.

Introducing Fall Veggies into Your Kitchen

Depending on what part of the world you are in, when you think of fall your mind might go to roasted root vegetables or warm soups and stews. Some people may think of butternut squash, sweet potatoes, or Brussel sprouts. Regardless of where you are, you can find something special about the fall season.

Aside from the memorable flavors, fall vegetables tend to be packed with vitamins, minerals, and antioxidants that support your health during colder months — just another reason why the fall season is so great.

Here I explore a few dishes that are perfect for a chilly fall day (you can also find other great veggie-focused side dishes in Chapter 17):

>> **Roasted Cabbage and Vegetables:** Roasting is one of the oldest cooking techniques used to transform the taste and texture of your vegetables. Roasting brings out the natural sweetness and adds depth, creating a contrast in textures and flavor.

>> **Oven-Roasted New Potatoes:** These small, thin-skinned potatoes are harvested before they reach full maturity, which creates a sweeter, creamier texture when they're cooked. Boiled or roasted, they add a tremendous value to any dish.

>> **White Bean and Swiss Chard Soup:** This soup is hearty, nutritious, and oh so delicious. Besides their amazing flavor, white beans are packed with beneficial nutrients like protein, dietary fiber, and vitamin C, just to name a few. This recipe, which pairs the beans with kale — also a superfood — creates one of the most power duos since Julia Child and Simone Beck.

>> **Corn Maque Choux:** This Corn Maque Choux recipe is a combination of vegetables, shrimp, and spicy meat that's closer to a meal than a side dish.

Roasted Cabbage and Vegetables

PREP TIME: 10 MIN	COOK TIME: 40 TO 50 MIN	YIELD: 10 SERVINGS

INGREDIENTS

1 teaspoon onion powder

½ teaspoon garlic powder

½ teaspoon smoked paprika

½ teaspoon salt

¼ teaspoon pepper

¼ teaspoon cumin

1 cup Brussel sprouts, cut in half lengthwise

1 cup baby carrots

1 cup cauliflower florets

1 cup pee wee potatoes, also known as Baby Dutch potatoes

¼ cup olive oil

½ head of green cabbage, cut in half, remove core, and slice into 1-inch pieces

2 tablespoons parsley, chopped

4 sprigs thyme, chopped

DIRECTIONS

1 Preheat the oven to 400 degrees. In a small bowl, add the onion powder, garlic powder, paprika, salt, pepper, and cumin to make a custom spice seasoning and mix well.

2 In a medium bowl, mix the Brussel sprouts, baby carrots, cauliflower, and potatoes with 2 tablespoons of olive oil and 2 teaspoons of seasoning from the small bowl and mix well. Taste and season accordingly.

3 Preheat your 12-inch cast iron skillet with 2 tablespoons of olive oil over medium heat for about 3 minutes. Add the mixed vegetables to the pan in a single layer, allowing them to roast for about 5 minutes and mix well. Add your cabbage to the skillet with the mixed vegetables.

4 Spread vegetables evenly across the pan. Place the skillet in the oven, allowing the vegetables to roast for about 20 to 25 minutes or until golden brown and fork tender. Remove from the oven and allow to cool for about 5 minutes. Finish with chopped parsley and thyme and serve.

NOTE: In Step 4, depending on the size of the skillet, you may need to do this in two batches.

PER SERVING: Calories 90(From FAT 40); Fat 6g (Saturated 1g); Cholesterol 0mg; Sodium 136mg; Carbohydrate 9g (Dietary Fiber 2g); Protein 1g.

⏀ Oven-Roasted New Potatoes

PREP TIME: 10 MIN	COOK TIME: 40 MIN	YIELD: 4 SERVINGS

INGREDIENTS

6 tablespoons butter

10 or 12 medium new potatoes, skin on (about 3 pounds)

½ teaspoon salt

¼ teaspoon pepper

½ teaspoon garlic salt

¼ teaspoon cayenne powder

Kosher salt (optional)

1 tablespoon chopped fresh parsley

DIRECTIONS

1 Preheat oven to 425 degrees. Put butter in 12-inch cast-iron skillet and put it into oven to heat.

2 Cut the potatoes in half. Sprinkle salt, pepper, garlic salt, and cayenne into the hot butter. Place the potatoes cut side down in hot butter. Bake for 25 minutes.

3 Turn the potatoes and bake an additional 15 minutes or until fork tender. Remove from oven, sprinkle with kosher salt, if desired, and garnish with parsley.

TIP: Look for *new potatoes* (the small, rounded potatoes with the reddish skin) that have thin, papery skin and are free of blemishes or any tint of green (a sign that the potato isn't ripe).

TIP: For this recipe, don't worry about the size of the potatoes; small or large work equally well. But select potatoes of roughly the same size so that they all get done about the same time.

PER SERVING: *Calories 369 (From Fat 157); Fat 17g (Saturated 11g); Cholesterol 46mg; Sodium 424mg; Carbohydrate 44g (Dietary Fiber 7g); Protein 9g.*

White Bean and Swiss Chard Soup

PREP TIME: 10 MIN	COOK TIME: 75 TO 80 MIN	YIELD: 2 SERVINGS

INGREDIENTS

½ cup dry white beans + 1 quart water (soak overnight)

2 tablespoons olive oil

1 shallot, sliced

1 onion, sliced

2 cloves garlic, minced

2 tablespoons butter

2 tablespoons flour

1 cup milk

4 cups vegetable stock

2 sprigs thyme

2 bay leaves

½ sprig rosemary (optional)

Salt and pepper to taste

2 cups Swiss chard, stems and ribs removed, halved and sliced

DIRECTIONS

1 Drain and rinse the beans and set aside. Preheat a Dutch oven with the olive oil over medium heat for about 2 minutes.

2 Add the shallots and onions and allow them to caramelize for about 8 to 10 minutes.

3 Add the garlic and butter and cook for about 1 minute. Add the flour, mix well, and cook for about 3 minutes.

4 Whisk in the milk until any lumps are dissolved. Add the stock, white beans, thyme, bay leaves, rosemary, salt, and pepper. Bring to a simmer, cover, and cook for about 45 minutes. Remove the lid and add the Swiss chard. Cover and cook for an additional 10 to 15 minutes. Adjust seasoning if needed and serve.

PER SERVING: *Calories 570 (From Fat 253); Fat 28g (Saturated 11g); Cholesterol 40mg; Sodium 1337mg; Carbohydrate 64g (Dietary Fiber 10g); Protein 19g.*

Corn Maque Choux

INGREDIENTS

8 ears fresh corn (about 4 cups)

2 to 4 tablespoons bacon drippings

1 cup chopped onions

½ cup chopped celery

½ cup chopped green bell pepper

½ cup chopped red bell pepper

¼ cup diced garlic

¼ cup finely diced andouille, or quality Polish sausage

2 cups coarsely chopped tomatoes

2 tablespoons tomato sauce

2 cups small shrimp, peeled and deveined

1 cup sliced green onions (about 10)

Salt and pepper

DIRECTIONS

1 Cut the corn kernels from the cobs and scrape each cob using the blade of the knife to remove all milk and additional pulp from the corn.

2 In a 3-quart cast-iron chicken fryer or deep-sided pan, melt the bacon drippings over medium-high heat. Sauté the corn, onions, celery, bell peppers, garlic, and andouille for approximately 15 to 20 minutes or until the vegetables are wilted and the corn begins to tenderize. Add the tomatoes and tomato sauce. Continue cooking until the juices from the tomatoes are rendered into the dish, approximately 15 to 20 minutes.

3 Add the shrimp, green onions, and salt and pepper. Continue to cook an additional 15 minutes or until the flavors of the corn and shrimp are fully developed.

TIP: Select tender, well-developed ears of corn and remove shucks and silk.

TIP: Using a sharp knife, cut lengthwise through the kernels to remove them from the cob. This is important because the richness of the dish depends on how much milk and pulp can be scraped from the cobs.

PER SERVING: *Calories 186 (From Fat 56); Fat 6g (Saturated 2g); Cholesterol 59mg; Sodium 237mg; Carbohydrate 26g (Dietary Fiber 5g); Protein 11g.*

Adding Vegetables to Your Side Dishes during the Winter

Like apples and oranges, winter and summer vegetables couldn't be more different. Summer vegetables thrive with plenty of rain, sun, and warm weather, whereas winter vegetables have to adapt to colder temperatures, which means they have slower growth rates, resulting in improved flavor and textures.

REMEMBER

When comparing winter vegetables grown in the summer versus in season, they tend to be sweeter, heartier, and more flavorful. Another great quality of winter vegetables is their shelf life. They can be stored for extended periods of time, which is great during a period of time where produce may be limited.

Here I explore sides dishes that accentuate the flavor and richness of beautiful winter dishes (you can also find other veggie-focused side dishes in Chapter 17):

>> **Acorn Squash and Cranberries:** Acorn squash has a distinctive sweet and nutty flavor that's rich and creamy. Its versatility lends itself well to cooking techniques like roasting, mashing, sautéing, or even stuffing. This side dish is a great way to add value to any meal.

>> **Southern-Style Turnip Greens:** Traditionally known in U.S. Southern cuisine, turnip greens have a slightly bitter taste, which adds complexity and balance when cooked with other ingredients. Another versatile ingredient, greens can be sautéed, steamed, braised, or added to soups or stews.

>> **Candied Sweet Potatoes:** Loved for its rich, indulgent taste, candied sweet potatoes are often served during the holiday season.

Acorn Squash and Cranberries

PREP TIME: 5 MIN	COOK TIME: 35 MIN	YIELD: 6 SERVINGS

INGREDIENTS

3 acorn squash

¼ cup butter

1 cup diced onion

½ cup brown sugar

½ cup fresh cranberries

¼ cup chopped fresh parsley

1 cup vegetable broth

½ teaspoon salt

½ teaspoon pepper

DIRECTIONS

1 Peel, seed, and dice squash into ½-inch cubes (about 4½ cups).

2 In a 12-inch cast-iron skillet, melt the butter over medium-high heat. Add the onions and sauté until translucent, about 5 minutes. Add the squash and continue cooking for 5 minutes. Add the sugar, cranberries, and parsley; cook for an additional 5 minutes.

3 Stir in the broth, scraping the sides to remove any browned bits. Add the salt and pepper, and simmer for 20 minutes.

TIP: Because the rind of an acorn squash (one of the winter squashes) is thick and hard, to remove the rind and seeds, cut the squash into quarters. Using a spoon, scrape the seeds from the flesh. Then take a sharp knife and carefully slice the flesh from the rind.

NOTE: This recipe is a great complement to poultry, pork, and game.

PER SERVING: *Calories 245 (From Fat 77); Fat 9g (Saturated 5g); Cholesterol 21mg; Sodium 377mg; Carbohydrate 44g (Dietary Fiber 4g); Protein 2g.*

Southern-Style Turnip Greens

PREP TIME: 45 MIN (10 MIN WITH PRECLEANED GREENS) | COOK TIME: 3 HRS | YIELD: 6 SERVINGS

INGREDIENTS

½ pound sliced salt pork (or thickly sliced bacon), chopped into 1-inch pieces (optional) sub smoked turkey neck

3 pounds turnip greens

½ cup chicken broth

½ teaspoon sugar

Salt and pepper

4 turnips, peeled and diced (optional)

DIRECTIONS

1 Clean the greens and tear into medium-size pieces.

2 In a large cast-iron Dutch oven (7 quarts or bigger), fry the salt pork over medium-high heat until cooked but not crisp. Add the greens, turning them over several times to coat with the pork drippings.

3 Add the broth, sugar, and salt and pepper. (You can adjust the salt and pepper to taste by adding more during the last part of cooking, so don't go crazy at this point.) Reduce the heat and cover the Dutch oven, simmering the greens very gently.

4 Greens release liquid as they cook but check occasionally to make sure the pan hasn't gone dry. You may have to add just enough water to keep it from scorching, but never cover the greens with water. Cook the greens until tender, about 2½ to 3 hours. If desired, add the diced turnips about halfway through the cooking time.

NOTE: This recipe calls for 3 pounds of greens. That's plenty of greens, but when cooked, they shrink to about one-quarter of their original volume.

PER SERVING: *Calories 310 (From Fat 266); Fat 30g (Saturated 10g); Cholesterol 32mg; Sodium 713mg; Carbohydrate 8g (Dietary Fiber 6g); Protein 5g.*

🍅 Candied Sweet Potatoes

PREP TIME: 10 MIN	COOK TIME: 30 MIN	YIELD: 4 SERVINGS

INGREDIENTS

2 to 3 tablespoons butter

¼ cup brown sugar

1 teaspoon cinnamon

3 or 4 medium sweet potatoes, peeled and sliced

1 cup water

DIRECTIONS

1 Heat the butter in a large (12- to 13-inch) cast-iron skillet on medium high.

2 Stir the sugar and cinnamon into the butter. Add the sweet potatoes and water. Cover, bring to a boil, and reduce the heat to medium. Continue to cook until the potatoes are fork tender, about 25 minutes, turning only to keep them from burning.

3 Remove the lid and cook until liquid thickens, about 5 minutes, watching carefully.

PER SERVING: *Calories 187 (From Fat 52); Fat 6g (Saturated 4g); Cholesterol 15mg; Sodium 98mg; Carbohydrate 33g (Dietary Fiber 3g); Protein 2g.*

Chapter **19**

Cornbreads, Biscuits, and Breads

This chapter delves into the fundamentals of baking, focusing on cornbread, biscuits, and various yeast breads. These classic staples are essential if you want to build a strong foundation in baking. Although you may find it easy to whip up delicious cornbread or biscuits, other home cooks may face challenges such as flat, tough, gritty, or dry results.

Here I present recipes that utilize some key techniques that are vital to cornbreads and biscuits. My goal is not only to enhance your understanding of these recipes but also to empower you to replicate the process with confidence, creating new memories and delightful culinary experiences.

Finding Some Comfort with Cornbread Recipes

Generally, southern folks prefer unsweetened cornbread with a crisp crust. They like white cornmeal. Northerners prefer sweeter cornbread with a more cake-like consistency. They go with yellow cornmeal. Whatever kind of cornmeal you go with, keep this tip in mind:

TIP

Always preheat your skillet or pan with shortening in it. The hot skillet and melted shortening gives your cornbread a crispier, tastier crust.

Cornbread purists like their cornbread plain, with a little (or a lot of) butter. Others like to experiment, tossing in a few herbs here or some cheese there, to create their own special breads. If you want the variety that flavored cornbread offers but aren't the kind to experiment yourself, try these recipes. They just may inspire you.

Here are the cornbread recipes in this section:

>> **Creamy Corn Pudding:** Not all corn recipes call for corn straight from the ear. This one uses cans of creamed and kernel corns. These canned corn varieties are readily available and offer a slightly different texture and flavor compared to fresh corn.

>> **Dilly Cornsticks:** Cornsticks are basically cornbread cooked in single-serving portions. The benefit of making cornsticks is that you end up with crispier edges.

>> **Buttermilk Cornsticks:** Another variation of a basic cornstick recipe, this one uses buttermilk.

>> **Jalapeño Cornbread:** Inspired by the flavors of Mexican cuisine, this recipe offers a nice balance of spice and cheese. This dish is great on its own and can also be served as a side dish. The combination of the spicy jalapeños and savory bacon creates a fantastic flavor profile, great with your favorite stew.

>> **Southern Cornbread:** Real southern cornbread isn't sweet. In fact, it uses little or no sugar. The tang in the buttermilk and the bacon grease give this cornbread its flavor.

>> **Sour Cream Cornbread:** The combination of white cornmeal, sour cream, and cream-style corn make this cornbread especially moist.

>> **Yankee Cornbread:** This recipe is for folks who like their cornbread yellow and sweet.

☙ Creamy Corn Pudding

PREP TIME: 10 MIN	COOK TIME: 1½ HRS	YIELD: 6 TO 8 SERVINGS

INGREDIENTS

3 tablespoons butter

3 tablespoons all-purpose flour

1 tablespoon sugar

¾ teaspoon salt

¾ cup milk

One 14-ounce can cream-style corn

One 14-ounce can whole corn

3 eggs, well beaten

DIRECTIONS

1 Preheat your oven to 350 degrees. In a 2-quart cast-iron serving pot, melt the butter over low heat. Add the flour, sugar, and salt, and stir until smooth. Cook 1 minute. Gradually add the milk and cook over medium low heat until thick and bubbly.

2 Remove from the heat and stir in the cream-style and whole corn. Gradually add ¼ of the hot mixture to the eggs. Then add the egg mixture back to the hot corn mixture, stirring constantly.

3 Bake for 1 hour or until set.

PER SERVING: Calories 168 (From Fat 70); Fat 8g (Saturated 4g); Cholesterol 94mg; Sodium 539mg; Carbohydrate 20g (Dietary Fiber 2g); Protein 5g.

⦿ Dilly Cornsticks

PREP TIME: 10 MIN	COOK TIME: 15 TO 18 MIN	YIELD: 15 CORNSTICKS

INGREDIENTS

1 cup all-purpose flour

1 cup yellow cornmeal

2 tablespoons sugar

1 tablespoon baking soda

½ teaspoon salt

1 teaspoon dill weed

1 tablespoon minced onion

2 eggs

1 cup plus 2 tablespoons milk

¼ cup olive oil

DIRECTIONS

1 Preheat your oven to 425 degrees. Place a greased cast-iron cornstick pan in the oven while preheating.

2 In a large mixing bowl, combine the flour, cornmeal, sugar, baking soda, salt, dill weed, and onion.

3 In another bowl, beat the eggs, milk, and oil together. Pour the liquid into the dry ingredients. Mix until just blended.

4 Fill the cornstick impressions a scant ¾ full.

5 Bake for 15 to 18 minutes or until golden brown. Serve hot and spread a little butter on it.

VARY IT! *Dill weed* (the leaves of the dill plant) has a milder flavor than *dill seed* (the seeds of the plant). If you want a stronger dill flavor, don't substitute dill seed. Instead increase the amount of dill weed slightly.

NOTE: A traditional favorite shape for cornstick molds is the ear of corn. But don't be bound by tradition. If you're whimsical, you can find cornstick molds with other shapes: stars, fish, cacti, and more. If you do use a specially molded pan, make sure that the batter fills the entire impression. After all, what good's a fish without its fin?

PER SERVING: *Calories 125 (From Fat 47); Fat 5g (Saturated 1g); Cholesterol 31mg; Sodium 347mg; Carbohydrate 16g (Dietary Fiber 1g); Protein 3g.*

Buttermilk Cornsticks

PREP TIME: 10 MIN	COOK TIME: 15 MIN	YIELD: 14 CORNSTICKS

INGREDIENTS

1 cup yellow cornmeal

1 cup all-purpose flour

2 teaspoons baking powder

¼ teaspoon baking soda

1 teaspoon salt

¼ cup margarine

1 cup buttermilk

2 eggs

DIRECTIONS

1 Preheat your oven and two well-greased cast-iron cornstick pans to 475 degrees.

2 In a mixing bowl, combine the cornmeal, flour, baking powder, baking soda, and salt. Cut in the margarine. Add the buttermilk and eggs, blending well.

3 Pour the batter into the hot pans. Bake at 475 degrees for 15 minutes.

PER SERVING: *Calories 115 (From Fat 39); Fat 4g (Saturated 1g); Cholesterol 31mg; Sodium 309mg; Carbohydrate 15g (Dietary Fiber 1g); Protein 3g.*

🍅 Jalapeño Cornbread

PREP TIME: 10 MIN	COOK TIME: 40 TO 45 MIN	YIELD: 12 PIECES

INGREDIENTS

1¼ cup white, self-rising cornmeal mix

2 eggs, beaten

¾ cup milk

¾ cup grated cheddar cheese

⅓ cup cooking oil

One 8-ounce can cream-style corn

½ green bell pepper, seeded and diced

¼ cup finely diced onion

1 small jalapeño pepper, seeded and chopped

½ teaspoon salt

½ teaspoon baking powder

DIRECTIONS

1 Preheat your oven to 400 degrees. Grease a 10-inch cast-iron skillet or spray it with cooking spray. Mix all the ingredients together.

2 Bake for 40 to 45 minutes or until golden brown.

VARY IT! You can make this cornbread as mild or as hot as you like by using more or fewer hot peppers.

PER SERVING: *Calories 180 (From Fat 94); Fat 11g (Saturated 3g); Cholesterol 45mg; Sodium 429mg; Carbohydrate 16g (Dietary Fiber 2g); Protein 5g.*

THE SELF-RISING CORNMEAL STORY

With *self-rising cornmeal mix* the flour, salt, and leavening (the stuff that makes the bread rise) is already added. If a recipe calls for self-rising cornmeal mix, and you have only plain cornmeal, you can make your own: Combine 1 cup cornmeal, 1 cup flour, 1 tablespoon baking powder, and 1 teaspoon salt; then cut in ¼ cup butter or shortening. In some regions of the country that are more cornbread crazy than others, *self-rising cornmeal* is available. Self-rising cornmeal (no *mix* on the end) contains cornmeal, salt, and the leavening agent but doesn't contain flour.

Southern Cornbread

PREP TIME: 10 MIN | **COOK TIME: 30 TO 40 MIN** | **YIELD: 8 PIECES**

INGREDIENTS

3 tablespoons bacon grease or vegetable oil

2 cups white, self-rising cornmeal mix

½ teaspoon baking soda

2 eggs, beaten

2 cups buttermilk

DIRECTIONS

1 Preheat your oven to 450 degrees. Put the bacon grease into a 9-inch cast-iron skillet and place it in the oven to get really hot.

2 Blend the cornmeal mix, baking soda, eggs, and buttermilk in a bowl, using a spoon or fork.

3 When the skillet and bacon grease are really hot, carefully remove the skillet from the oven and pour the hot bacon grease into the batter. Quickly stir the bacon grease into the batter. Pour the batter into the hot skillet. It should sizzle and may splatter. Bake for 30 to 40 minutes or until golden brown.

4 Remove from the oven and let it cool 5 to 10 minutes. Invert onto a plate, revealing crispy brown crust. Cut into wedges and serve hot (with plenty of butter).

PER SERVING: *Calories 204 (From Fat 58); Fat 6g (Saturated 2g); Cholesterol 60mg; Sodium 692mg; Carbohydrate 29g (Dietary Fiber 2g); Protein 7g.*

TENNESSEE MILKSHAKE

Forget the ice cream. In Tennessee, you can make a milkshake with just cornbread and milk. Here's how:

1. Fill a glass a little over half full of milk.

2. Crumble plain, old cornbread into the milk until the glass is almost full.

3. Stir it around a little to get the bread saturated.

Pretty simple. In fact, this recipe has no science or precise measurement. If you like your shake thicker, use less milk and more cornbread. Want it thinner? More milk and less cornbread. You can even be daring and add a little sugar to the mix.

⟡ Sour Cream Cornbread

PREP TIME: 10 MIN	COOK TIME: 45 MIN	YIELD: 8 PIECES

INGREDIENTS

½ cup vegetable oil

One 8-ounce can cream-style corn

1 cup sour cream

1 cup white, self-rising cornmeal mix

3 eggs, beaten

¾ teaspoon salt

DIRECTIONS

1 Preheat your oven to 400 degrees. Place ¼ cup of the oil in a 9-inch cast-iron skillet and place the skillet in the oven to heat. Mix the rest of the oil with the corn, sour cream, cornmeal mix, eggs, and salt.

2 When the skillet and oil are really hot, remove the skillet from the oven and carefully pour the hot oil into the batter. Mix well.

3 Pour the batter into the hot skillet. Bake for about 45 minutes or until golden brown.

PER SERVING: *Calories 314 (From Fat 205); Fat 23g (Saturated 5g); Cholesterol 92mg; Sodium 339mg; Carbohydrate 22g (Dietary Fiber 2g); Protein 6g.*

QUICK BREADS

Cornbread is considered a quick bread, just as muffins and biscuits are, because you don't have to use yeast as a *leavener* (rising agent): The upshot? You can mix all the ingredients in the time it takes to preheat your oven. These breads, unlike yeast breads, don't take hours to rise. The leaveners that you use in quick breads are baking soda and baking powder. If you use self-rising cornmeal mix, you can do so without these leaveners entirely, because the cornmeal contains them already.

🍅 Yankee Cornbread

INGREDIENTS

2½ cups yellow self-rising cornmeal mix

¼ cup sugar

1 cup milk

¼ cup vegetable oil

2 eggs, slightly beaten

DIRECTIONS

1 Preheat your oven to 425 degrees. Grease a 10-inch cast-iron skillet.

2 In a large bowl, combine the cornmeal mix, sugar, milk, oil, and eggs and blend well with a spoon; pour into skillet.

3 Bake for 20 to 25 minutes or until a toothpick inserted in the center comes out clean.

NOTE: You can influence how sweet your cornbread is by experimenting with the amount of sugar you add. If this recipe is just a touch too sweet, add less sugar — 2 tablespoons instead of the ¼ cup, for example.

VARY IT! For corn muffins, grease muffin cups, fill with batter about ⅔ full and bake for 15 to 20 minutes.

PER SERVING: *Calories 290 (From Fat 94); Fat 10g (Saturated 2g); Cholesterol 57mg; Sodium 491mg; Carbohydrate 43g (Dietary Fiber 2g); Protein 6g.*

Baking the Best Biscuit

Everyone has their own preference of biscuit based on their upbringing and personal taste. It's fascinating how people often associate their mothers or grandmothers with making the best biscuits. Here you can create your own version of the best biscuits (refer to Chapter 10 for some tricks and tips).

You can start making some flaky biscuits in your cast iron with just a little practice. I include the following biscuit recipes in this section:

>> **Bacon Biscuits:** Savory yet smoky, fluffy and buttery, these flavors are a match made in heaven. Whether you're enjoying them for breakfast, snack, or a side, these biscuits won't disappoint.

>> **Baking Powder Biscuits:** You can say plenty about plain biscuits. They're delicious and go with anything. And you can't beat them when you have some butter and honey that you're anxious to get rid of. These biscuits are also great topped with sausage gravy.

>> **Buttermilk Biscuits:** In this recipe buttermilk is a key ingredient. It adds flavor and makes a lighter, airier biscuit than regular milk does.

>> **Buttermilk Drop Biscuits:** Drop biscuits are perhaps the easiest to make. Simply mix the ingredients and then drop the spoonful of dough into your pan.

>> **Cheese Biscuits:** These biscuits offer a bit of nostalgia, especially when they're warm, right out of the oven. The beautiful golden-brown color and the slightly crispy exterior paired with the often flakey interior is life changing.

>> **Cornmeal Biscuits:** This recipe combines all-purpose flour and cornmeal to create a light and airy biscuit that can stand up to any broth or gravy. These biscuits are perfect for soups and stews.

REMEMBER

Many people go no further when flavoring biscuits than spreading butter and jam or honey on them. But flavored biscuits like the Bacon Biscuits and Cheese Biscuits — that special breed of biscuit with special flavors cooked right in — are a treat not to be missed. In fact, flavored biscuits can stand on their own: No butter needed.

Bacon Biscuits

INGREDIENTS

8 slices bacon

2 cups all-purpose flour

½ teaspoon salt

2 teaspoons baking powder

4 tablespoons vegetable shortening

¾ cup milk

DIRECTIONS

1 Place a medium cast-iron skillet on a stovetop burner on medium heat. Fry the bacon until crisp and drain on paper towels. Crumble and set aside. Preheat your oven to 450 degrees.

2 Sift the flour, salt, and baking powder together in a large bowl. Cut in the shortening with a fork or pastry blender until the mixture resembles coarse crumbs. Stir in the cooked bacon. Stir in the milk with a fork just until the dough pulls away from bowl.

3 Turn onto a lightly floured surface and knead it for about 30 seconds or just until smooth. Cut out the biscuits with a floured biscuit cutter.

4 Place on a lightly greased medium cast-iron skillet or griddle. Bake for 10 to 12 minutes or until golden brown.

TIP: To enhance the bacon flavor of these biscuits, cook them in the skillet that you used to fry the bacon. Pour out the excess bacon grease (save it for other recipes if you want), wiping the sides of the pan with just enough grease to keep the biscuits from sticking.

PER SERVING: *Calories 126 (From Fat 54); Fat 6g (Saturated 2g); Cholesterol 5mg; Sodium 210mg; Carbohydrate 14g (Dietary Fiber 1g); Protein 3g.*

THE BIRTH OF THE BISCUIT

The soft-wheat flours of the South didn't (and still don't) bond well with yeast. To make yeast breads, southern cooks had to import good bread flour from the North. Folks couldn't afford to purchase it. Biscuits were born when commercially prepared baking powder and baking soda became readily available to the southern cook. These ingredients could be combined with the South's soft flour to make biscuits, a yummy substitute for the yeast breads that were common in the North.

When the leavening agents of baking soda and baking powder became available, biscuits became as much a part of southern meals as cornbread and hoe cakes had been before that time.

Baking Powder Biscuits

PREP TIME: 10 MIN | COOK TIME: 12 MIN | YIELD: 12 BISCUITS

INGREDIENTS

2 cups all-purpose flour

2 teaspoons baking powder

¾ teaspoon salt

Dash of sugar

3 tablespoons vegetable shortening

⅔ cup milk

DIRECTIONS

1 Preheat your oven to 450 degrees.

2 In a large bowl, sift together the flour, baking powder, salt, and sugar. Work in the shortening with a pastry cutter or your fingers, until the mixture resembles coarse crumbs. Gradually add the milk, mixing it in with a spoon.

3 Turn the dough onto a lightly floured board and knead for about 30 seconds. Roll out to ½-inch thickness. Cut with a floured biscuit cutter or a can with both ends cut away.

4 Bake in a medium cast-iron skillet or griddle coated with cooking spray for about 12 minutes.

NOTE: In Step 2 when you add the milk, the dough should be as soft as can be handled without sticking.

PER SERVING: *Calories 113 (From Fat 35); Fat 4g (Saturated 1g); Cholesterol 2mg; Sodium 216mg; Carbohydrate 17g (Dietary Fiber 1g); Protein 3g.*

🍅 Buttermilk Biscuits

PREP TIME: 10 MIN	COOK TIME: 12 MIN	YIELD: 12 TO 14 BISCUITS

INGREDIENTS

2 cups all-purpose flour

½ teaspoon salt

½ teaspoon baking soda

2 teaspoons baking powder

4 tablespoons vegetable shortening

1 cup buttermilk

DIRECTIONS

1 Preheat your oven to 450 degrees.

2 In a large bowl, sift together the flour, salt, baking soda, and baking powder. Work in the shortening with a pastry blender or your fingers, until the mixture resembles coarse meal. Slowly stir in the buttermilk until the dough pulls away from the bowl.

3 Turn the dough onto a lightly floured surface, knead for about 30 seconds, and roll to ½-inch thickness. Cut with a floured biscuit cutter, and place on a medium cast-iron griddle or skillet coated with cooking spray.

4 Bake for about 12 minutes until golden brown on top.

PER SERVING: *Calories 104 (From Fat 36); Fat 4g (Saturated 1g); Cholesterol 1mg; Sodium 201mg; Carbohydrate 15g (Dietary Fiber 1g); Protein 2g.*

HIGH-RISE BISCUITS NEED GAS

For biscuits to rise, the fat needs to be evenly distributed throughout the dough. When your biscuits cook, two actions take place at the same time. The leavener, as it warms, releases gas, and the shortening, as it warms, melts. If the shortening and leavener are evenly distributed, the melting shortening gives the released gas a place to go. This combination of events — the gas releasing into little bubbles that pop in the spaces that the melting shortening has opened up — is what causes your biscuits to rise.

If the shortening isn't mixed in very well, the gas doesn't have anywhere to go and just dissipates. If you overmix the shortening (and end up with a paste instead of crumbs), the dough is too heavy and collapses around the gas pockets.

Buttermilk Drop Biscuits

PREP TIME: 10 MIN	COOK TIME: 15 TO 18 MIN	YIELD: 14 BISCUITS

INGREDIENTS

2 cups all-purpose flour

1 tablespoon baking powder

¼ teaspoon baking soda

2 teaspoons sugar

½ teaspoon cream of tartar

¼ teaspoon salt

½ cup butter or vegetable shortening

1¼ cups buttermilk

2 tablespoons chopped fresh parsley (optional)

DIRECTIONS

1 Preheat your oven to 450 degrees.

2 In a medium bowl, stir together the flour and the baking powder, baking soda, sugar, cream of tartar, and salt. Cut in the butter with a fork or pastry blender, until the mixture resembles coarse crumbs. Add the buttermilk (and parsley, if desired) and stir until just blended.

3 Using a spoon, drop the dough into a greased cast-iron drop biscuit pan (fill quite full) or onto a medium cast-iron skillet or griddle.

4 Bake for 15 to 18 minutes or until golden brown. Serve while hot.

NOTE: Refer to the color insert for a photo of this recipe.

PER SERVING: *Calories 134 (From Fat 62); Fat 7g (Saturated 4g); Cholesterol 18mg; Sodium 170mg; Carbohydrate 15g (Dietary Fiber 1g); Protein 3g.*

Cheese Biscuits

| PREP TIME: 10 MIN | COOK TIME: 12 MIN | YIELD: 12 TO 14 BISCUITS |

INGREDIENTS

2 cups all-purpose flour

3 teaspoons baking powder

¾ teaspoon salt

4 tablespoons vegetable shortening

1 cup finely shredded sharp cheddar cheese

½ teaspoon dry mustard

Scant ¾ cup milk

DIRECTIONS

1 Preheat your oven to 450 degrees.

2 Sift the flour, baking powder, and salt together in a bowl. With a pastry blender or fork, cut in the shortening until the mixture resembles coarse crumbs. Stir in the cheese and dry mustard. Stir in the milk with a fork until the dough pulls away from the sides of the bowl.

3 Turn onto a lightly floured surface and knead about 10 times or just until the dough is smooth. Roll out the dough to a ½-inch thickness. Cut out the biscuits with a floured biscuit cutter.

4 Place on lightly greased cast-iron skillet or griddle. Bake for about 12 minutes or until golden brown.

NOTE: Pair these flavorful biscuits with a nice dinner salad or bowl of soup for a (relatively) light meal.

PER SERVING: *Calories 139 (From Fat 63); Fat 7g (Saturated 3g); Cholesterol 10mg; Sodium 263mg; Carbohydrate 14g (Dietary Fiber 1g); Protein 4g.*

Cornmeal Biscuits

PREP TIME: 10 MIN	COOK TIME: 12 TO 15 MIN	YIELD: 8 BISCUITS

INGREDIENTS

1¼ cups all-purpose flour

¾ cup cornmeal

1 teaspoon salt

2 teaspoons sugar

3 teaspoons baking powder

4 tablespoons vegetable shortening

⅔ cup milk

DIRECTIONS

1 Preheat your oven to 375 degrees.

2 In a large bowl, sift together the flour, cornmeal, salt, sugar, and baking powder. Cut in the shortening with a pastry blender or fork until the mixture resembles coarse crumbs. Stir in the milk with a fork until the dough just pulls away from the bowl.

3 Turn onto lightly floured surface and roll out to ½-inch thickness. Cut out the biscuits with a floured biscuit cutter.

4 Place on a lightly greased cast-iron skillet or griddle. Bake for 12 to 15 minutes.

PER SERVING: *Calories 145 (From Fat 66); Fat 7g (Saturated 2g); Cholesterol 3mg; Sodium 444mg; Carbohydrate 17g (Dietary Fiber 1g); Protein 3g.*

Creating Flavorful Bread Recipes

Baking flavored bread is a great way to infuse a burst of taste into any bread recipe. Whether you're making hoecakes (also known as *Johnnycakes*), dill bread, or even your favorite spoonbread, each dish adds a layer of depth and complexity to every bite. Cast-iron pans are regarded as the best vessel to cook in thanks to their exceptional heat retention and even distribution, which helps ensure that your flavored bread bakes evenly and develops a satisfying crust.

You can discover a wide array of bread recipes here that you can try with your cast iron:

» **Hoecakes (Johnnycakes):** Hoecakes are known by various names around the world. In different regions, they may be called journey cakes, hoecakes, Johnnycakes, ashcakes, or corn pones. These names may vary based on local dialects and culinary traditions.

This dish is thought to have originated in West Africa; the introduction of hoecakes to the Caribbean can be traced back to the slave trade. Over time, the recipe has evolved, incorporating local ingredients and culinary techniques to make it what it is today. People worldwide love hoecakes, and they're frequently enjoyed for breakfast, as a delicious snack, or as a versatile side dish with a meal.

» **Spoon Rolls:** This recipe gives you the distinctive taste of yeast rolls without all the prep work. No kneading, rising, rolling, or shaping required. Simply prepare your dough and drop it by spoonful into your muffin pan. Because the batter can be kept in the refrigerator for a week, make as many rolls as you want and save the rest of the batter for your next dinner.

» **Savory Dill Bread:** The combination of dill's distinct taste and the savory notes of the bread make this a mouthwatering culinary experience.

» **Sheepherders Bread:** This classic dish, was originally designed for sheepherders who spent long periods of time out and needed durable bread. Known for its simplicity and hearty flavor, this bread is the perfect side to soak up the liquid from any stew.

» **Spoon Bread:** Spoon bread is a cross between cornbread and a soufflé, rising sky high when you cook it and falling when you remove it from the oven.

» **Quick Pizza Dough:** If you're running short on time, skip making your own dough: Just buy ready-made dough from your grocer's freezer or refrigerator section.

Hoecakes (Johnnycakes)

INGREDIENTS

1 cup white cornmeal

½ cup all-purpose flour

1¼ teaspoons baking powder

¼ teaspoon baking soda

1 teaspoon salt

1 tablespoon sugar

About 1⅓ cup buttermilk

DIRECTIONS

1 Heat your cast-iron griddle to medium-high heat on your stovetop.

2 In a medium bowl, combine cornmeal, flour, baking powder, baking soda, salt, and sugar. Add buttermilk to the desired consistency — think of a thin, cornmeal pancake batter.

3 Grease a hot griddle with solid vegetable shortening. Test the griddle for correct temperature by splashing a few drops of water onto the surface. If the water dances in beads, the griddle is hot enough.

4 Pour ¼ cup of the batter onto the hot griddle. Turn when the surface is full of bubbles. Fry until the second side is golden brown as well. Keep griddle well-greased and hot with each batch. Serve hot with butter.

NOTE: Not as common as they once were, hoecakes are still a hit with outdoor enthusiasts because they don't require an oven. Indoors, you can serve them as a bread for dinner just like you would cornbread. And you can serve them for breakfast with honey or jam in place of pancakes, toast, or biscuits.

PER SERVING: *Calories 43 (From Fat 7); Fat 1g (Saturated 0g); Cholesterol 1mg; Sodium 144mg; Carbohydrate 8g (Dietary Fiber 1g); Protein 1g.*

SOME HOECAKE HISTORY

The precursor to pancakes, hoecakes, which are sometimes called *Johnnycakes,* go back to colonial times. According to legend, the name *Johnnycake* may have come from *journey cakes,* which people would pack to snack on during long journeys on horseback. And the name *hoecake* could have come from a preferred cooking method — on a hoe over the fire — but that history is difficult to confirm. Johnnycakes were a favorite of President William McKinley's — along with bacon and eggs — all fried in cast iron.

◔ Spoon Rolls

INGREDIENTS

1 package dry yeast

¼ cup sugar

1 egg, beaten

¾ cup butter, melted

4 cups self-rising flour

DIRECTIONS

1 Preheat your oven to 400 degrees.

2 Using a bowl large enough to hold all the ingredients, dissolve the yeast in 2 cups warm water and let stand for about 20 minutes for yeast to swell.

3 With a wooden spoon, mix in the sugar, egg, butter, and flour.

4 Spoon the batter into a well-greased cast-iron drop biscuit pan or muffin pan until each well is slightly over ½ full. Bake for 20 minutes.

PER SERVING: Calories 233 (From Fat 94); Fat 11g (Saturated 6g); Cholesterol 42mg; Sodium 460mg; Carbohydrate 30g (Dietary Fiber 1g); Protein 4g.

Savory Dill Bread

PREP TIME: 2 TO 3 HRS INCLUDING RISING TIME	COOK TIME: 40 TO 50 MIN	YIELD: 12 TO 14 SLICES

INGREDIENTS

1 package yeast

1 cup creamed cottage cheese

2 tablespoons sugar

1 tablespoon butter

1 teaspoon salt

1 unbeaten egg

1 tablespoon dried dill weed

¼ teaspoon soda

1 tablespoon instant onion

2½ cups bread flour

Kosher salt

DIRECTIONS

1 Combine the yeast with ¼ cup warm water in a bowl large enough to hold all the ingredients and double in size. Let stand about 10 minutes until bubbly.

2 Mix the cottage cheese, sugar, butter, salt, egg, dill weed, soda, and instant onion into the yeast and water.

3 Gradually add the flour, beating well after each addition. The dough will be a little sticky at this point, but it's more manageable after the first rise.

4 Let the dough rise in a warm place until doubled in size, about 1 to 1½ hours. Stir down dough.

5 Preheat your oven to 350 degrees. Turn the dough into a well-greased 3-inch-deep cast-iron skillet. Let rise until doubled in size again, about 1 hour.

6 Bake for 40 to 50 minutes. The finished loaf makes a hollow sound when you thump it. Brush with melted butter. Sprinkle with kosher salt. Makes one round, 10-inch loaf.

NOTE: The sugar in the recipe isn't strictly for taste; it actually affects how your loaf rises. This little bit of added sugar gives the yeast more sugar to act on, creating more rise.

PER SERVING: Calories 126 (From Fat 21); Fat 2g (Saturated 1g); Cholesterol 20mg; Sodium 257mg; Carbohydrate 21g (Dietary Fiber 1g); Protein 6g.

HOW YEAST WORKS

Yeast, the leavening agent in many breads, is a living organism that feeds on sugar and starch in the flour, converting these substances into carbon dioxide and alcohol. The carbon dioxide gas gives yeast bread its rise, and the alcohol gives it its characteristic flavor. Kneading is important because it distributes the yeast evenly throughout the bread dough.

So, when you bite into a dinner roll, are you eating tiny little live organisms? No. You're eating tiny little dead organisms. The heat of the oven kills the yeast.

Sheepherders Bread

PREP TIME: 2½ HRS INCLUDING RISING TIME	COOK TIME: ABOUT 1 HR	YIELD: 14 TO 16 SLICES

INGREDIENTS

3 cups warm tap water

2½ teaspoons salt

1 stick butter, slightly melted

½ cup sugar

2 packages (¼ ounce each) dry yeast

8 to 10 cups bread flour

DIRECTIONS

1 Put the water (no hotter than 120 degrees), salt, butter, and sugar into a bowl and stir. Add the yeast and let it stand for 15 minutes, until bubbly.

2 Using a wooden spoon, add 5 cups of the flour, beating it into batter a little at a time. Add 3 more cups of the flour and beat well with a wooden spoon.

3 Turn the dough onto a floured surface and knead, adding up to 1 more cup of flour, until the dough feels smooth and elastic. Turn into a large, greased bowl and let it rise in a warm place until it's doubled in size (about ½ hour).

4 Punch down and place into a 6- or 7-quart cast-iron Dutch oven lined with nonstick aluminum foil or aluminum foil that's greased with shortening or butter. Leave enough aluminum foil to make handles for removing the bread from the Dutch oven when the baking process is complete. Cover with a lid that's also been greased. Let it rise until doubled (about 1½ hours) in a warm place.

5 Bake, covered, in a 350-degree oven for 12 minutes. Remove the lid and continue to bake for 45 to 60 minutes longer. Bread should be brown on top and sound hollow when thumped.

6 Lift the bread from the Dutch oven with the aluminum foil and let it cool. Makes one large round loaf of bread, 12 inches in diameter.

NOTE: Sheepherders Bread calls for bread flour, which is processed to have more gluten, a type of flour protein that traps bubbles that form when the yeast feeds on the sugars in the dough. More gluten means higher rise and a better structure, which is ideal for any yeast bread.

PER SERVING: Calories 324 (From Fat 62); Fat 7g (Saturated 4g); Cholesterol 15mg; Sodium 366mg; Carbohydrate 56g (Dietary Fiber 2g); Protein 8g.

🍅 Spoon Bread

INGREDIENTS

2 cups whole milk

½ cup cornmeal

1 teaspoon salt

2 tablespoons melted butter

2 eggs, separated

½ teaspoon baking powder

DIRECTIONS

1 Preheat your oven to 400 degrees. Grease a 12-inch, deep, cast-iron skillet and place it in your hot oven.

2 In a 3-quart saucepan, heat the milk until simmering. Gradually add the cornmeal and salt to the hot milk, stirring constantly. Continue to blend until the cornmeal has absorbed the milk and becomes stiff. Add the butter, blend well, and remove from the heat.

3 Using an electric mixer, beat the egg yolks and baking powder in a separate bowl until well blended.

4 Pour the egg mixture into the cornmeal batter. Blend well and set aside.

5 In a separate mixing bowl, beat the egg whites until stiff. Using a large serving spoon, gently fold the egg whites into the batter.

6 Pour the batter into a preheated 12-inch skillet and bake for 35 minutes. The bread will be done when firm to the touch and golden brown.

TIP: The key to good spoon bread is a lump-free mush. Pour the meal into the hot liquid quickly and stir like crazy, using a wire whisk; then keep stirring until the mush begins to thicken.

NOTE: So named because you serve it with a spoon and eat it with a fork, spoon bread is great as a side dish in place of potatoes or rice.

VARY IT! Add shredded cheese when you add the butter in Step 2.

NOTE: Refer to the color insert for a photo of this recipe.

PER SERVING: *Calories 90 (From Fat 45); Fat 5g (Saturated 3g); Cholesterol 55mg; Sodium 287mg; Carbohydrate 8g (Dietary Fiber 1g); Protein 4g.*

Quick Pizza Dough

PREP TIME: 30 MIN | YIELD: DOUGH FOR ONE 13-INCH PIZZA CRUST

INGREDIENTS

3 cups bread flour, divided

1 package dry rapid-rise yeast

1 teaspoon salt

1½ teaspoons honey

1¼ cups lukewarm water

1 tablespoon olive oil

DIRECTIONS

1 In a large bowl, mix ½ cup of the flour with the yeast and salt. Dissolve the honey in 1¼ cups of lukewarm water and add to the dry mixture.

2 Add the olive oil and mix for 3 minutes with a wooden spoon. Mix in the remaining flour. (The dough should be only slightly sticky.) Turn the dough onto a floured surface and knead for about 5 minutes, until smooth.

3 Place the dough in a lightly oiled bowl and cover with the plastic wrap. Let it relax for 10 minutes in a warm place.

4 Punch down the dough. Allow to relax for another 10 minutes. Punch down.

PER SERVING: *Calories 207 (From Fat 23); Fat 3g (Saturated 0g); Cholesterol 0mg; Sodium 292mg; Carbohydrate 39g (Dietary Fiber 1g); Protein 7g.*

Chapter **20**

Pancakes, Muffins, and More

nlike cooking, where you often rely on ratios, baking is more of an exact science. For instance, replacing a tablespoon for a teaspoon can have disastrous consequences. However, fear not, because making delicious pancakes, muffins, and other baked goods isn't a mystical process. Here I guide you through recipes that can inspire you to venture outside your culinary comfort zone.

This chapter explores an array of my favorites, including pancakes, muffins, and more. There is nothing like the irresistible aroma of perfectly caramelized crust created in a cast-iron pan. Each bite carries whispers of vanilla, nutmeg, and cinnamon, transporting you to a world of pure indulgence through each dish.

Flipping over Pancake Recipes

Pancakes have a long history and are one of the oldest forms of bread. Throughout different cultures, they have different names — in France, they're called crepes and in Russia, they're known as blinis. Begin your day using your cast iron with these pancake recipes. I include the following pancake recipes in this section:

>> **Buttermilk Pancakes:** Hot off the griddle, these moist and delicious pancakes will stir up memories of days gone by.

>> **German Pancakes:** German pancakes, also called *Dutch pancakes, puff pancakes, apple pancakes,* and quite a few other names, are the giants of the pancake world that you cook in a skillet in the oven rather than in a griddle on the stovetop.

>> **Corncakes:** Sturdier than traditional pancakes and flavored with bacon grease, these corncakes have much in common with a quick bread.

>> **Dutch Pancakes:** In Germany, the Dutch pancakes are also referred to as baby pancakes. It's interesting to see how such a simple concept has evolved and taken on different forms across the globe.

Buttermilk Pancakes

PREP TIME: 5 MIN	COOK TIME: 1 TO 2 MIN EACH SIDE	YIELD: 8 PANCAKES

INGREDIENTS

1 egg

1 cup buttermilk

2 tablespoons vegetable oil

1 scant cup all-purpose flour

½ tablespoon sugar

1 teaspoon baking powder

½ teaspoon baking soda

½ teaspoon salt

DIRECTIONS

1 Heat a cast-iron griddle to medium-high heat.

2 In a bowl, beat the egg. Stir in the buttermilk and oil. Add the flour, sugar, baking powder, baking soda, and salt and stir. Some small lumps will remain.

3 Grease your hot griddle. Sprinkle a few drops of water on the griddle. If the drops dance in beads, the griddle is at the correct temperature.

4 Pour ¼ cup of the batter onto the hot griddle. Turn the pancake when to top is full of bubbles. Cook until golden brown. Continue until all batter is used. Be sure that the griddle is still greased and hot between batches.

VARY IT! For fruit pancakes, gently stir ½ cup cut-up fruit or berries into your batter.

PER SERVING: Calories 112 (From Fat 41); Fat 5g (Saturated 1g); Cholesterol 28mg; Sodium 312mg; Carbohydrate 14g (Dietary Fiber 0g); Protein 3g.

KOSHER SALT VERSUS TABLE SALT

Many cooks prefer kosher salt to table salt, and some recipes specifically call for kosher salt. Some important differences between the two types of salt are that table salt is a finer grained salt with additives to make it pour freely. Kosher salt is usually additive-free and has a courser grain. In addition, kosher salt has a milder salt flavor than table salt.

When you cook with kosher salt, remember that kosher salt has less salt per volume (due to the coarser grains) than table salt does. For that reason, you need to use more kosher salt to attain the same level of saltiness that table salt yields. Similarly, if you're substituting table salt in a recipe that specifically calls for kosher salt, you use less. The difference in saltiness depends on the brands that you're comparing; sometimes kosher salt is half as salty as table salt. If you're substituting salts and the recipe doesn't include the alternative quantity, season to taste.

German Pancakes

INGREDIENTS

6 tablespoons butter

1 cup all-purpose flour

1 teaspoon salt

6 eggs

1 cup milk

½ lemon

Powdered sugar

Cinnamon

1½ cups applesauce or fried apples

DIRECTIONS

1 Preheat your oven to 400 degrees. Spread the bottom and sides of a 12-inch cold cast-iron skillet with the butter.

2 Sift the flour and salt together and set aside. Beat the eggs until very light. Add the milk to the eggs. Add the dry ingredients to the eggs and milk.

3 Pour the batter into a skillet and bake for 30 to 35 minutes, or until cooked through and golden brown. Remove from the oven.

4 Squeeze the juice of ½ lemon over the top. Top with a sprinkle of powdered sugar and cinnamon. Serve with applesauce or fried apples.

NOTE: These pancakes don't use leaveners (baking powder or soda). Instead the combination of the eggs and high oven temperature causes them to rise.

TIP: Depending on the season, the best apples for cooking are Granny Smith and Honey Crisp, although you can use other apples you may have on hand. The more intentional you are about your ingredients, the bigger the opportunity to enhance your flavors and textures.

PER SERVING: *Calories 495 (From Fat 244); Fat 27g (Saturated 14g); Cholesterol 373mg; Sodium 712mg; Carbohydrate 49g (Dietary Fiber 2g); Protein 15g.*

🍅 Corncakes

INGREDIENTS

1 cup white cornmeal

1 cup white cornmeal mix

1 teaspoon baking soda

2 teaspoons baking powder

1 teaspoon salt

2 eggs

2 cups buttermilk

4 tablespoons butter, melted

DIRECTIONS

1 In a large bowl, combine the cornmeal, cornmeal mix, baking soda, baking powder, and salt. Set aside.

2 In a smaller bowl, beat the eggs, the buttermilk, and butter. Pour the liquid into the dry ingredients and beat together hard.

3 Heat a cast-iron griddle to medium-high on your stovetop. Grease the hot griddle. Pour about ¼ cup of the batter onto the hot griddle and turn when bubbles appear, about 3 minutes. Cook until the other side is golden brown, about 2 minutes. Continue until all the batter is used. Be sure that the griddle is still greased and hot between batches.

TIP: When you make corncakes, be sure to keep your griddle hot and grease it with each batch.

TIP: For my vegan friends, you can use vegan butter.

PER SERVING: *Calories 83 (From Fat 39); Fat 4g (Saturated 2g); Cholesterol 30mg; Sodium 321mg; Carbohydrate 8g (Dietary Fiber 1g); Protein 3g.*

Dutch Pancakes

PREP TIME: 10 MIN | COOK TIME: 15 MIN | YIELD: 4 SERVINGS

INGREDIENTS

½ cup powdered sugar

½ teaspoon cinnamon

4 strawberries, quartered

½ cup blueberries

½ cup blackberries, halved

4 leaves mint, sliced

¼ teaspoon vanilla extract

1 lemon zest and juice

1 cup flour

2 tablespoons brown sugar

¼ teaspoon salt

¼ teaspoon nutmeg

4 eggs

1 cup milk

4 tablespoons butter

DIRECTIONS

1 Preheat your oven to 400 degrees. In a small bowl mix the powdered sugar, ¼ teaspoon cinnamon, strawberries, blueberries, blackberries, mint, vanilla, and lemon zest and juice. Reserve.

2 In a large bowl add the flour, brown sugar, salt, nutmeg, and ½ teaspoon cinnamon and mix well. While mixing, add the eggs and milk. Mix until smooth.

3 Preheat a 10-inch cast-iron skillet in the oven for about 3 to 5 minutes. Remove the skillet from the oven and add the butter. Swirl the butter in the pan on both the bottom and the sides until the butter has melted. Add about ½ cup of batter from the large mixing bowl to the skillet, rotating the pan so the batter completely coats the bottom and sides.

4 Place the skillet in the oven and bake for about 8 to 10 minutes or until puffy and golden brown. Remove the skillet from the oven. Serve with a scoop of berries. Repeat the process to cook the rest of the batter.

TIP: In Step 2, don't burn your butter when putting the pan in the oven. I recommend setting a timer or keeping an eye on the skillet.

NOTE: This dish is also great with savory items like eggs, prosciutto, and soft cheeses. Experiment with the garnish and make this dish your own.

PER SERVING: *Calories 420 (From Fat 164); Fat 18g (Saturated 10g); Cholesterol 247mg; Sodium 329mg; Carbohydrate 53g (Dietary Fiber 3g); Protein 12g.*

Tackling Tasty Muffin Recipes

Seeing how different foods can vary throughout the world is interesting. Muffins have an interesting history. They made their way to the Americas from Europe through English settlers who brought their culinary traditions with them. Muffins originally were more like bread rolls, but they gradually transformed into the delightful, small, and sweet baked goods enjoyed today. Food can evolve and adapt to different cultures and tastes over time.

These muffin recipes are great for so many purposes: Pack a couple in your lunch, grab one for an afternoon or evening snack, and share some with a sick friend or loved one. Here are some of my faves:

» **Breakfast Muffins:** Breakfast muffins are usually quick and easy to make; they lend themselves well to flavors like banana, blueberry, and even bacon. Muffins are a great item to have around, especially for a quick grab'n'go item.

» **Chocolate Muffin Cakes:** You can call this a breakfast muffin if you want to, but the richness of the sour cream and the melted chocolate make this muffin suitable for an after-dinner dessert — if you can keep the children away from it that long.

» **Mini-Muffins:** Essentially a smaller version of regular muffins, these bite-sized portions pack a punch. They're great for folks who don't want to eat a whole portion or who want a quick snack.

» **Pumpkin Muffins:** These muffins are a seasonal treat. Made with pumpkin purée, they're paired with flavors like cinnamon, nutmeg, and ginger that scream fall. They're also good on the holiday brunch menu.

» **Sugar Muffins:** Sugar Muffins, whose tops are given a brush of melted butter and then rolled in sugar, are the next best thing to a streusel topping — without the work.

REMEMBER

Breads baked in cast iron have a nicer crust. Papering a cast-iron muffin pan defeats the purpose of using cast iron. If getting the muffin out the pan is your main concern, just make sure that each compartment of your cast-iron pan is well greased. Also, make sure to grease around the top rim so that the muffin crown releases, too.

Breakfast Muffins

INGREDIENTS

2 cups all-purpose flour

2 tablespoons sugar

3 teaspoons baking soda

½ teaspoon salt

2 eggs

1 cup milk

2 tablespoons melted vegetable shortening

DIRECTIONS

1 Preheat your oven and well-greased cast-iron muffin pans to 450 degrees.

2 In a bowl, combine the flour, sugar, baking soda, and salt.

3 In a separate bowl, beat the eggs; then add the milk and shortening. Blend with dry ingredients.

4 Spoon into muffin cups. Carefully fill each cup ⅔ full. Bake at 450 degrees for 15 minutes.

VARY IT! To make buttermilk muffins, use 2 teaspoons baking powder and ½ teaspoon baking soda. Substitute buttermilk for the milk.

To make nut muffins, add ½ cup of chopped pecans or walnuts to the batter.

To make blueberry muffins, fold 1½ cups of dry berries into the batter.

To make banana muffins, add 1 cup mashed bananas to the batter.

To make bran muffins, mix 1 cup bran with milk before adding it to the mixture.

PER SERVING: *Calories 85 (From Fat 23); Fat 3g (Saturated 1g); Cholesterol 26mg; Sodium 142mg; Carbohydrate 13g (Dietary Fiber 0g); Protein 3g.*

Chocolate Muffin Cakes

PREP TIME: 10 MIN	COOK TIME: 30 MIN	YIELD: 16 MUFFINS

INGREDIENTS

½ cup butter

½ cup vegetable shortening

2 cups sugar

3 eggs

1 teaspoon vanilla

3 cups all-purpose flour

½ teaspoon salt

¼ teaspoon baking soda

1 cup sour cream

1 package (12 ounces) chocolate chips

3 ounces German chocolate, melted

DIRECTIONS

1 Preheat your oven and well-greased, cast-iron muffin pan to 325 degrees.

2 Blend the butter, shortening, and sugar until fluffy. Add the eggs, one at a time, and the vanilla.

3 In a separate bowl, stir together the flour, salt, and soda until blended. Add to the butter mixture alternating with sour cream. Stir in both chocolates.

4 Spoon the batter into the greased muffin pan and bake for 30 minutes. Be careful with the hot muffin pan.

PER SERVING: *Calories 461 (From Fat 217); Fat 24g (Saturated 12g); Cholesterol 62mg; Sodium 116mg; Carbohydrate 60g (Dietary Fiber 2g); Protein 5g.*

🍅 Mini-Muffins

INGREDIENTS

1¾ cups all-purpose flour

⅓ cup sugar

2 teaspoons baking powder

¼ teaspoon salt

1 beaten egg

¾ cup milk

¼ cup oil

¼ cup sugar

1 teaspoon cinnamon

3 tablespoons melted butter

DIRECTIONS

1 Preheat your oven and well-greased cast-iron muffin pan to 400 degrees.

2 Combine the flour, sugar, baking powder, and salt. Make a well in the center.

3 Combine the egg, milk, and oil. Pour it into the well of the flour mixture all at once. Mix until blended. Batter will be lumpy.

4 Fill the preheated and greased muffin pan ⅔ full. Bake at 400 degrees 16 to 18 minutes (until golden brown). Let the muffins sit for 10 minutes and then remove from the pan.

5 In a small bowl, combine the sugar and cinnamon. Brush the tops with butter. Sprinkle a mixture of sugar and cinnamon on the tops. Serve warm.

NOTE: The touch of cinnamon-sugar, added after baking, gives these muffins a little additional sweetness. If you want more pronounced sweetness, add a dollop of jam or jelly — any flavor — to the top of each uncooked muffin and then let it bake right in.

VARY IT! Add ¾ cup fresh or frozen blueberries to the batter.

Add 1 cup coarsely chopped cranberries and 2 tablespoons sugar.

Add ⅔ cup chopped dates and ⅓ cup chopped nuts.

Add ½ cup shredded cheese.

Add 1 medium, finely chopped apple.

Reduce milk to ½ cup and add ¾ cup mashed banana and ½ cup chopped nuts.

PER SERVING: *Calories 124 (From Fat 52); Fat 6g (Saturated 2g); Cholesterol 18mg; Sodium 84mg; Carbohydrate 16g (Dietary Fiber 0g); Protein 2g.*

Pumpkin Muffins

PREP TIME: 10 MIN	COOK TIME: 20 MIN	YIELD: 12 MUFFINS

INGREDIENTS

⅔ cup sugar

1 egg

¼ cup vegetable shortening

½ cup cooked fresh or canned pumpkin

2 tablespoons milk

1 cup all-purpose flour

2 teaspoons baking powder

¼ teaspoon salt

1 teaspoon ground cinnamon

⅛ teaspoon ground cloves

Lemon Glaze

DIRECTIONS

1 Preheat your oven and well-greased cast-iron muffin pan to 350 degrees.

2 In a large bowl, cream together the sugar, egg, and shortening. Add the pumpkin and milk.

3 In another bowl, blend the flour, baking powder, salt, cinnamon, and cloves. Mix the dry ingredients into the wet.

4 Carefully spoon the batter into the cast-iron muffin pan, ½ to ⅔ full. Bake at 350 degrees for 20 minutes until a toothpick inserted into the center comes out clean.

5 Drizzle with the Lemon Glaze.

Lemon Glaze

1½ tablespoons melted butter

½ cup powdered sugar

1 tablespoon lemon juice

⅛ teaspoon grated lemon rind

DIRECTIONS

1 In a small bowl, combine the butter, powdered sugar, lemon juice, and lemon rind and mix.

NOTE: Fresh pumpkin imparts a milder flavor than its canned cousin. To prepare fresh pumpkin, cut a small pumpkin in half and remove the seed and fiber — the stringy stuff. Place the pumpkin, cut side up, in a baking dish filled with ¼-inch of water. Cover and bake for 1 hour at 400 degrees. Scoop the tender pumpkin from the shell and mash. Store the unused portion in the refrigerator.

PER SERVING: *Calories 163 (From Fat 57); Fat 6g (Saturated 2g); Cholesterol 22mg; Sodium 119mg; Carbohydrate 25g (Dietary Fiber 1g); Protein 2g.*

Sugar Muffins

PREP TIME: 10 MIN	COOK TIME: 20 TO 25 MIN	YIELD: 9 MUFFINS

INGREDIENTS

⅓ cup vegetable shortening

½ cup sugar

1 egg

1½ cups cake flour

1½ teaspoon baking powder

½ teaspoon salt

¼ teaspoon cinnamon

½ cup milk

½ cup melted butter

½ cup sugar

DIRECTIONS

1 Preheat your oven and the well-greased cast-iron muffin pan to 325 degrees.

2 Cream the shortening and sugar. Add the egg. Combine the flour, baking powder, salt, and cinnamon. Add to the creamed sugar mixture alternating with the milk.

3 Carefully fill the preheated and greased muffin pan ⅔ full. Bake at 325 degrees for 20 to 25 minutes or until golden.

4 Cool 3 to 4 minutes. Brush the top with the melted butter and roll in the sugar. Serve warm.

VARY IT! For a different flavor, roll the muffin top in cinnamon sugar.

PER SERVING: *Calories 324 (From Fat 169); Fat 19g (Saturated 9g); Cholesterol 53mg; Sodium 208mg; Carbohydrate 37g (Dietary Fiber 0g); Protein 3g.*

Creating Other Cast-Iron Treats

One of the reasons I love cooking with cast iron is the versatility it offers. It opens up a world of culinary possibilities. These dishes are fantastic additions to any meal, whether it's a Sunday dinner, a special occasion, or just a late-night snack:

>> **Raspberry Dazzler Cornbread:** I include this recipe in this chapter because it's more of a cake than a traditional cornbread. You can serve it in place of coffeecake for breakfast or after dinner as dessert.

>> **Old-Time Banana Bread:** This recipe is a wonderful way to use overripe bananas.

>> **Basic Popovers:** Popovers are a fun pastry that earned their name due to their unique baking process. When placed in the oven, the pastries rapidly rise and pop over the top of the cast-iron muffin tin, resulting in a light and hollow delicacy. Because of the high heat, the batter puffs up and develops a crispy exterior while maintaining a soft and airy texture on the inside. What makes popovers even more versatile and exciting is that you can fill them with various fillings, whether you prefer something sweet or savory.

>> **Hushpuppies:** Popularized in the American South, hushpuppies are savory fritters made from a mixture of cornmeal, buttermilk, and eggs. These tasty morsels are then deep-fried to perfection until they become crispy and golden brown. They're often served as a delicious side dish that pairs well with seafood, barbecue, and other beloved southern dishes.

☕ Raspberry Dazzler Cornbread

PREP TIME: 10 MIN	COOK TIME: 30 MIN	YIELD: 18 PIECES

INGREDIENTS

1 cup self-rising flour

1 cup self-rising cornmeal mix

¾ cup sugar

1½ tablespoons finely grated lemon zest

1 egg

2 egg yolks

1½ sticks butter, melted and cooled

¾ cup milk

1½ cups fresh raspberries

2 to 3 tablespoons sugar

DIRECTIONS

1 Preheat your oven to 400 degrees. Grease a 9-inch cast-iron skillet with shortening.

2 In a large bowl, mix the flour, cornmeal mix, sugar, and lemon zest.

3 In another bowl, beat the egg and egg yolks, butter, and milk. Stir it into the flour mixture. Gently stir in the raspberries.

4 Pour the mixture into the skillet and bake in the middle of the oven for 25 minutes. Sprinkle the top with sugar and bake for an additional 5 minutes.

PER SERVING: *Calories 179 (From Fat 81); Fat 9g (Saturated 5g); Cholesterol 57mg; Sodium 202mg; Carbohydrate 22g (Dietary Fiber 2g); Protein 3g.*

Old-Time Banana Bread

PREP TIME: 10 MIN	COOK TIME: 55 TO 60 MIN	YIELD: 12 TO 14 SLICES

INGREDIENTS

½ teaspoon baking soda

¼ cup buttermilk

¼ cup vegetable shortening

¾ cup sugar

1 egg

⅔ cup bananas (2 medium) mashed

2 cups all-purpose flour

½ teaspoon baking powder

¼ teaspoon salt

½ cup walnuts chopped (optional)

DIRECTIONS

1 Preheat your oven and well-greased cast-iron loaf pan to 350 degrees.

2 Add the baking soda to the buttermilk in a measuring cup and let it stand.

3 In a large bowl, combine the shortening and sugar, beating it until fluffy. Add the egg and bananas. Beat until mixed. In a small bowl, combine the flour, baking powder, and salt. Add the dry ingredients and buttermilk mixture alternately to the shortening, sugar, egg, and banana mixture. Stir in the nuts.

4 Carefully pour the batter into the preheated and greased loaf pan and bake at 350 degrees for 55 to 60 minutes or until bread tests done — a toothpick inserted into the center comes out clean.

5 Remove from the oven and place on wire rack until cooled.

TIP: To get a nice rise out of your banana bread, don't overstir the batter. Good banana-bread batter should be thick and chunky.

VARY IT! If you or a loved one is allergic to nuts, you can leave them out.

VARY IT! You can substitute pecans for the walnuts.

PER SERVING: *Calories 190 (From Fat 63); Fat 7g (Saturated 1g); Cholesterol 15mg; Sodium 110mg; Carbohydrate 29g (Dietary Fiber 1g); Protein 3g.*

🍅 Basic Popovers

PREP TIME: 5 MIN | COOK TIME: 20 MIN | YIELD: 6 POPOVERS

INGREDIENTS

1 cup all-purpose flour

¼ teaspoon salt

2 eggs

1 cup milk

1 tablespoon vegetable shortening

DIRECTIONS

1 Preheat your oven and well-greased cast-iron muffin pan to 450 degrees.

2 In a mixing bowl, sift together the flour and salt.

3 Make a well in the center of the flour and break the eggs into it. Add your milk and shortening to the well and stir with a wooden spoon until smooth.

4 Pour the batter into a hot muffin pan ⅔ full. Bake at 450 degrees for 20 minutes.

5 Split the popovers when baked and fill with butter or jam or serve with roast beef and gravy.

NOTE: Popovers are best served piping hot, straight from the oven. If you let them sit long enough to cool, they lose the texture that makes them so delectable.

VARY IT! Change a regular popover into Yorkshire pudding: Put about ¼ to ½ cup drippings from any roasted beef into a 10-inch skillet or casserole dish and heat in a hot oven until very hot but not smoking. Pour your popover batter into the hot skillet and bake in a 425-degree oven for 25 to 30 minutes. Serve immediately.

NOTE: Turning up the heat is especially important for popovers, which lack leavening ingredients in the mix and rely on the combination of heat and eggs to make them rise.

PER SERVING: *Calories 145 (From Fat 48); Fat 5g (Saturated 2g); Cholesterol 76mg; Sodium 138mg; Carbohydrate 18g (Dietary Fiber 1g); Protein 6g.*

Hushpuppies

INGREDIENTS

1 cup self-rising flour

1 cup self-rising cornmeal mix

½ teaspoon salt

1 teaspoon sugar

1 egg, beaten

1 cup buttermilk

½ cup chopped green onions

DIRECTIONS

1 In a cast-iron deep fryer, preheat the oil to 375 degrees.

2 Combine the flour, cornmeal mix, salt, and sugar in a mixing bowl. Add the egg and ½ cup of the buttermilk to mix to a stiff batter. Stir in the onions.

3 Add more buttermilk a little at a time until the batter is well mixed and let it stand for 10 minutes.

4 Drop it by spoonful into the hot oil and fry until golden brown.

PER SERVING: *Calories 266 (From Fat 139); Fat 15g (Saturated 1g); Cholesterol 28mg; Sodium 617mg; Carbohydrate 27g (Dietary Fiber 2g); Protein 5g.*

THE ALLEGED HISTORY OF HUSHPUPPIES

Legend has it that the Ursuline nuns developed the hushpuppy in the early 1700s. Native Americans gave the nuns some cornmeal, which the nuns converted into a delicious fritter called *croquettes de maise.* The name *hushpuppy* came about when an old Creole cook was frying a batch of catfish and croquettes. His hungry dogs began to howl in anticipation of a chance to savor some of the catfish. The innovative Creole instead tossed a few of the croquettes de maise to the dogs and yelled, "Hush, puppies!" The name has since been associated with this cornmeal delicacy.

Chapter **21**
Satisfying Desserts

Many people often associate desserts with a positive memory or a special occasion. Indulging in a sweet bite of your favorite pleasure is also a form of self-care or a way to reward yourself after a hard day.

This chapter shows how you can use your cast iron to create your next favorite dessert. I include everything from some cake and pie recipes to other types of desserts. No matter what the dessert, if you have a sweet tooth, these dishes live up to their names. They're also a great way to finish a family dinner with your favorite warm beverage or share with friends.

Taking a Stab at Cake Recipes

Celebrating with cake is ingrained in today's cultural traditions. The act of sharing and enjoying cake is at the center of memorable gatherings — holidays, birthdays, weddings, and even sometimes the celebration of life. This section combines delicious flavors and textures, which help you create your next favorite memory. Here are the cake recipes in this section:

» **Almond Star Cakes:** The name refers to the decorative use of sliced almonds in the shape of stars on top of the cake. Cast iron evenly heats the cake, which results in a more consistent bake, giving you the best texture and flavor.

» **Easy Pineapple Upside Down Cake:** The key to a great pineapple upside down cake is caramelized fruit and brown-sugar topping. Started on the stovetop in a cast-iron skillet and finished in the oven, this cake is a contrast in delicious things: the rich, buttery topping and the moist, sweet cake.

» **January 1900 Jam Cake:** This recipe was handed down from generation to generation, as so many cast-iron recipes are.

» **Nutty Funnel Cakes:** A summertime fairground favorite, funnel cakes can be topped with cinnamon-sugar, as this recipe specifies, or powdered sugar, fruit, and just about anything else you feel like putting on top. They're even delicious served plain.

» **Double Cherry Tea Cake:** The beautiful blend of cherries in this tea cake complements a cup of tea or coffee perfectly. The texture of a tea cake is light, moist, and delicate, making it perfect for any part of your day.

🍅 Almond Star Cakes

INGREDIENTS

½ cup water

½ cup butter or margarine

1 cup all-purpose flour

1 cup sugar

1 teaspoon salt

1 teaspoon baking powder

¼ cup sour cream

2 eggs, beaten

1 teaspoon almond extract

Almond Cake Glaze

¼ cup chopped sliced almonds (optional)

5 maraschino cherries, halved (optional)

DIRECTIONS

1 Preheat the oven and your well-greased cast-iron muffin pan to 375 degrees.

2 Bring the water and butter to a boil in a large saucepan. Remove from the heat. Stir in the flour, sugar, salt, baking powder, sour cream, eggs, and almond extract until smooth. Pour into a preheated and greased muffin pan. Carefully fill the molds ¾ full.

3 Bake at 375 degrees for 20 minutes. Cool for 20 minutes. Remove the muffins from the pan. Spread the Almond Cake Glaze on top of the cakes. If desired, sprinkle each with the nuts or top with maraschino cherry halves.

Almond Cake Glaze

2 cups confectioners' sugar

2 to 3 tablespoons water

¼ to ½ teaspoon almond extract

DIRECTIONS

1 Mix the confectioners' sugar, 2 to 3 tablespoons of water, and the almond extract to make a glaze.

NOTE: This recipe calls for an All-Star pan, which is really a cast-iron muffin pan with star-shaped molds. You can use a regular muffin pan instead or any fun-shaped muffin pan you have.

PER SERVING: *Calories 327 (From Fat 103); Fat 11g (Saturated 7g); Cholesterol 70mg; Sodium 376mg; Carbohydrate 54g (Dietary Fiber 0g); Protein 3g.*

Easy Pineapple Upside Down Cake

PREP TIME: 15 MIN | COOK TIME: 45 MIN | YIELD: 8 SERVINGS

INGREDIENTS

3 tablespoons butter

1 cup light brown sugar

7 slices canned pineapple

½ cup pineapple juice reserved

7 candied cherries

10 to 12 pecan halves (optional)

¼ cup raisins (optional but makes a prettier and tastier cake)

3 eggs

1½ cups white sugar

1 teaspoon vanilla

1½ cups all-purpose flour

1½ teaspoons baking powder

¼ teaspoon salt

DIRECTIONS

1 Preheat oven to 350 degrees. Melt butter in 10-inch cast-iron skillet over low heat. Sprinkle the brown sugar over the butter. Remove the skillet from heat.

2 Arrange the pineapple rings in the skillet, cutting a few in half, if necessary, to fit all the rings in the pan. Place candied cherries in the center of each pineapple ring. Place the pecan halves and raisins, if desired, between pineapple rings.

3 In a mixing bowl, beat the eggs. Stir in the sugar. Add the vanilla and reserved pineapple juice and blend well.

4 In a separate bowl or on parchment paper, combine the flour, baking powder, and salt. Add the dry ingredients to the egg mixture and blend.

5 Pour batter over brown sugar and pineapple rings in a skillet. Bake for 45 minutes or until nicely brown. Invert onto a platter while warm.

NOTE: When you use cast iron, you can determine how caramel-y your topping is. Leave it on the stovetop just long enough to melt the butter; or leave it a couple minutes longer so that the brown sugar begins to melt, too. Either way, you're creating a classic cast-iron dessert.

PER SERVING: *Calories 445 (From Fat 58); Fat 6g (Saturated 3g); Cholesterol 91mg; Sodium 184mg; Carbohydrate 94g (Dietary Fiber 1g); Protein 5g.*

🍅 January 1900 Jam Cake

PREP TIME: 15 MIN	COOK TIME: 30 MIN	YIELD: 10 SERVINGS

INGREDIENTS

½ cup butter

2 cups sugar

6 egg yolks

2 cups buttermilk

2 teaspoons baking soda

3 cups all-purpose flour

2 teaspoons cinnamon

2 teaspoons ground cloves

2 teaspoons nutmeg

2 teaspoons allspice

3 tablespoons cocoa

2 cups jam, usually blackberry

1 cup raisins

Old-Time Icing

DIRECTIONS

1 Preheat your oven to 325 degrees. Line two 10-inch cast-iron skillets with wax paper because the jam can make the cake stick. In a large bowl, cream the butter and sugar and then add the egg yolks, one at a time. Set aside.

2 In another small bowl, mix the buttermilk and the baking soda and let stand for 3 minutes. To the creamed butter, sugar, and egg yolks mixture, add the flour alternately with the buttermilk mixture. Add the cinnamon, cloves, nutmeg, allspice, cocoa, jam, and raisins.

3 Divide the batter evenly into two skillets and bake at 325 degrees for 30 minutes. Remove the skillets from the oven and place the Old-Time Icing between the two layers and on top of the cake.

Old-Time Icing

2 cups milk

4 cups sugar

1 cup butter

⅛ teaspoon baking soda

DIRECTIONS

1 Combine the milk, sugar, butter, and baking soda in a deep cast-iron skillet. Cook for about 20 minutes until the mixture reaches the hard-ball stage on a candy thermometer (250 to 265 degrees). At this point the mixture will form thick threads from the spoon and form a hard ball when dropped into cold water.

PER SERVING: Calories 1143 (From Fat 297); Fat 33g (Saturated 20g); Cholesterol 207mg; Sodium 293mg; Carbohydrate 209g (Dietary Fiber 3g); Protein 11g.

Nutty Funnel Cakes

PREP TIME: 10 MIN	COOK TIME: 2 MIN PER CAKE	YIELD: 8 TO 10 CAKES

INGREDIENTS

¾ cup powdered sugar, sifted

1 teaspoon cinnamon

⅔ cup pecans

2½ cups self-rising flour

¼ cups sugar

1⅓ cup milk

2 eggs

½ teaspoon vanilla

Vegetable oil for frying

DIRECTIONS

1 Combine the powdered sugar and cinnamon in a small bowl and set aside.

2 With the knife blade in a food processor bowl, add pecans and chop until fine. Add the flour, sugar, milk, eggs, and vanilla. Process for 30 seconds or until smooth.

3 In your cast-iron deep skillet or Dutch oven, heat the vegetable oil to 375 degrees.

4 Using a measuring cup or a funnel to make a thin stream of batter, pour ¼ cup batter in a circle to form a spiral in the oil. Fry 1 minute until edges are golden brown. Turn and fry until golden, about 1 minute. Drain on paper towels.

5 Sprinkle with sugar-cinnamon mixture. Serve immediately. Continue making funnel cakes in batches. If the remaining batter gets thick while standing, stir in 1 to 2 tablespoons of additional milk about halfway through the process.

PER SERVING: Calories 401 (From Fat 22); Fat 22g (Saturated 3g); Cholesterol 48mg; Sodium 430mg; Carbohydrate 41g (Dietary Fiber 2g); Protein 6g.

Double Cherry Tea Cake

| PREP TIME: 15 MIN | COOK TIME: 25 TO 30 MIN | YIELD: 10 TO 12 CAKES |

INGREDIENTS

1¼ cups all-purpose flour

2 cups candied red and green cherries, chopped

1 cup walnuts, chopped

½ cup butter

½ cup sugar

½ teaspoon baking powder

½ teaspoon salt

3 eggs

¼ cup drained crushed pineapple

Orange Glaze

DIRECTIONS

1 Preheat the oven and the well-greased cast-iron muffin pan to 350 degrees.

2 Combine the flour with the cherries and nuts. Set aside.

3 Cream the butter. Add the sugar, baking powder, and salt. Cream thoroughly for about 5 minutes. Add the eggs, one at a time. Stir in the flour mixture and pineapple.

4 Carefully spoon into a greased muffin pan, ½ full. Bake at 350 degrees for 25 to 30 minutes or until golden brown.

5 Cool and frost with Orange Glaze.

Orange Glaze

2 cups confectioners' sugar

1 teaspoon orange rind

2 to 3 tablespoons orange juice

1 Mix the confectioners' sugar and orange rind. Blend in the orange juice until the mixture has a glaze consistency.

TIP: Be sure to drain the crushed pineapple well for this recipe. Too much moisture produces a soggy cake.

PER SERVING: Calories 373 (From Fat 140); Fat 16g (Saturated 6g); Cholesterol 74mg; Sodium 145mg; Carbohydrate 56g (Dietary Fiber 1g); Protein 5g.

Trying Cast-Iron Pie Recipes

Excellent for heat retention and even heat distribution, cast iron is the perfect pan for baking a pie. The high heat distribution also gives the pan the ability to create a golden-brown crust on the bottom and sides of the pie, which is great if you need to precook your pie crust before filling. The following recipes are sure to inspire you to bake more:

>> **Apple Maple Tart Tatin:** This recipe is essentially an upside-down pie. The filling is on the bottom, and the crust is on top. To get it right-side up again, carefully invert it onto a large serving platter.

>> **Skillet Chocolate Pie:** This pie adds a bit of nostalgia to your pie recipe repertoire. Resembling more of a chocolate pudding, this dish is a great way to switch it up.

THE TATIN SISTERS AND THEIR TART

Here's one of the stories behind the origins of Tart Tatin: Stephanie and Caroline Tatin, French sisters who ran their father's hotel after his death in the late 19th century, were in a hurry to prepare an apple tart for their hungry guests returning from a hunt. Behind schedule and rushed, Stephanie threw together the apple mixture for the tart and then tossed the mixture into the pan and the pan into the oven. To her horror, about halfway through the baking time, Stephanie realized that she had forgotten the crust. The two sisters pulled the half-cooked concoction from the oven and, desperate, added the crust on top. Hoping to hide their mistake, they inverted the upside-down apple tart onto a plate and served it to their guests. Although perhaps not the traditional *tarte aux pommes* they'd been expecting, the guests nonetheless devoured the hot, golden, caramel-y tart: A dessert was born.

Less exciting versions of the dessert's origins? The sisters got the recipe from their father or they got it from the chef who worked for some French count.

Apple Maple Tart Tatin

INGREDIENTS

6 Cortland or Fuji apples

2 tablespoons lemon juice

¼ cup butter

½ cup sugar

¾ cup maple syrup

¼ cup all-purpose flour

½ teaspoon cinnamon

Dough for Apple Maple Tart Tatin

DIRECTIONS

1 Preheat your oven to 400 degrees. Peel and core the apples. Cut the apples into quarters and sprinkle with lemon juice. Set aside.

2 In a 12-inch cast-iron skillet, melt the butter over medium-high heat. Dust the bottom of the skillet with ½ cup sugar until completely covered. Remove from the heat and set aside.

3 In a large mixing bowl, place the apples, syrup, flour, and cinnamon. Toss the apples, coating completely with the syrup mixture. Line the bottom of the skillet with the apples in a decorative fashion.

4 Top with the Dough for Apple Maple Tart Tatin and trim away the excess dough. Place the skillet over medium heat. When the edges of the pan begin to bubble, about 3½ to 4 minutes, remove skillet.

5 Place the tart in the oven and bake for 15 minutes or until the crust is brown. Carefully turn hot tart over onto a large serving platter. Allow tart to cool slightly before serving.

(continued)

Dough for Apple Maple Tart Tatin

2 cups all-purpose flour

½ cup butter

1 egg

pinch of sugar

½ teaspoon salt

3 teaspoons milk

1 Place the flour on a flat surface. Cut in the butter. Add the egg, sugar, and salt. Knead the dough until it forms a ball. Add the milk and knead several times until smooth. Roll the dough into a ¼–inch–thick circle, large enough to cover the skillet.

PER SERVING: *Calories 472 (From Fat 166); Fat 18g (Saturated 11g); Cholesterol 73mg; Sodium 160mg; Carbohydrate 74g (Dietary Fiber 3g); Protein 5g.*

Skillet Chocolate Pie

PREP TIME: 15 MIN	COOK TIME: 30 MIN	YIELD: 8 SERVINGS

INGREDIENTS

1 cup sugar

1 rounded tablespoon flour

3 tablespoons cocoa

3 egg yolks (reserve the whites for The Best Meringue)

1 cup milk

1 heaping tablespoon butter

1 tablespoon pure vanilla extract

1 deep 8-inch pie shell, baked

The Best Meringue

DIRECTIONS

1 Mix together the sugar, flour, and cocoa and set aside. In another bowl, beat the egg yolks and add the milk. Preheat your oven to 350 degrees.

2 In a 3-inch-deep cast-iron skillet, melt the butter over medium heat. Stir in the sugar, flour, and cocoa mixture. Remove from the heat and stir in the milk and egg yolk mixture. Place the skillet back on the burner and cook on medium heat until very thick. This should take about 15 to 20 minutes.

3 Remove from the heat and stir in the vanilla. Pour into a baked pie crust.

4 Top with The Best Meringue and bake at 350 degrees until the meringue peaks are slightly brown. Don't leave the kitchen because it only takes 10 to 15 minutes.

The Best Meringue

3 egg whites

¼ teaspoon cream of tartar

¼ teaspoon vanilla extract

¼ teaspoon almond extract

⅛ teaspoon salt

½ cup sugar

1 In a bowl, beat the egg whites at high speed with an electric mixer until the egg whites are foamy.

(continued)

2 Sprinkle the cream of tartar, vanilla extract, almond extract, and salt over the egg whites. Continue beating until soft peaks form.

3 Gradually add the sugar, 1 tablespoon at a time, beating until stiff peaks form. Spread over the hot pie filling or, using a pastry bag, pipe the meringue onto the pie in desired shapes, being sure to spread or pipe it all the way to the pie crust.

PER SERVING: *Calories 368 (From Fat 132); Fat 15g (Saturated 4g); Cholesterol 88mg; Sodium 216mg; Carbohydrate 55g (Dietary Fiber 1g); Protein 5g.*

Eyeing Other Tasty Dessert Recipes

This section presents an array of delicious recipes that showcase the versatility of your cast iron. From the crispy Beignets to the indulgent Blueberry French Toast Cobbler, my mouth is watering just talking about it! These sweet delights not only offer a chance to experiment and get creative in the kitchen but also to reimagine the endless possibilities of cooking with your favorite cast iron.

Although the following recipes are a hodgepodge of desserts that aren't cakes or pies, they're still so tasty:

» **North Carolina Apple Sonker:** *Sonker* is an Appalachian term for a deep-dish fruit pie. In areas outside Appalachia, it's better known as a cobbler. Spooned on individual serving plates and topped with whipped cream, this dessert is called delicious in any part of the country.

» **Beignets:** Beignets are deep-fried pastries. Although they can be savory (including ingredients like crab meat and herbs), most beignets are sweet. This recipe calls for a generous dusting of confectioners' sugar.

» **Blueberry French Toast Cobbler:** The tart blueberries when cooked burst with flavors. This dish captures the essence of summer and is perfect for family gatherings and summer picnics.

» **Aebleskiver (Pancake Balls):** These tasty treats are perfect for snacking or a gathering with friends.

» **Skillet Caramel Frosting:** Skillet Caramel Frosting makes an old-time golden, hard caramel frosting that's great on cupcakes and pound cakes.

TIP

Depending on what season you're in, I encourage you to try substituting in-season fruit in fruit recipes.

🍎 North Carolina Apple Sonker

| PREP TIME: 15 MIN | COOK TIME: 1 HR TO 1 HR 15 MIN | YIELD: 8 SERVINGS |

INGREDIENTS

6 large or 12 small apples, peeled, cored, and sliced

2 tablespoons butter

2½ cups sugar

½ cup all-purpose flour

½ teaspoon cinnamon

Dough for North Carolina Hillbilly Apple Sonker

1 cup whipping cream

1 teaspoon vanilla

DIRECTIONS

1 Preheat your oven to 350 degrees. Grease a 10-inch cast-iron skillet with butter. Place the apples, 2 cups of the sugar, flour, and cinnamon in a large mixing bowl. Toss lightly to coat the apples with the sugar mixture.

2 Place the apple mixture into the preheated skillet and top with the Dough for North Carolina Hillbilly Apple Sonker. (The recipe follows.) Using a paring knife, cut 1-inch steam holes in the top of the pastry for ventilation.

3 Bake the sonker for 1 hour to 1 hour and 15 minutes, or until crust is golden brown and flaky. Remove from your oven and cool slightly.

4 Place the whipping cream, ½ cup sugar, and vanilla in the bowl of an electric mixer. Beat on high speed until soft peaks form. Using a serving spoon, place a generous portion of the sonker in the center of an 8-inch plate and top with fresh whipped cream.

Dough Mixture

1 egg

2 teaspoons vinegar

3 cups all-purpose flour

1 teaspoon salt

¾ cup vegetable shortening or butter

1 Beat the egg, 10 tablespoons tap water, and vinegar together in the bowl of an electric mixer. Sift together the flour and salt in a large mixing bowl.

2 Using your hands, crumble the shortening or butter into the flour mixture, blending thoroughly until mixture resembles the texture of cornmeal. Pour in the water mixture and blend until the dough forms.

3 Turn the dough out onto a lightly floured surface and knead until smooth. Divide into 3 equal portions and roll each crust into a circle until ¼ inch thick.

PER SERVING: *Calories 831 (From Fat 312); Fat 35g (Saturated 14g); Cholesterol 75mg; Sodium 312mg; Carbohydrate 127g (Dietary Fiber 4g); Protein 7g.*

🍅 Beignets

| PREP TIME: 1 HR 40 MIN | COOK TIME: 2½ MIN | YIELD: 4 DOZEN BEIGNETS |

INGREDIENTS

1 package dry yeast

3½ cups all-purpose flour

1 teaspoon salt

¼ cup sugar

1¼ cups milk

3 eggs beaten

¼ cup melted butter

Oil for deep-frying

1 cup confectioners' sugar

DIRECTIONS

1 Dissolve the yeast in 4 tablespoons of warm water or according to package directions. Set aside.

2 In a mixing bowl, combine the flour, salt, and sugar and mix well to ensure proper blending. Fold in the dissolved yeast, milk, eggs, and butter. Continue to blend until the beignet dough is formed.

3 Place the dough in a metal, glass, or ceramic bowl, cover with a towel, and allow to rise for 1 hour. Remove to a well-floured surface and roll out to ¼-inch thickness. Cut into rectangular shapes, cover with a towel, and allow dough to rise for 30 minutes.

4 In a deep-sided (3 to 4 inches) cast-iron skillet or pot, preheat the oil to 375 degrees.

5 Deep-fry, turning once, until the beignet is golden brown, about 2½ minutes. Drain and dust generously with confectioners' sugar.

PER SERVING: *Calories 106 (From Fat 56); Fat 6g (Saturated 1g); Cholesterol 17mg; Sodium 56mg; Carbohydrate 11g (Dietary Fiber 0g); Protein 2g.*

Blueberry French Toast Cobbler

INGREDIENTS

1 loaf French bread, sliced ¾-inch thick

5 eggs

¼ cup sugar

¼ teaspoon baking powder

1 teaspoon vanilla

¾ cup milk

3 tablespoons butter

4½ cups blueberries

½ cup sugar

1 teaspoon cinnamon

1 teaspoon cornstarch

Powdered sugar

¼ cup blueberries for garnish

DIRECTIONS

1 Place the bread slices in a single layer in a large dish.

2 In a large mixing bowl, combine the eggs, ¼ cup sugar, baking powder, and vanilla. Using a wire whisk, blend all the ingredients thoroughly. Slowly add the milk until all is incorporated.

3 Pour the egg mixture over the bread, turning once to coat evenly. Cover and allow to set for 1 hour at room temperature.

4 Preheat your oven to 450 degrees. In a 14-inch cast-iron skillet, melt butter over medium-high heat.

5 In another large mixing bowl, combine the blueberries, sugar, cinnamon, and cornstarch. Pour the blueberry mixture into the skillet. Using a spatula, place the bread, wettest side up, on top of the blueberries.

6 Bake for 25 minutes or until the blueberries are bubbling around the bread, and the bread is golden brown.

7 Remove from the oven and sprinkle with the powdered sugar. Top with additional fresh blueberries.

NOTE: French bread has the perfect texture and weight for French toast, but it isn't the only bread you can use. If you don't have French bread, substitute any bread with solid texture. The solid texture is key. Fresh, brand-name white sandwich breads are too soft; they fall apart in the egg mixture.

PER SERVING: *Calories 353 (From Fat 89); Fat 10g (Saturated 4g); Cholesterol 147mg; Sodium 350mg; Carbohydrate 58g (Dietary Fiber 4g); Protein 9g.*

Aebleskiver (Pancake Balls)

INGREDIENTS

2 cups all-purpose flour

2 tablespoons sugar

1 teaspoon baking soda

1 teaspoon cardamom

¾ teaspoon salt

1 cup sour cream

⅔ cup milk

3 egg yolks, beaten

2 tablespoons melted butter

3 egg whites, beaten

2 tablespoons melted butter or vegetable oil

DIRECTIONS

1 Set the aebleskiver pan on the stove burner on medium-low heat.

2 In a large bowl, sift the flour, sugar, baking soda, cardamom, and salt together and set aside. In a smaller bowl, combine the sour cream, milk, egg yolks, and 2 tablespoons melted butter.

3 Make a well in the center of the dry ingredients and add the liquid mixture, stirring until well blended.

4 Gently fold the beaten egg whites into the batter.

5 Test the pan by dropping a few drops of water on it. If the drops dance in small beads, then the temperature is correct.

6 Add about ½ teaspoon of melted butter or vegetable oil into the wells and heat. Pour the batter into the wells, filling slightly over ½ full. (Re-oil the wells with each batch.)

7 With knitting needles or fork, turn the aebleskiver frequently to brown evenly. Do not pierce.

8 Aebleskivers are done when a wooden pick inserted in the center comes out clean.

9 Remove from the pan and sprinkle immediately with the confectioners' sugar. Serve with jam.

NOTE: To make this recipe, you really need a specialty pan called a *Danish cake pan*, an *aebleskiver pan*, or a *munk pan*. With several rounded wells, this pan is designed for stovetop use — a necessity because you have to turn the pancake balls as they cook.

VARY IT! Pare and dice 2 medium apples. Sprinkle about 1 teaspoon diced apple over the batter in each well while cooking.

PER SERVING: *Calories 63 (From Fat 39); Fat 4g (Saturated 3g); Cholesterol 24mg; Sodium 47mg; Carbohydrate 5g (Dietary Fiber 0g); Protein 1g.*

🍅 Skillet Caramel Frosting

PREP TIME: 15 MIN	COOK TIME: 5 MIN	YIELD: FROSTS ABOUT 12 CUPCAKES OR AN 8-INCH LAYER CAKE

INGREDIENTS

½ cup butter

1 cup firmly packed light brown sugar

¼ cup dark corn syrup

2 teaspoons cream of tartar

3 cups powdered sugar, sifted

3 tablespoons whipping cream

2 teaspoons vanilla

DIRECTIONS

1 Melt the butter in a 3-inch-deep cast-iron skillet over medium-high heat. Make sure that you use a deep skillet because the frosting will bubble up and can boil over the sides of a regular skillet.

2 Stir in the brown sugar, corn syrup, and cream of tartar. Bring to a boil and boil for 5 minutes without stirring. When the mixture is thick and brown, remove the skillet from the heat.

3 Stir in the powdered sugar, whipping cream, and vanilla. Be careful when adding the cream to the hot mixture — it can splatter. Beat at medium speed in the pan with an electric mixer for 2 minutes. Spread immediately on cupcakes or cake.

NOTE: As with all frosting, be sure to measure the ingredients carefully. Even a tad too much or too little liquid can make the frosting too hard or impossible to spread. With this kind of hard frosting, altitude and humidity can also factor into the end result. For example, in the South, making this frosting is difficult on rainy days.

PER SERVING: *Calories 288 (From Fat 81); Fat 9g (Saturated 6g); Cholesterol 26mg; Sodium 21mg; Carbohydrate 53g (Dietary Fiber 0g); Protein 0g.*

Chapter 22
Campfire Recipes

Nothing compares to cooking over an open fire. The intense heat helps to enhance the flavors and textures of every dish, and the charred smokiness from the fire adds taste and aroma to any dish. The trick is having the right pan. Besides its durability and sturdiness, cast iron has the ability to distribute heat evenly, which makes it the perfect pan for cooking outdoors. Here I explore a few classic and modern recipes that will fit in perfectly on your next outdoor adventure.

Appetizing Your Friends with Starters

Here are the starter recipes in this section that you can make when camping with family and friends:

>> **Dutch Oven Veggies:** Many people cook their vegetables first and add any seasoning or butter afterward. The result is bland vegetables that get perked up as an afterthought. This recipe adds the seasoning and butter during the cooking process.

>> **Slow-Simmered Black Beans:** This recipe puts a little spin on the traditional soup bean. Instead of navy beans, it uses black beans.

>> **Herb-Roasted New Potatoes:** This recipe is great for outdoor cooking. Pack the bag containing the seasoned potatoes with the rest of your outdoor cooking gear, and about an hour before you want to eat, place the seasoned potatoes in a cast-iron skillet or on a griddle and cook over hot coals until they're golden brown and tender.

FINDING OTHER FOLKS WHO LIKE TO COOK OUTDOORS

If you discover that outdoor cooking is your thing, you have quite a bit of company. You can find several Dutch oven societies across the United States and in other places in the world. Here are a few:

- **International Dutch Oven Society:** Based in Utah, the IDOS has chapters in Texas, Southern California, New York, Pennsylvania, and Ontario, Canada. For information, visit www.dutchovensociety.com.

- **Lone Star Dutch Oven Society:** Based in San Antonio, Texas, the LSDOS has local chapters throughout the state of Texas. For information about the LSDOS, visit www.lsdos.com.

- **Northwest Dutch Oven Society:** Based in Tacoma, Washington, the NWDOS has chapters throughout Washington. For information, contact the society at https://nwdos.com.

- **Suncoast Dutch Oven Society:** Based in Tampa Bay, Florida, the Suncoast DOS has local chapters throughout Florida. For information, contact the society at www.oocities.org/suncoastidos/recipies.html.

Regardless of which region they serve, all these societies — and the many others out there — promote the fun and skill of Dutch oven cooking, sponsor events and gatherings, and publish newsletters containing society news, recipes, and cooking tips for their members.

Dutch Oven Veggies

PREP TIME: 20 MIN	COOK TIME: 20 TO 30 MIN	YIELD: 8 SERVINGS

INGREDIENTS

1 cup broccoli florets

1 cup cauliflower florets

1 cup baby carrots

1 cup mushrooms

1 cup onions, cut into bite-size pieces

1 cup bite-size bell pepper pieces

1 cup bite-size zucchini pieces

1 cup bite-size butternut squash pieces

Salt and pepper

¼ pound butter

2 cups shredded sharp cheddar cheese

2 cups grated fresh Parmesan cheese

DIRECTIONS

1 Put ¼ inch of water into a 12-inch cast-iron camp oven and add the veggies. Season generously with the salt and pepper — more than seems enough. Place the slices of butter on top of the veggies.

2 Put the camp oven over 24 hot coals until the vegetable mixture is steaming, then pull out at least half of the coals. Steam the veggies until the carrots are tender.

3 Take the oven off the coals, remove the water with a baster, cover the veggies with the grated cheeses, and put the lid on the oven. Serve when the cheese is melted.

TIP: Even without the cheese (which is a favorite of grown-ups and kids alike), the vegetables can stand on their own merits. Also keep in mind that, in a pinch, you can substitute pre-grated Parmesan cheese, but if you do, you'll sacrifice flavor. Freshly grated Parmesan beats pre-grated Parmesan hands down.

VARY IT! You can use virtually any vegetables you want with this recipe; simply make sure that you use 8 cups of veggies total and that you cut them into bite-size pieces.

VARY IT! To make a lighter version of this recipe, use cheese made with part skim rather than whole milk and use light butter. To make it lighter yet, take away the cheese entirely.

PER SERVING: *Calories 344 (From Fat 244); Fat 27g (Saturated 17g); Cholesterol 77mg; Sodium 639mg; Carbohydrate 9g (Dietary Fiber 3g); Protein 17g.*

Slow-Simmered Black Beans

PREP TIME: 10 MIN | COOK TIME: 2½ HRS | YIELD: 6 SERVINGS

INGREDIENTS

1 pound canned black beans, rinsed and drained

¼ pound salt pork, sliced, or 4 to 5 slices thick bacon, cut into bite-size pieces

1 medium onion, chopped

2 cloves garlic, chopped

1 carrot, peeled and sliced

10 cups (2.5 quarts) chicken stock

Salt to taste

DIRECTIONS

1 Preheat your Dutch oven over medium heat (about 20 hot coals) for about 3 minutes.

2 Add the salted pork or the bacon and allow it to render for about 5 to 7 minutes. Reduce the heat to medium low (about 15 hot coals), add the onions and carrots, and cook for 5 minutes or until the onions are transparent. Add the garlic and cook for about 1 minute or until fragrant.

3 Add the beans and stock, bring to a simmer, cover with the lid, and place about 5 hot coals on top of the lid. Cook for about 30 minutes, stirring occasionally.

4 Remove the lid and taste. Adjust the seasoning with salt and pepper. Serve.

PER SERVING: *Calories 388 (From Fat 139); Fat 16g (Saturated 5g); Cholesterol 16mg; Sodium 635mg; Carbohydrate 46g (Dietary Fiber 16g); Protein 18g.*

🍅 Herb-Roasted New Potatoes

PREP TIME: 20 MIN | COOK TIME: 45 MIN TO 1 HR | YIELD: 2 SERVINGS

INGREDIENTS

1 pound new potatoes, medium diced

Salt and pepper

2 tablespoons olive oil

½ cup onion, sliced very thick

½ cup red bell pepper, sliced very thick

½ cup yellow bell pepper, sliced very thick

2 tablespoons garlic, minced

2 tablespoons fresh thyme, chopped

2 tablespoons fresh rosemary, chopped

2 tablespoons butter, melted

2 tablespoons red wine vinegar

2 teaspoons Creole seasoning

DIRECTIONS

1 Add the potatoes, salt, and pepper to a bowl and mix well. Preheat your 12-inch cast-iron skillet with olive oil for 3 minutes over about 20 hot coals. Add the potatoes, turning every 3 minutes, allowing them to cook until they're golden brown, about 10 to 15 minutes.

2 Add the butter, onions, and bell peppers and mix well. Allow everything to cook for about 5 minutes or until the onions start to slightly brown.

3 Add the garlic and herbs and mix well. Cook for about 1 minute.

4 Finish with red wine vinegar and Creole seasoning and serve.

PER SERVING: *Calories 514 (From Fat 232); Fat 26g (Saturated 9g); Cholesterol 31mg; Sodium 386mg; Carbohydrate 62g (Dietary Fiber 7g); Protein 7g.*

Focusing on Campsite Main Dishes

Here I switch up cooking techniques and focus on braising, which is the perfect technique for cooking outside because it allows you to cook for longer periods of time, capturing the maximum amount of flavor and achieving the ultimate texture.

The following main dish recipes are perfect for camping trips and sitting around a campfire:

» **Campsite Beef Stroganoff:** When you make traditional beef stroganoff, you prepare everything in stages, cooking the meat first, adding the sauce mixture next, and adding the sour cream last. The noodles you cook entirely separately, and then you combine everything during serving. In this recipe, after you brown the meat, you cook everything (including the noodles) together. The result is stroganoff that's as yummy and delicious as the original — without the work or attention.

» **Corned Beef and Cabbage:** Also called New England boiled dinner, this dish — or the beef used in it — doesn't have anything to do with corn, the vegetable. *Corning* means to salt with brine (saltwater) as a way of preserving the meat.

» **Hunters' Venison Bourguignon:** This recipe has a fancy name, but the technique is actually simple. *Bourguignon* (boor-gee-*nyon*) is the French term for *prepared in Burgundy.* Although Burgundy *is* a region in France, the term speaks more to the technique of braising meat in red wine, which comes from Burgundy.

» **Mountain Breakfast:** Technically a breakfast, when you're camping, you can eat breakfast food anytime. This hearty recipe gives you your meat, eggs, and hash browns without the hassle of cleaning separate pans.

Campsite Beef Stroganoff

PREP TIME: 5 MIN | COOK TIME: 50 MIN TO 1 HR | YIELD: 4 TO 6 SERVINGS

INGREDIENTS

2 pounds extra-lean ground beef

1 medium onion, chopped

¼ teaspoon celery salt

¼ teaspoon garlic salt

Salt and pepper

Three 8-ounce cans tomato sauce

1 teaspoon Worcestershire sauce

½ cup sour cream

One 12-ounce bag egg noodles

DIRECTIONS

1 Brown together the meat, onion, celery salt, garlic salt, salt, and pepper in a 12-inch cast-iron camp oven over 25 hot coals.

2 While the meat is browning, mix together 1½ cups of water, the tomato sauce, Worcestershire sauce, and sour cream in a medium bowl.

3 When the meat and onion are browned, spread the uncooked noodles evenly over the meat and onion. Pour the liquid mixture evenly over the noodles to moisten all the noodles well.

4 Cover with the lid and place 15 briquettes on top, leaving 10 briquettes on the bottom.

5 Cook for approximately 30 to 45 minutes, or until the noodles are fully cooked.

NOTE: In Step 2, the sour cream won't be completely blended, and the mixture will have a few lumps.

PER SERVING: *Calories 462 (From Fat 149); Fat 17g (Saturated 7g); Cholesterol 95mg; Sodium 1,032mg; Carbohydrate 46g (Dietary Fiber 4g); Protein 32g.*

Corned Beef and Cabbage

| PREP TIME: 20 MIN | COOK TIME: 3 TO 4 HRS | YIELD: 8 TO 10 SERVINGS |

INGREDIENTS

4 pounds corned beef brisket

2 teaspoons sugar

1 tablespoon whole black peppercorn

3 to 4 sprigs fresh parsley

6 carrots, peeled and quartered

1 medium onion, quartered

8 medium potatoes, peeled and halved

1 cabbage, cored and cut into 6 wedges

Salt to taste

DIRECTIONS

1 Place the brisket in a 7-quart cast-iron Dutch oven and cover with water.

2 Add the sugar, peppercorn, and parsley and bring to a boil. Cover, place over 20 hot coals, and simmer for 2¾ hours. Check the water level once an hour throughout, and add additional water, if necessary, to cover the brisket.

3 Add the carrots, onion, and potatoes. Cover and simmer for 30 minutes.

4 Add the cabbage; cover and simmer for 15 minutes or until the cabbage is tender. Salt to taste. Place the corned beef in the middle of a serving platter and surround it with vegetables.

VARY IT! You can use other root vegetables in addition to or in place of the carrots, onion, and potatoes. Try turnips, brussels sprouts, parsnips, or rutabagas.

NOTE: You can buy brisket that's already been corned (the easier option), or you can buy fresh brisket and corn it yourself. The process is fairly easy (rubbing the meat with salt and other spices, wrapping it securely, pressing it down with weights, and letting it sit in your refrigerator for five days), but it takes so long that I recommend buying it ready to go.

PER SERVING: *Calories 494 (From Fat 237); Fat 26g (Saturated 9g); Cholesterol 133mg; Sodium 1,594mg; Carbohydrate 35g (Dietary Fiber 6g); Protein 29g.*

Hunters' Venison Bourguignon

PREP TIME: 10 MIN | **COOK TIME: ABOUT 2 HRS** | **YIELD: 4 TO 6 SERVINGS**

INGREDIENTS

3 pounds venison, cut into 2-inch cubes

Salt and pepper

2 tablespoons butter

1 onion, chopped

¼ pound Virginia ham, chopped or finely diced

2 cloves garlic, minced

2 bay leaves

1 quart beef stock or bouillon

1 cup dry red wine

1 pound fresh mushrooms, sliced

DIRECTIONS

1 Salt and pepper the venison. In a 5-quart cast-iron Dutch oven, heat the butter over 24 hot coals. Add the venison and cook slowly for about 10 minutes, at which point the venison should have a little color. Add the onion and cook until tender.

2 Add the ham, garlic, bay leaves, marjoram, and thyme. Stir and simmer for about 3 minutes. Add the flour and cook and stir for another 3 minutes.

3 Add the beef stock and wine. Cover with the lid and simmer for about 1 hour.

4 Remove the lid, add the mushrooms, and adjust seasoning, if necessary. Simmer another 45 minutes. Remove the bay leaves before serving.

NOTE: When you think of venison, the first — and only — animal that probably comes to mind is deer. But the venison category includes elk, moose, reindeer, caribou, and antelope.

TIP: Serve this dish over egg noodles or alongside simply prepared potatoes.

PER SERVING: Calories 461 (From Fat 188); Fat 21g (Saturated 7g); Cholesterol 203mg; Sodium 1,108mg; Carbohydrate 8g (Dietary Fiber 2g); Protein 58g.

Mountain Breakfast

PREP TIME: 5 MIN	COOK TIME: 45 MIN	YIELD: 8 SERVINGS

INGREDIENTS

2 pounds breakfast sausage

2 pounds frozen hash brown potatoes

10 to 12 eggs, beaten with ¼ cup water

2 cups grated cheddar cheese

DIRECTIONS

1 Fry and crumble the sausage in a 12-inch cast-iron camp oven over 24 hot coals. Remove the cooked sausage and drain on the paper towels.

2 Using the sausage drippings in the pan, brown the potatoes and spread them evenly in the bottom of the camp oven. Place the cooked sausage over the potatoes.

3 Pour the eggs over the sausage layer. Sprinkle the top with cheese.

4 Cook with 8 coals underneath the camp oven and 16 on top for 20 to 25 minutes, until the eggs are cooked.

PER SERVING: Calories 482 (From Fat 284); Fat 32g (Saturated 11g); Cholesterol 364mg; Sodium 887mg; Carbohydrate 21g (Dietary Fiber 2g); Protein 31g.

Finishing with Campsite Desserts

The combination of the wood fire and the seasoned cast iron creates the perfect environment for outdoor baking. Just because you're camping doesn't mean you have to sacrifice dessert. These rustic dessert recipes are tasty and perfect for camping:

>> **Apple Crisp:** This is a great recipe for fall when apples are in season and at local produce stands. Of course, it's (almost) equally appetizing any time of year with store-bought apples. The key is the apple.

>> **Almost Pumpkin Pie:** Less of a pie and more of crisp, this dish gives you the best of both worlds.

>> **Baked Pears:** The slightly caramelized edge is just one of the things I love about the marriage of pear and cast iron. The low slow cooking allows the natural sweetness of the pear to develop, creating a harmonic balance that goes perfectly with the background of crickets and frogs.

🍅 Apple Crisp

PREP TIME: 10 MIN   COOK TIME: 1 HR   YIELD: 8 TO 10 SERVINGS

INGREDIENTS

10 cups peeled and
sliced apples

¼ cup lemon juice

3 tablespoons lemon zest

¾ cup sugar

½ cup golden raisins

¾ cup butter

1½ cups brown sugar

1¼ cups all-purpose flour

1½ cups oats

1 tablespoon cinnamon

1 teaspoon nutmeg

1 teaspoon cardamom

DIRECTIONS

1 Combine the apples, lemon juice, 1 tablespoon lemon zest, sugar, and raisins in a bowl. Spread the apple mixture in the bottom of a 12-inch cast-iron camp oven.

2 In a medium bowl, combine the butter and brown sugar. In another bowl, cut the butter mixture into the flour. Stir in the oats, cinnamon, nutmeg, cardamom, and the remaining 2 tablespoons lemon zest. Top the apple mixture with this topping mixture.

3 Place 8 coals under the oven and 16 on top of the lid. Continue cooking until the apples are cooked and the topping is brown, about 1 hour. Serve warm.

NOTE: Good cooking apples, which don't turn mushy or gritty, are Rome apples, Golden Delicious, and Winesap, varieties that are widely available.

NOTE: Refer to the color insert for a photo of this recipe.

PER SERVING: *Calories 500 (From Fat 135); Fat 15g (Saturated 9g); Cholesterol 37mg; Sodium 18mg; Carbohydrate 91g (Dietary Fiber 5g); Protein 4g.*

🍅 Almost Pumpkin Pie

PREP TIME: 10 MIN | **COOK TIME: 1 HR** | **YIELD: 12 SERVINGS**

INGREDIENTS

One 29-ounce can pumpkin

1 tablespoon pumpkin pie spice

3 eggs

1 cup sugar

½ teaspoon salt

1 teaspoon vanilla

1 cup evaporated milk

1 cup butter

One 18.25-ounce package yellow cake mix

1 cup chopped pecans

DIRECTIONS

1. In a large bowl, mix together the pumpkin, pumpkin pie spice, eggs, sugar, salt, vanilla, and evaporated milk. Pour this mixture into your greased 12-inch cast-iron camp oven.

2. Cut the butter into the cake mix with a pastry blender, then mix in the pecans. Sprinkle over the top of the pumpkin mixture.

3. Bake for 1 hour with 8 hot coals on the bottom of the camp oven and 16 on top of the camp oven.

TIP: If you don't have a pastry cutter, you can use a fork, two knives, or even your fingers. Whatever you use, don't stop until the cake mix-butter-pecan mixture is well blended and crumbly.

PER SERVING: *Calories 528 (From Fat 273); Fat 30g (Saturated 12g); Cholesterol 102mg; Sodium 425mg; Carbohydrate 60g (Dietary Fiber 4g); Protein 7g.*

⚬ Baked Pears

INGREDIENTS

2 tablespoons butter

6 tablespoons light brown sugar

1 tablespoon cinnamon

6 crumbled butter cookies

½ cup pecan pieces

6 firm Bartlett pears

Ground cloves

12 pecan halves (optional)

DIRECTIONS

1 Preheat a 12-inch cast-iron camp oven with the butter using 8 to 10 hot coals under the oven.

2 In a bowl, combine the brown sugar, cinnamon, crumbled cookies, and pecan pieces.

3 Cut the pears in half and gently scoop out the seeds, core, and stem. Sprinkle a pinch of ground cloves onto each pear half, being careful not to use too much. Stuff each pear half with the brown sugar mixture.

4 Place pear halves cut-side up in the camp oven. Dot with butter and place a pecan half on each pear.

5 Cover with the lid and add 12 to 14 hot coals on top of the oven. Cook until hot, about 20 to 30 minutes. Serve while hot.

NOTE: Unlike many fruits, pears should ripen off the tree. The only time that you want a tree-ripened pear is if the tree is in your front yard, and you're picking the pear yourself. A tree-ripened pear that's been boxed and shipped across the country will be unpleasantly mushy by the time it hits your grocer's produce section.

TIP: When you're buying pears, select the ones that feel firm but give slightly at the stem. You can leave them at room temperature to ripen the rest of the way. You'll know they're ready when the skin lightens, and the aroma becomes noticeable.

PER SERVING: *Calories 291 (From Fat 126); Fat 14g (Saturated 4g); Cholesterol 16mg; Sodium 4mg; Carbohydrate 45g (Dietary Fiber 6g); Protein 2g.*

Chapter **23**

Ready for the Game — Great Tailgating Recipes

Seeing tailgaters hanging out in parking lots before football games as well as other sporting events is a common occurrence in the United States. Canadians have their own tradition of gathering before hockey games, whereas in Australia they have footy BBQs as a similar tradition. Regardless of the sporting event, the sense of camaraderie and celebration before a game is universal.

This chapter has the perfect recipes for these moments, whether you're having friends over to watch a big a game or going to a tailgating event to support your favorite team play in person. From dips to savory appetizers, all cooked in your favorite cast-iron pan, these recipes are sure to become a hit at your next event.

Appetizing Your Fans with Dips

What makes dips so enticing? The first few things that come to mind are versatility, sociability, and international appeal. They have the power to transform a simple dish into something memorable. Whether you're hosting a game night or simply enjoying a quick snack with friends, adding a delicious dip can take a dish from good to great.

This section explores some mouthwatering baked dips that you can serve before cheering on your favorite team to victory:

>> **Jalapeño Bacon Dip:** This dip brings the bold smokiness of bacon together with the spicy heat of a jalapeño. This savory dish is baked until the dip is hot and bubbly and can be served with your favorite tortilla chips, crackers, or even sliced toasted baguette.

>> **Spinach and Artichoke Dip:** Creamy deliciousness is the only way to describe this dip! The earthy spinach and tangy artichokes blended with cream cheese and sour cream creates the ultimate crowd-pleaser dish for your next event.

>> **Guacamole:** Okay, I admit. This isn't really a cast-iron recipe, but every tailgate needs guac. So sue me! You need guac to go with the Fabulous Fajitas recipe later in this chapter.

>> **Pico de Gallo:** Yes, I know this recipe isn't a cast-iron recipe, but pico goes right up there with guac. You also need pico to go with the Fabulous Fajitas recipe later in this chapter.

Jalapeño Bacon Dip

PREP TIME: 5 TO 10 MIN | COOK TIME: 20 MIN | YIELD: 6 SERVINGS

INGREDIENTS

½ pound bacon, small diced

1 onion, small diced

2 cloves garlic, minced

8 ounces cream cheese, soft

½ cup sour cream

¼ cup mayo

1 teaspoon onion powder

½ teaspoon garlic powder

½ teaspoon cayenne powder

½ teaspoon smoked paprika

1 tablespoon apple cider vinegar

Salt and pepper to taste

½ cup pickled jalapeño (jar), chopped

2 green onions, sliced

DIRECTIONS

1 Preheat a cast-iron skillet over medium for about 2 minutes. Add the bacon, allowing it to render until crispy and golden brown, about 8 to 10 minutes. Add the onion and cook for about 5 minutes or until soft. Add the garlic and cook until fragrant, about 1 minute.

2 Remove the skillet from the heat and allow it to cool for about 5 minutes. Next, add the cream cheese, sour cream, mayo, onion powder, garlic powder, cayenne powder, paprika, apple cider vinegar, and salt and pepper. Mix well, taste, and adjust seasoning as needed. Finish with the jalapeños and green onions. Serve warm.

TIP: If you're not a big fan of bacon grease, drain half off before moving on to Step 2.

PER SERVING: *Calories 459 (From Fat 354); Fat 39g (Saturated 16g); Cholesterol 98mg; Sodium 1191mg; Carbohydrate 9g (Dietary Fiber 1g); Protein 18g.*

🍅 Spinach and Artichoke Dip

PREP TIME: 10 MIN	COOK TIME: 30 MIN	YIELD: 8 SERVINGS

INGREDIENTS

2 tablespoons olive oil

2 shallots, minced

2 garlic cloves, minced

1 cup white wine

2 tablespoons apple cider vinegar

1 sprig tarragon (optional)

2 sprigs thyme

8 ounces cream cheese, soft

½ cup sour cream

¼ cup mayo

1 cup pepper jack cheese, grated

¼ teaspoon cayenne

1 teaspoon Worcestershire sauce

Salt and pepper to taste

2 cups frozen spinach, defrosted, squeezed, and chopped

½ cup artichokes (jar or canned), drained, and quartered

½ cup Parmesan cheese, grated

DIRECTIONS

1 Preheat a cast-iron skillet with olive oil over medium heat for 2 minutes. Also preheat your oven to 375 degrees.

2 Add the shallots and cook for about 2 minutes or until soft. Next, add the garlic and cook until fragrant, about 1 minute. Add the white wine, apple cider vinegar, tarragon, and thyme and reduce for about 3 minutes. Remove the skillet from the heat.

3 Add the cream cheese, sour cream, mayo, pepper jack cheese, cayenne, and Worcestershire sauce and mix well. Season to taste with salt and pepper.

4 Fold in the spinach and artichokes and mix well. Finish with Parmesan cheese.

5 Place the skillet in the oven and cook for 20 minutes. Then remove the skillet and rest for 5 minutes before serving.

PER SERVING: *Calories 328 (From Fat 249); Fat 28g (Saturated 12g); Cholesterol 61mg; Sodium 357mg; Carbohydrate 6g (Dietary Fiber 2g); Protein 10g.*

🍅 Guacamole

INGREDIENTS

3 medium, ripe avocados, peeled, pitted and mashed

¼ small onion, grated

1 small ripe tomato, peeled, seeded and chopped

4 slices jalapeño pepper, seeded and chopped

1 tablespoon lime juice

½ teaspoon salt

2 tablespoons chopped fresh cilantro

Juice from 1 lemon

DIRECTIONS

1 Combine the avocado, onion, tomato, jalapeño, lime juice, salt, and the cilantro in a medium bowl.

2 Add the lemon juice. Taste the combined ingredients and adjust the seasoning as necessary.

3 Place plastic wrap directly on the surface of the mixture and let it stand for a few minutes.

4 Refrigerate in an airtight container until it's time to serve.

NOTE: The most important ingredient in guacamole is the avocado. Fresh avocado is best, but if avocados aren't in season, aren't available in your area, or aren't ripe, your best bet is buying canned avocado.

PER SERVING: *Calories 220 (From Fat 170); Fat 19g (Saturated 4g); Cholesterol 0mg; Sodium 294mg; Carbohydrate 15g (Dietary Fiber 12g); Protein 4g.*

PITTING AND MASHING AN AVOCADO

To prepare the avocado for guacamole, you have to first pit it and then mash it. Follow these steps (you need a cutting board and a paring knife):

1. Cut the avocado lengthwise down to the pit and slide your knife all the way around; then twist to separate the halves.

2. Keeping your fingers well out of the way, swing the blade of a knife (preferably a heavy one) down into the pit, then twist the knife to remove the pit

3. Slide a large spoon between the skin and the flesh and scoop out the flesh.

4. Using a fork or potato masher, mash the avocado.

Pico de Gallo

PREP TIME: 5 MIN	COOK TIME: 3 TO 5 MIN CHILL TIME: OVERNIGHT	YIELD: 4 ¼-CUP SERVINGS

INGREDIENTS

1 cup peeled, seeded, and diced tomatoes

2 tablespoons olive oil

2 cloves garlic, minced

1 poblano pepper, seeded and finely chopped

¼ to ½ small onion, grated

2 tablespoons lime juice

DIRECTIONS

1 Place the tomatoes in a medium bowl.

2 Combine the olive oil, garlic, and pepper in a small saucepan over medium heat for 3 to 4 minutes, stirring constantly. Pour over the tomatoes.

3 Add the onion and lime juice. Chill overnight or until cold.

PER SERVING: *Calories 89 (From Fat 67); Fat 7g (Saturated 1g); Cholesterol 0mg; Sodium 7mg; Carbohydrate 6g (Dietary Fiber 2g); Protein 1g.*

Entertaining with Other Greats

When tailgating, different people have different tastes and dietary preferences, so having a variety of food available is essential. Offering a range of menu options ensures that everyone can find something they enjoy.

I hope to inspire you to think outside the box the next time you host a tailgating event. Here are some other fan-favorite appetizers:

» **Berbere-Spiced Pan-Fried Okra:** Pan-fried okra is a favorite of many folks. If you're lucky, your assistants in the kitchen won't have snatched it all away, and you'll still have some left to take to the table.

» **BBQ Dry Rub Skillet Wings:** Dry rub wings are perfect for outdoor events because they give you all the flavor without the mess of a sauce.

» **Bacon and Sausage Monkey Bread:** Perfect for the early morning tailgating event, this delicious dish combines both savory and sweet. It's also the perfect early morning dish to serve in a cast-iron skillet.

» **Classic Fries:** The use of cast iron's high heat and even heat distribution helps fries achieve a crispy exterior while keeping the inside tender.

» **Fabulous Fajitas:** Most fajita recipes include marinated strips of beef or chicken. Although this recipe calls for marinated beef, you can substitute marinated chicken or pork for the beef.

Berbere-Spiced Pan-Fried Okra

| PREP TIME: 5 MIN | COOK TIME: 7 TO 10 MIN | YIELD: 6 SERVINGS |

INGREDIENTS

1½ pounds fresh okra

1 to 2 tablespoons olive oil

1 teaspoon yellow mustard seeds

2 garlic cloves, minced

1 teaspoon grated fresh ginger root

1 onion, sliced

2 fresh tomatoes, chopped

¼ teaspoon ground cumin

1 teaspoon turmeric

Salt

DIRECTIONS

1 Wash the okra and cut it into ¾-inch diagonal slices, discarding the ends.

2 Heat the oil in a 12-inch cast-iron skillet or a cast-iron wok on medium high. Add the mustard seeds, cooking and stirring until the mustard seeds pop, about 2 minutes. If necessary, briefly cover and remove the skillet from heat until the mustard seeds stop popping. Return the skillet to heat.

3 Add the garlic, ginger root, onion, and okra and sauté for 2 minutes. Stir in the tomatoes, cumin, and turmeric. Cook and stir until the okra becomes slightly tender, 3 to 5 minutes, turning the heat down if necessary. Salt to taste.

PER SERVING: *Calories 85 (From Fat 26; Fat 3g (Saturated 0g); Cholesterol 0mg; Sodium 106mg; Carbohydrate 14g (Dietary Fiber 4g); Protein 3g.*

BBQ Dry Rub Skillet Wings

PREP TIME: 10 MIN	COOK TIME: 20 MIN	YIELD: 6 SERVINGS

INGREDIENTS

2 quarts canola oil

2 tablespoons flour

1 tablespoon cornstarch

1 teaspoon onion powder

½ teaspoon garlic powder

1 teaspoon cayenne powder

1 teaspoon salt

1 pound chicken wings

½ cup Frank's Red Hot Sauce

2 teaspoons apple cider vinegar

3 tablespoons butter

DIRECTIONS

1 Preheat the oil over medium heat in a 6-quart Dutch oven until it reaches 350 degrees. In a large bowl, add the flour, cornstarch, onion powder, garlic powder, ½ teaspoon cayenne, and salt and mix well.

2 Add the chicken wings to the flour mixture and gently toss.

3 Carefully add the chicken wings to the oil in batches of 6 to 8 without overcrowding the pan, and cook for about 8 to 10 minutes or until golden brown.

4 In a small cast-iron skillet, add the hot sauce, ½ teaspoon cayenne, and apple cider vinegar and bring to a simmer over medium heat. After it's simmering, turn off the heat and whisk the butter, 1 tablespoon at a time, until all has been incorporated. Reserve.

5 To serve, add 6 to 8 wings to a large bowl. Add ½ cup of sauce and toss to combine. Serve immediately.

TIP: You can pat dry any excess oil from the chicken wings after Step 3.

PER SERVING: Calories 276 (From Fat 203); Fat 23g (Saturated 7g); Cholesterol 73mg; Sodium 527mg; Carbohydrate 3g (Dietary Fiber 0g); Protein 14g.

Bacon and Sausage Monkey Bread

PREP TIME: 15 MIN	COOK TIME: 30 MIN	YIELD: 8 SERVINGS

INGREDIENTS

1 teaspoon onion powder

½ teaspoon garlic powder

¼ teaspoon Italian seasoning

½ teaspoon brown sugar

¼ teaspoon salt

One 16-ounce can of flaky layer biscuit dough

4 tablespoons butter, room temperature

½ pound of bacon, cooked and chopped

½ pound of breakfast sausage, cooked and chopped

1 cup shredded cheddar cheese

DIRECTIONS

1 Preheat your oven to 350 degrees. In a small bowl, add the onion powder and garlic powder, Italian seasoning, brown sugar, and salt. Mix well and reserve.

2 Take each biscuit, cut it into 4 pieces, and roll each piece into a ball.

3 Brush a cast-iron skillet with 2 tablespoons of butter and season the skillet with the spice blend. Cook half of the dough balls, evenly dispersing them in the pan. Layer the bacon and sausage and top with cheese. Drizzle some of the melted butter on top of the cheese and season again with the seasoning. Repeat the process until the remaining amount of ingredients has been incorporated.

4 Cover the skillet with a lid and cook in the oven for 30 to 40 minutes or until golden brown. Remove and rest for about 5 minutes. Before serving, turn the skillet over on a plate or platter.

NOTE: Serve directly out of the pan or invented on to a plate for a dish that looks and tastes great.

PER SERVING: *Calories 455 (From Fat 307); Fat 34g (Saturated 12g); Cholesterol 56mg; Sodium 1107mg; Carbohydrate 22g (Dietary Fiber 0g); Protein 14g.*

Classic Fries

PREP TIME: 10 MIN	COOK TIME: 7 MIN	YIELD: 6 SERVINGS

INGREDIENTS

1 quart canola oil

3 russet potatoes, cut into ¼-inch strips

Salt and pepper to taste

DIRECTIONS

1 Using a medium bowl, rinse the potatoes under cold water for about 15 to 20 seconds to rinse off some of the starch. In a cast-iron skillet, preheat the oil over medium heat for about 3 minutes or until the oil reaches 350 degrees.

2 Carefully place about 1 cup of the potatoes into the oil, allowing them to cook for about 10 to 15 minutes or until golden brown. Use a slotted spoon to remove the fries and place them on a baking tray with a rack. Finish with salt and pepper and serve.

TIP: Do Step 2 in two to three batches so that you don't overcrowd the skillet. Overcrowding causes the temperature of the oil to go down, resulting in soggy fries.

TIP: Wait about 2 to 3 minutes between batches, which gives the oil time to return to the original temperature and ensures that each batch is cooked evenly.

NOTE: Serve these fries with the Lomo Saltado (Beef Stir Fry) recipe in Chapter 24.

PER SERVING: *Calories 146 (From Fat 64); Fat 7g (Saturated 1g); Cholesterol 0mg; Sodium 5mg; Carbohydrate 19g (Dietary Fiber 1g); Protein 2g.*

Fabulous Fajitas

| PREP TIME: 20 MIN | COOK TIME: 30 MIN | YIELD: 4 SERVINGS |

INGREDIENTS

8 10-inch flour tortillas

2 to 2½ pounds marinated flank steaks, pounded to ¼-inch thickness

4 tablespoons butter

2 large onions, sliced and separated into rings

2 green bell peppers, sliced and separated into rings

2 limes, halved

DIRECTIONS

1 Place the top rack of the oven 4 inches below broiler. Place the bottom oven rack in the lowest position. Place a cast-iron griddle on the bottom rack. Set your oven to 425 degrees. Heat your cast iron for 30 minutes.

2 Heat another cast-iron griddle or skillet on the stovetop on high heat for a few minutes; then reduce the heat to medium.

3 Place one tortilla on the griddle; cook until the bottom blisters (about 30 seconds). Turn with tongs and repeat until the second side is blistered. Stack the tortillas on foil and wrap to keep warm.

4 Set your oven to broil — one griddle is still on the bottom rack. Place the meat in a pan on the top rack and broil for approximately 5 to 6 minutes on each side.

5 While the meat is cooking, melt the butter in a cast-iron skillet. Add the vegetables and sauté until the onions are translucent. Season with the salt and pepper. Remove from the heat but leave in the pan to keep warm.

6 Remove the meat from the broiler and cut it against the grain into finger length strips.

7 Using potholders, remove the griddle from the bottom rack of the oven and place it on wooden liners or a hot pad. Place the meat and vegetables on the griddle to serve. Serve with tortillas and lime halves, Pico de Gallo, and Guacamole.

Marvelous Fajita Marinade

PREP TIME: 5 MIN	CHILL TIME: UP TO 2 HRS	YIELD: 4 SERVINGS

INGREDIENTS

1 large orange

1 lemon

¼ cup pineapple juice

¼ cup white wine

1 tablespoons soy sauce

1 clove garlic, minced

1 teaspoon pepper

1 dried chile pepper, left whole

3 tablespoons butter, melted

DIRECTIONS

1 Grate 1 tablespoon of the peel from the orange and 2 teaspoons of the peel from the lemon and set it aside. Squeeze the orange and lemon to get ¼ cup of juice from each.

2 Combine the zest, orange juice, lemon juice, pineapple juice, wine, soy sauce, garlic, pepper, chile pepper, and butter in a large resealable plastic bag.

3 Place approximately 2 to 2½ pounds flank steak, pork tenderloin, or chicken breast (pounded to ½-inch thickness) in the marinade and seal the bag.

4 Place the bag in the refrigerator to marinate for at least 30 minutes and up to 2 hours, turning occasionally.

NOTE: Serve with the Guacamole and Pico de Gallo recipes from earlier in this chapter.

PER SERVING: *Calories 791 (From Fat 290); Fat 32g (Saturated 16g); Cholesterol 59mg; Sodium 1311mg; Carbohydrate 104g (Dietary Fiber 8g); Protein 18g.*

Chapter **24**

One-Pot World Favorites

With all the focus on complex cooking techniques and unique culinary experiences, you can easily overlook the beauty of simplicity in cooking. Sometimes, all it takes is the perfect combination of a few select ingredients in a single pot to create something truly legendary.

This chapter offers an exciting journey around the globe, showcasing a variety of flavorful dishes. Although some may appear exotic at first, they're actually quite approachable, and even novice cast-iron home cooks can them. These recipes are designed to be enjoyed by both family and friends, making them a delightful experience to explore new flavors and expand your culinary repertoire.

Seeing What the Americas Have to Offer

When I hear about food from the Americas, a few things come to mind: rich and vibrant flavors, cultural diversity, and a wide variety of ingredients and culinary traditions. From the spicy and flavorful dishes of Mexico to the hearty and comforting cuisine of the United States, the Americas offer a vast range of culinary experiences that reflect the history, geography, and traditions of the different regions.

Whether it's succulent barbecue, zesty escovitch, or indulgent desserts like apple pie or churros, the food of the Americas is sure to inspire you to explore new cultures and flavors within this melting pot of cultural diversity.

Focusing on North America

North American cuisine is incredibly diverse, as it incorporates the culinary traditions of various cultural influences. Native American, European, African, and Asian cuisines have all contributed to the unique flavors found in North American dishes.

North American cuisine often emphasizes comfort food and hearty flavors, with an abundance of ingredients like beef, pork, poultry, corn, potatoes, and various vegetables. Each region has its own specialties and local ingredients, making the cuisine diverse and exciting to explore. These recipes highlight some classics you can create in your cast iron:

>> **Gullah Rice:** The origins of this dish rest with the men, women, and children brought as slaves from West Africa to work the rice plantations on the coastal islands off of South Carolina and Georgia. Isolated from the mainland and eventually outnumbering their often-absent owners, these people preserved the language, religious practices, music, and social customs of their homeland. The result is a uniquely and literally African-American culture. These people and their descendants are known as the Gullah (in South Carolina) and Geechee (in Georgia) people. *Gullah* is also the name of their language, which is made up of English and over 4,000 words from many different African languages.

» **Arroz con Pollo:** Popular in many Spanish-speaking countries, this dish is a wonderful example of the flavorful and comforting cuisine found in these regions. Inspired by the flavors of Mexico, this dish includes spices and herbs that lend a distinct flavor profile to the dish.

» **Jambalaya:** A standard in Louisiana in the United States, this dish is a true representation of Creole and Cajun cuisine. Known for its rich and bold flavors, this one-pot meal showcases the culinary heritage and diverse flavors of Louisiana.

» **Caribbean Escovitch Fish:** From the Caribbean, this tangy and spicy dish is full of vibrant flavors that will make your mouth water. This dish offers a combination of textures and taste, making it a favorite among locals and visitors alike.

» **Calabasa Skillet Soufflé:** This squash soufflé is an Old Mexico recipe brought from a home kitchen in Chihuahua, Mexico. This dish is a great way to enjoy the flavors of calabasa squash in a unique, delicious way.

Gullah Rice

INGREDIENTS

2 pounds smoked sausage, sliced ½-inch thick

2 tablespoons vegetable oil, if necessary

1 cup chopped onion

1 cup chopped red bell pepper

1 or 2 chopped jalapeño peppers, seeded

2 cups uncooked rice

1 teaspoon brown sugar

1 teaspoon salt

1 cup chopped tomatoes

2½ to 3 cups chicken stock

1 cup cooked black beans

DIRECTIONS

1 In a 10-quart cast-iron Dutch oven, brown the sausage over medium-high heat. Remove the sausage and set aside; reserve the fat. Add enough of the vegetable oil so that the pan contains approximately 4 tablespoons of fat/oil.

2 Add the onion, bell pepper, and hot peppers. Cook over medium heat until the vegetables are wilted, approximately 10 minutes.

3 Add the rice and stir to coat the grains with the vegetable mixture. Stir in the sausage, sugar, salt, and tomatoes. Pour in 2½ cups of the chicken stock, one ladle at a time, blending well.

4 Bring the mixture to a rolling boil, reduce the heat to a simmer, and cover. Cook for about 20 minutes, or until the rice is tender and the stock is absorbed. Check occasionally and, if necessary, add up to ½ cup additional stock as the rice cooks.

5 Remove the Dutch oven from the heat. Stir in the black beans, cover, and let it stand for 10 minutes. Serve warm.

NOTE: Standard long-grain rice is ideal for this recipe, but you can use brown or white rice, too. If you use brown, just add 5 minutes cooking time to Step 4. Don't use instant rice; it cooks too quickly and will break down before the rest of the ingredients are done.

PER SERVING: Calories 838 (From Fat 435); Fat 48g (Saturated 16g); Cholesterol 103mg; Sodium 2,437mg; Carbohydrate 70g (Dietary Fiber 5g); Protein 29g.

Arroz con Pollo

PREP TIME: 20 MIN | **COOK TIME: 2 HRS** | **YIELD: 8 SERVINGS**

INGREDIENTS

4 pounds of your favorite chicken pieces

Salt and pepper

2 strips bacon

½ pound sausage

½ cup peanut oil or canola oil

2 cloves garlic, minced

2 medium onions, finely sliced

1 green bell pepper, seeded and finely sliced

2 cups long grain rice

2 cups peeled, seeded, and chopped fresh tomatoes

One 4-ounce can chopped green chiles, drained

2 teaspoons wine or balsamic vinegar

2 teaspoons salt

1 teaspoon pepper

2 bay leaves

⅛ teaspoon saffron (optional)

2 cups chicken broth

1 cup vermouth or dry white wine

1 cup frozen peas (optional)

DIRECTIONS

1 Preheat your oven to 325 degrees. Wash the chicken and pat dry. Lay on the wax paper and salt and pepper both sides of the chicken. In a 12-inch cast-iron skillet, fry the bacon over medium-high heat and then drain on paper towels and crumble into your 7-quart cast-iron Dutch oven.

2 Fry the sausage in the bacon grease until it's brown. Remove the sausage to a Dutch oven with a slotted spoon to leave the drippings in a skillet. Add the peanut oil to the bacon and sausage drippings in the skillet. Add a few pieces of the chicken at a time to the skillet and brown on both sides. With tongs, remove the chicken pieces to the Dutch oven as they're browned.

3 In the same skillet and drippings, sauté the garlic, onions, and bell pepper until slightly tender. Remove to the Dutch oven with a slotted spoon to leave the drippings in the skillet. In the skillet drippings, brown the rice and add it to the Dutch oven. Also add the tomatoes, green chiles, vinegar, salt, pepper, bay leaves, saffron (if desired), chicken broth, and vermouth.

4 Place the cover on the Dutch oven and bake for about 2 hours, checking every 30 minutes to add more chicken broth if necessary. The mixture should not be soupy, but neither should it be dry. Add the peas (if desired) during the last 15 minutes. Remove the bay leaves before serving.

PER SERVING: *Calories 683 (From Fat 324); Fat 36g (Saturated 8g); Cholesterol 133mg; Sodium 1,332mg; Carbohydrate 49g (Dietary Fiber 3g); Protein 39g.*

Jambalaya

PREP TIME: 10 MIN	COOK TIME: 50 MIN	YIELD: 8 SERVINGS

INGREDIENTS

2 tablespoons olive oil

1 pound chicken thigh, boneless, skin off, medium diced

½ pound andouille sausage, medium diced

1 cup onion, medium diced

1 green bell pepper, medium dice

2 stalks celery, medium dice

2 cloves garlic, minced

2 cups Roma tomato or canned tomato, medium diced

1 tablespoon smoked paprika

1 teaspoon cumin

½ teaspoon oregano

½ teaspoon basil

3 sprigs thyme

¼ teaspoon cayenne powder

1 teaspoon salt

2 cups long grain rice, rinsed and drained

3½ cups chicken broth

½ pound shrimp, peeled and deveined

2 green onions, sliced (optional)

DIRECTIONS

1 Preheat a Dutch oven over medium heat with the olive oil, about 2 minutes. Add the chicken and sear on all sides until golden brown, about 5 minutes. Then add the sausage, cooking until browned and crispy, about 3 minutes.

2 Add the onion and bell pepper and cook until the onions are golden brown, stirring about every 5 minutes. Then add the celery and garlic. Mix well and cook for another 2 minutes. Next add the tomato, smoked paprika, cumin, oregano, basil, thyme, cayenne, and salt. Cook until the sides start to turn a rusty color, about 5 to 7 minutes.

3 Stir in the rice, add the chicken broth, and bring the mixture to a simmer. Cover with a lid and reduce the heat to a medium low, cooking for about 15 minutes.

4 Remove the lid and add the shrimp on the rice in a single layer. Cover and cook for an additional 5 minutes or until the shrimp is cooked. Remove from the heat, remove the lid and the thyme, and top with green onions. Serve warm.

VARY IT! You can substitute brown rice. If you do, you'll need to add more stock and increase your cooking time. Refer to the cooking instructions on your brown rice bag for cooking time and liquid ratios.

NOTE: This dish gets its dark brown color from the caramelization of the protein, onions, and tomatoes, which also provides a depth of flavor that provide a beautiful balance of roasted flavors, heat, and spice.

PER SERVING: *Calories 420 (From Fat 139); Fat 15g (Saturated 4g); Cholesterol 109mg; Sodium 830mg; Carbohydrate 43g (Dietary Fiber 3g); Protein 26g.*

Caribbean Escovitch Fish

PREP TIME: 10 MIN | **COOK TIME: 20 MIN** | **YIELD: 2 SERVINGS**

INGREDIENTS

2 pounds whole red snapper or any medium-sized white fish

Salt and pepper to taste

½ cup olive oil

1 cup onion, sliced

1 red bell pepper, sliced

1 yellow bell pepper, sliced

1 carrot, julienned

1 clove garlic, minced

½ teaspoon ginger

2 sprigs thyme

1 teaspoon Worcestershire sauce

¼ teaspoon allspice

1 tablespoon sugar

2 bay leaves

½ cup apple cider vinegar

DIRECTIONS

1 Season both sides of the fish with salt and pepper on a baking tray.

2 Preheat a large cast-iron skillet over medium heat with the olive oil for about 2 minutes. Then add the fish to the hot skillet and cook each side for about 5 or 7 minutes or until golden brown (with an internal temperature of 145 degrees or the fish is completely cooked with a flaky texture). After the fish is cooked, remove the fish from the skillet and rest on a clean baking sheet with a rack.

3 Add the onions, bell peppers, and carrots to the skillet and cook for about 3 to 5 minutes. Add the garlic, ginger, and thyme and cook for about 1 minute. Then add the Worcestershire, allspice, sugar, bay leaves, and vinegar. Allow to simmer, about 3 to 5 minutes. Adjust seasoning with salt and pepper. Remove the bay leaves and thyme and serve on top of the fish.

NOTE: This classic dish is traditionally served whole, skin on, and garnished with peppers and onions. Don't be afraid to make it your own by removing the skin or cooking fish fillets instead of the whole fish.

PER SERVING: *Calories 496 (From Fat 282); Fat 32g (Saturated 4g); Cholesterol 0mg; Sodium 36mg; Carbohydrate 15g (Dietary Fiber 2.5g); Protein 37g.*

Calabasa Skillet Soufflé

INGREDIENTS

½ cup vegetable oil

½ cup diced chayote squash

½ cup diced summer squash

½ cup diced zucchini

½ cup diced onion

½ cup diced whole kernel corn

7 egg yolks

2½ cups heavy whipping cream

1 teaspoon salt

1 teaspoon white pepper

DIRECTIONS

1 Preheat your oven to 350 degrees.

2 In a 12-inch cast-iron skillet, heat the oil over medium-high heat. Add the chayote squash, summer squash, zucchini, onions, and corn. Sauté until the vegetables are wilted, about 10 minutes.

3 In a medium mixing bowl, combine the egg yolks and cream. When the vegetables are wilted, remove the skillet from the heat and pour the egg mixture into the vegetables, blending thoroughly. Season to taste using the salt and pepper.

4 Cover the skillet and bake in the oven until the soufflé is set, about 35 to 40 minutes.

5 Remove from the heat and let rest for 10 minutes before serving.

NOTE: For information on types of squash and the difference between summer and winter squash, head to Chapter 9.

TIP: If you have trouble finding the chayote squash, check out natural food stores.

PER SERVING: *Calories 600 (From Fat 554); Fat 62g (Saturated 26g); Cholesterol 384mg; Sodium 437mg; Carbohydrate 8g (Dietary Fiber 1g); Protein 6g.*

Creating dishes from South America

South American cuisine offers a vibrant and diverse range of flavors. Fish and seafood play significant roles in coastal regions. Each country within the region has its own unique dishes, ingredients, and culinary traditions, resulting in an exciting culinary landscape.

These recipes highlight dishes from the region that embody the culture, allowing you to create a unique and memorable family dinner:

» **Lomo Saltado (Beef Stir-Fry):** Lomo Saltado brings together the perfect blend of Asian flavors and Latin flair with the end result of pure goodness. In Peru this dish is served with a side of white rice.

» **Chicken Curry:** Chicken curry is a popular dish in Guyana, a country located in South America. Guyanese chicken curry is known for its rich and aromatic flavors. This dish is loved for its combination of tender chicken and deeply spiced curry, making it a wise choice for curry enthusiasts.

» **Acarejé:** Acarejé is a popular street food in Brazil, particularly in the northeastern region where it originated. This dish is served with Vatapá (see the next recipe).

» **Vatapá:** Renowned for its rich and complex taste, Vatapá is a staple in Afro-Brazilian cuisine and showcases the diverse influences and culinary traditions of Brazil's northeastern region.

Lomo Saltado (Beef Stir-Fry)

PREP TIME: 8 MIN	COOK TIME: 20 MIN	YIELD: 2 SERVINGS

INGREDIENTS

2 tablespoons olive oil

8 ounces sirloin steak, cut into ¼-inch strips

Salt and pepper to taste

1 cup red onion, julienned

2 Roma tomatoes, quartered

2 garlic cloves, minced

1 tablespoon aji amarillo paste

2 tablespoons soy sauce

1 tablespoon apple cider vinegar

8 to 12 ounces french fries, cooked (see Chapter 23 for the Classic Fries recipe)

1 tablespoon cilantro, chopped

DIRECTIONS

1 Preheat a cast-iron skillet with 1 tablespoon olive oil over medium heat for about 3 minutes. While preheating, season the steak with salt and pepper on a baking tray.

2 Place the steak strips into pan, making sure the steak gets a good sear and allowing the steak to caramelize on all sides. Use tongs or a spoon to turn the steak. After all the meat has browned — about 4 to 8 minutes — remove it from the skillet and set on a baking tray with a rack to rest.

3 Using the same pan without cleaning it, add 1 tablespoon olive oil and preheat for about 30 seconds. Add the onions and allow them to sweat for about 5 minutes, or until they're soft. Then add the tomatoes, garlic, and aji amarillo paste, allowing the mixture to cook for about 5 minutes or until the tomatoes start to caramelize. Add the soy sauce and vinegar, and season with salt and pepper to taste. Allow the mixture to cook for about 1 minute.

4 Add the steak, fries, and cilantro to the skillet. Use a set of tongs or a wooden spoon to mix. Serve immediately.

VARY IT! You aren't limited to using sirloin. The most important thing about your steak is that it's tender. Other options include lower-end cuts like flank or skirt steak or higher-end cuts like strip steak or my favorite, rib-eye.

NOTE: Depending on how you like your steak cooked, the cook time can vary. For a more medium steak cook on high for about 4 minutes and for a more medium-well, cook for 6 minutes over high heat. Remember, one of the most important parts of cooking meat is making sure that you rest it properly after it's cooked.

PER SERVING: *Calories 715 (From Fat 377); Fat 42g (Saturated 9g); Cholesterol 46mg; Sodium 1226mg; Carbohydrate 54g (Dietary Fiber 7g); Protein 32g.*

Chicken Curry

PREP TIME: 1 HR 15 MIN | COOK TIME: 45 MIN | YIELD: 4 SERVINGS

INGREDIENTS

2 pounds chicken thighs and/or drumstick (bone-in/skin-on)

Chicken Marinade

2 tablespoons olive oil

Curry Paste

1 quart chicken stock

2 bay leaves

2 large russet potatoes, large diced

DIRECTIONS

1 Add the chicken to the marinade in a medium bowl, mix well, cover, and refrigerate for at least 1 hour.

2 Using a Dutch oven with a lid, add the olive oil and preheat over medium heat for about 2 minutes. Add the curry paste, allowing it to cook for about 5 minutes or until it starts to thicken and slightly brown.

3 Reduce the heat to medium low. Remove the chicken from marinade and discard the liquid. Add the chicken and mix well, allowing the curry to completely coat each piece of chicken. Add the stock and bay leaves. Cover and allow it to cook for about 20 minutes

4 Remove the lid, add the potatoes, and mix well. Cover again, allowing it to cook for an additional 15 to 20 minutes or until the chicken is falling off the bone and the potatoes are fork tender. Adjust the seasoning if necessary with salt and pepper.

Chicken Marinade

1 lemon zest and juice

1 tablespoon olive oil

1 teaspoon onion powder

1 teaspoon garlic powder

1 teaspoon salt

2 scallions, thinly sliced

3 sprigs cilantro, remove thick stems and chop

3 sprigs parsley, remove thick stems and chop

1 medium sweet onion, julienned

1 to 2 Wiri Wiri peppers, minced (optional)

(continued)

1 In a medium bowl, add the lemon zest and juice, olive oil, onion and garlic powder, salt, scallions, cilantro, parsley, onion, and Wiri Wiri peppers.

Curry Paste

3 tablespoons yellow curry

1 teaspoon cumin

½ teaspoon mustard powder

½ teaspoon coriander

½ teaspoon turmeric

½ teaspoon smoked paprika

¼ teaspoon garam masala

½ cup chicken stock

1 In a small bowl add the curry, cumin, mustard powder, coriander, turmeric, smoked paprika, garam masala, and stock. Mix well to form a paste.

NOTE: The trick to a good Guyanese curry is the pepper. Traditional dishes use a Wiri Wiri pepper, which produces a medium heat. If you can't find this pepper, a great substitute is a scotch bonnet chili or a habanero pepper.

TIP: To mitigate the spiciness, remove the pepper seeds.

NOTE: You can serve with a cup of steamed rice.

PER SERVING: *Calories 444 (From Fat 179); Fat 20g (Saturated 4g); Cholesterol 56mg; Sodium 893mg; Carbohydrate 45g (Dietary Fiber 3g); Protein 21g.*

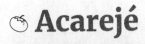 # Acarejé

INGREDIENTS

2 cups black-eye peas, soaked overnight

1 cup onion, minced

½ teaspoon salt

2 quarts peanut oil or neutral cooking oil

DIRECTIONS

1 Remove the outer skin on the peas by gently rubbing them in your hands. After you remove the skin, rinse and strain off the skin and water.

2 Add the beans, onion, and salt to a food processor and blend until the mixture is slightly smooth. Use a rubber spatula to scrape down the sides of the bowl. Adjust seasoning with salt and pepper.

3 Using a Dutch oven, add about 2 quarts of oil and preheat to 350 degrees. Scoop the batter and carefully drop it in the oil. Allow the Acarajé to cook for about 3 minutes on each side, or until golden brown. Remove and rest on a baking tray with a rack.

NOTE: When blending in Step 2, the mixture should have a paste consistency, which doubles in size as it blends.

PER SERVING: *Calories 284 (From Fat 88); Fat 10g (Saturated 2g); Cholesterol 0mg; Sodium 169mg; Carbohydrate 38g (Dietary Fiber 6g); Protein 14g.*

Vatapá

PREP TIME: 15 MIN | COOK TIME: 30 MIN | YIELD: 6 SERVINGS

INGREDIENTS

½ cup dried shrimp
(soak for about 2 minutes in
1 cup water)

¼ cup cashews, unsalted

¼ cup peanuts, unsalted

1 cup onion, small diced

1 red bell pepper, small diced

2 tablespoons ginger, minced

3 garlic cloves, minced

1 red chile, minced (optional)

4 tablespoons olive oil

1 tablespoon flour

3 cups vegetable broth
or shrimp stock

1 cup coconut milk

1 pound shrimp (steamed
or grilled)

1 sprig flat parsley, chopped

2 sprigs cilantro, chopped

Salt and pepper to taste

DIRECTIONS

1 Preheat a Dutch oven over medium heat for about 2 minutes.

2 Add the dried shrimp, cashews, and peanuts, allowing them to toast until fragrant, using a wooden spoon to mix while cooking, about 2 to 4 minutes. Remove them from the heat and allow to cool, about 5 minutes. Blend the ingredients in a food processor until a smooth powder. Remove and reserve.

3 Blend the onion, bell pepper, ginger, garlic, and chile in a food processor or blender until smooth. Remove and reserve.

4 In a 12-inch cast-iron skillet add the olive oil and preheat over medium heat for about 2 minutes. Add the vegetable purée to the skillet and allow it to cook for about 5 minutes. Add the flour, dried shrimp, and nuts mixture. The flour needs to cook for 3 to 5 minutes.

5 Add the stock and coconut milk and mix with a wooden spoon. Bring to a simmer and cook for about 8 minutes. As soon as the mixture starts to pull away from the sides reduce the heat to medium low.

6 Finish the dish with the fresh shrimp and a blend of parsley, cilantro, and green onions.

PER SERVING: *Calories 346 (From Fat 218); Fat 24g (Saturated 10g); Cholesterol 135mg; Sodium 656mg; Carbohydrate 13g (Dietary Fiber 2g); Protein 21g.*

Introducing Some African Dishes to Your Repertoire

When I hear about food from Africa, a few things come to mind: bold and complex flavors, a focus on fresh and locally sourced ingredients, and the influence of diverse ethnic groups and traditions. Africa has a rich culinary heritage that varies greatly across different regions and countries. From the aromatic spices of North African cuisine to the hearty stews and grilled meats of West Africa, and the injera and spicy dishes of East Africa, the food of Africa is known for its vibrant flavors and unique combinations.

Here you can discover some of my favorite dishes that beautifully represent Africa's diverse and rich traditions and cuisines:

>> **Potjiekos:** This word means *small pot food.* In South Africa, they use a round, three-legged pot called a potjie, which is traditionally used for cooking outdoors.

>> **Jollof Rice:** Jollof is a popular rice dish in many African countries. This dish resembles more of a Nigerian-style rice, which uses a bit more spice.

>> **Chicken Tagine:** Originating from Morocco, this traditional North African stew showcases the region's use of spices, aromatic ingredients, and slow-cooking techniques, combining tender chicken with a variety of spices, herbs, and vegetables. The term *tagine* refers to both the dish itself and the cooking vessel used to prepare it. This dish includes *ras el hanout*, which is a secret jewel used to add a ton of flavor value to Moroccan dishes. The literal translation is *head of the shop,* but in reality it means *top shelf,* implying that it's the very best.

>> **Ambasha (Sweet Flatbread):** This traditional Ethiopian delicacy is flavored with spices such as cardamom, cinnamon, or nutmeg. It's commonly enjoyed during holidays and celebrations in Ethiopian culture, including Christmas and Easter.

Potjiekos

INGREDIENTS

¼ cup olive oil

2 pounds lamb shoulder or braising meat like chuck, large dice

Salt and pepper, to taste

2 cups onion, julienned

1 teaspoon ginger, chopped

3 garlic cloves, chopped

2 cups tomato, chopped

2 cups red wine

2 bay leaves

2 to 3 sprigs thyme

2 quarts broth, vegetable or beef

2 cups potato, skin on, medium dice

1 cup carrots, chopped

1 cup green beans

1 cup zucchini, medium dice

DIRECTIONS

1 Preheat your cast-iron Dutch oven over medium heat with the olive oil, about 3 minutes.

2 Place the lamb on a baking tray and season both sides with salt and pepper. Carefully add the lamb to the oil and cook for 5 to 7 minutes, allowing it to brown on all sides.

3 Add the onions and cook for 3 minutes or until translucent and soft. Add the ginger and garlic and cook for 1 minute. Then add the tomatoes and cook for 3 minutes or until they start to stick to the bottom slightly. Add the red wine and reduce by half.

4 Add the bay leaves, thyme, and broth. Cover and cook for 45 minutes.

5 Remove the lid and add the potatoes, carrots, and green beans. Cover and cook out for another 15 to 20 minutes or until the meat is tender. During the last 10 minutes of cooking add the zucchini. Adjust the seasoning with salt and pepper. Serve over rice.

NOTE: In South Africa they call zucchini baby marrow.

NOTE: In cooking, *reducing* refers to the process of simmering or boiling a liquid, such as a stock, wine, or sauce, to remove some of the water content and concentrate the flavors. By evaporating the liquid, the flavors become more intense and, in the case of a sauce, thicken.

PER SERVING: *Calories 469 (From Fat 164); Fat 18g (Saturated 5g); Cholesterol 94mg; Sodium 1415mg; Carbohydrate 29g (Dietary Fiber 4g); Protein 33g.*

🍅 Jollof Rice

PREP TIME: 15 MIN	COOK TIME: 30 MIN	YIELD: 6 SERVINGS

INGREDIENTS

1 tablespoon curry powder (Jamaican-style)

½ teaspoon cayenne powder

3 cups onion, small diced, divided

2 bell peppers (red or yellow), small diced

¼ cup olive oil

1 scotch bonnet, small diced (optional)

1 teaspoon ginger, minced

2 garlic cloves, minced

4 tablespoons tomato paste

1 teaspoon salt

2 cups long-grain rice (rinsed and drained)

2 bay leaves

2 sprig thyme, remove leaves and chop

3½ cups vegetable broth

2 cups Roma tomato, small diced

¼ cup butter, melted

Salt and pepper to taste

DIRECTIONS

1 Preheat your Dutch oven over medium heat for about 2 minutes. Add the curry powder and cayenne, allowing it to toast for about 2 to 3 minutes, or until fragrant. Add 2 cups onions, bell peppers, and olive oil. Allow the onions to cook until translucent and soft.

2 Add the scotch bonnet, ginger, and garlic, and cook for about 1 minute. Add the tomato paste, salt, and rice. Cook the mixture until the edges start to become rusty, about 4 minutes.

3 Add the bay leaves, thyme, and broth and bring to a simmer. Cover and reduce heat to medium low and cook for about 20 minutes. Turn off the heat and allow it to rest for about 8 minutes before removing the lid. Cover and cook for about 20 minutes.

4 After it's cooked, remove the lid and add the tomatoes, 1 cup onions, butter, and salt. Use a fork to mix well. Serve warm.

NOTE: West African food has been gaining popularity over the past decade, especially in the Americas. Every year Washington, D.C., and Toronto hold a jollof food festival to celebrate World Jollof Day.

PER SERVING: *Calories 475 (From Fat 172); Fat 19g (Saturated 7g); Cholesterol 20mg; Sodium 1025mg; Carbohydrate 70g (Dietary Fiber 6g); Protein 8g.*

Chicken Tagine

PREP TIME: 10 MIN	COOK TIME: 45 MIN	YIELD: 4 SERVINGS

INGREDIENTS

½ cup olive oil

1 pound chicken thighs, bone in and skin on

Salt and pepper to taste

2 cups onion, medium diced

2 cloves garlic, minced

2 tablespoons ras en hanout

One 12-ounce can chickpeas, drained

1 cup Roma tomato, chopped

½ cup fresh apricot, chopped

2 tablespoons honey

1 lemon, zest and juice

1 cup chicken stock

¼ cup black olives

2 sprigs cilantro, chopped

DIRECTIONS

1 Preheat the olive oil in a Dutch oven over medium heat for about 2 minutes.

2 Place the chicken in skin side down and season well on both sides with salt and pepper. Allow it to cook slowly, rendering the skin until golden brown, about 5 to 8 minutes. Remove the chicken and hold on a clean baking tray with rack.

3 Add the onions and cook until translucent. Then add the garlic and ras en hanout. Mix well and cook for 1 minute. Add the chickpeas, tomatoes, apricots, honey, and lemon zest and juice. Mix well. Add the chicken back and then add the stock and cover with a lid. Simmer for 30 minutes. Add the olives and cilantro. Mix well and serve.

Ras en hanout

1 teaspoon ginger, ground

1 teaspoon garlic powder

1 teaspoon turmeric, ground

½ teaspoon cardamom, ground

½ teaspoon cinnamon, ground

½ teaspoon coriander, ground

½ teaspoon black pepper, ground fine

¼ teaspoon anise, ground

¼ teaspoon allspice, ground

¼ teaspoon nutmeg, ground

¼ teaspoon mace, ground

¼ teaspoon cayenne

¼ teaspoon cloves, ground

1 Mix all the ingredients well and store in an airtight container.

PER SERVING: *Calories 612 (From Fat 357); Fat 40g (Saturated 6g); Cholesterol 50mg; Sodium 400mg; Carbohydrate 48g (Dietary Fiber 8g); Protein 19g.*

Ambasha (Sweet Flatbread)

PREP TIME: 12 MIN	COOK TIME: 30 MIN	YIELD: 8 SERVINGS

INGREDIENTS

2 cups all-purpose flour

3 tablespoons sugar

2 teaspoons instant yeast

½ teaspoon salt

1 teaspoon black sesame seeds (optional)

½ teaspoon cardamom powder

¼ cup raisins

2 tablespoons olive oil

½ cup water (warm)

2 tablespoons milk

DIRECTIONS

1 Add the flour, sugar, yeast, salt, sesame seed, and cardamom and mix well using a kitchen mixer. Add the raisins and oil and continue to mix well.

2 While continuing to mix, slowly add the warm water to make a soft dough. After the dough is formed, place the dough on a lightly floured surface and knead for about 5 to 7 minutes or until the dough is no longer sticky. Then cover the dough and place in a warm environment and let it rest for about 1½ hours or until it doubles in size.

3 While the dough is resting, preheat your oven to 350 degrees.

4 After the dough has risen, punch it gently and then spread it evenly in your cast-iron skillet. Cover the skillet and allow the dough to rest for another 30 minutes or until the dough is puffy.

5 Before baking, use a knife to make the traditional wheel pattern on the dough.

6 Brush the dough with milk and bake for 20 to 30 minutes or until it's golden brown. After baking, remove from the oven, allowing it to cool for about 5 minutes. Cut and serve.

PER SERVING: *Calories 182 (From Fat 35); Fat 4g (Saturated 1g); Cholesterol 0mg; Sodium 149mg; Carbohydrate 33g (Dietary Fiber 1g); Protein 4g.*

Mastering Some Asian Recipes

Asian cuisine is a vibrant and diverse culinary landscape encompassing many cultures, flavors, and influences. It's characterized by the abundant use of fresh ingredients, vibrant flavors, and aromatic spices. One of the key aspects that makes this cuisine so unique is its strong emphasis on balance, not just in terms of flavors but also in textures. The diverse cultures within Asia, shaped by thousands of years of history and regional variations, have had a profound impact on the evolution of their beautiful cuisines. This section includes some Asian recipes you can experiment with your cast iron:

>> **Beef and Broccoli:** Commonly found in Chinese-American cuisine, this dish was developed in the United States as a way to adapt Chinese flavors and ingredients to suit American tastes. Beef and Broccoli is typically cooked using the stir-frying technique. Stir-frying involves quickly cooking ingredients in a hot pan or wok over high heat, allowing them to retain their texture, flavor, and nutritional value.

>> **Chicken Katsu with Tonkatsu Sauce:** Chicken Katsu or "Katsu" is a Japanese take on deep-fried breaded chicken cutlets, similar to German schnitzel. But instead of using pork or veal, this recipe uses tender, juicy chicken breast. Katsu with tonkatsu sauce is a popular dish in Japanese cuisine and is loved for its crispy exterior, tender chicken, and rich flavor.

Beef and Broccoli

| PREP TIME: 20 MIN | COOK TIME: 20 MIN | YIELD: 4 SERVINGS |

INGREDIENTS

4 tablespoons seasoned rice vinegar

2 tablespoons soy sauce

1 tablespoon brown sugar

4 tablespoons cornstarch

½ teaspoon salt

¼ teaspoon black pepper

1 pound flank or skirt steak, sliced thin

½-inch piece of ginger, minced

2 cloves garlic, minced

2 scallions, sliced (separate tops from bottoms)

½ cup water

2 teaspoons oyster sauce

1 tablespoon chili oil (optional)

2 tablespoons soy sauce

4 tablespoons olive oil

2 cups broccoli florets

DIRECTIONS

1 Add and mix well the rice vinegar, soy sauce, brown sugar, cornstarch, salt, and pepper in small bowl. Add the sliced steak, allowing it to marinate for about 10 to 20 minutes.

2 In another bowl add the ginger, garlic, and scallion bottoms. Using a third bowl mix the water, oyster sauce, chili oil, and soy sauce. Reserve.

3 Using a cast-iron wok or 10-inch skillet, preheat over medium-high heat with about 2 tablespoons of olive oil for about 3 minutes.

4 Add half of your marinated steak and cook on high for about 2 to 3 minutes or until the meat is brown and completely cooked. Remove and set on a clean baking tray. Wipe out your wok and repeat the process until all the meat has been sautéed. After wiping clean the wok, add 2 tablespoons of olive oil and preheat the wok over medium heat for about 3 minutes.

5 Add the broccoli and slightly sauté for about 3 minutes. Then add and cook the ginger and garlic mixture, for about 1 minute. Return the steak to the wok and add the oyster sauce mixture. Cook for about 5 minutes or until thick. Remove and serve with sliced scallion tops

TIP: The longer you marinate the meat, the better the taste. If you have the time, prepare the marinade the night before, soak the meat, and refrigerate.

PER SERVING: *Calories 374 (From Fat 187); Fat 21g (Saturated 5g); Cholesterol 48mg; Sodium 1463mg; Carbohydrate 18g (Dietary Fiber 1g); Protein 28g.*

Chicken Katsu with Tonkatsu Sauce

INGREDIENTS

½ cup all-purpose flour

2 eggs

1 cup panko breadcrumbs

1 teaspoon salt

1 tablespoon sesame oil (optional)

2 boneless, skinless chicken breasts

Salt and pepper to taste

1 cup peanut oil or canola oil

DIRECTIONS

1 Place the flour, eggs, and breadcrumbs in three separate bowls. Add ½ teaspoon of salt in the flour and another ½ teaspoon of salt in the breadcrumbs. Add the sesame oil to the eggs and mix each bowl with a fork.

2 Butterfly the chicken by cutting it in half crosswise, then pound to about ¼-inch thick. Season with salt and pepper. To bread the chicken, take one piece at a time; dip both sides into the flour, next into the egg, and last coat in the breadcrumbs, pressing the breadcrumbs into the chicken. Place all the coated chicken on a baking tray.

3 Using a 12-inch skillet add the oil and preheat over medium heat until the oil has reached about 350 degrees. Add the chicken one piece at a time into the skillet (you should be able to fit three comfortably.) Allow them to cook for about 2 to 3 minutes on each side or until they become golden brown, or reach 165 degrees internal cooking temperature. Remove and place the cooked chicken on either a baking tray with a rack or a plate with a few paper towels to rest for about 3 minutes before serving.

Tonkatsu Sauce

¼ cup ketchup

1 tablespoon Worcestershire sauce

1 teaspoon seasoned rice wine vinegar

1 teaspoon sugar

1 teaspoon soy sauce

1 Whisk together all the ingredients in a medium bowl.

(continued)

NOTE: The sauce for this dish can serve as a dip or can be drizzled directly on top of your beautiful Katsu. Shaking off the excess flour after each dip is an important part of the breading process. It allows you to have more cohesive binding on your chicken.

NOTE: Cast iron regulates the temperature, so all you have to do is just wait for the chicken to turn golden brown; refer to the color insert for a photo.

PER SERVING: *Calories 322 (From Fat 92); Fat 10g (Saturated 2g); Cholesterol 45mg; Sodium 1154mg; Carbohydrate 36g (Dietary Fiber 2g); Protein 21g.*

Turning to the Old World — Europe — for Inspiration

European cuisine is a diverse and rich culinary tradition that has developed over centuries across the continent. The cuisine encompasses a wide range of flavors, techniques, and ingredients that vary from country to country. From the delicate sauces and pastries of French cuisine to the hearty stews and sausages of German cuisine, each region offers its own unique culinary identity. Here are some classic European recipes you can try with your cast iron:

>> **Paella:** Paella is a traditional Spanish dish that originated in the Valencia region. It's a flavorful one-pot rice dish that's known for its vibrant colors and rich flavors.

>> **Cassoulet:** Cassoulet is a rich and hearty French dish hailing from the region of Southwest France. It's a slow-cooked casserole-like dish made with white beans, various types of meat, and a flavorful sauce.

>> **Pot-au-Feu:** Pot-au-Feu is a classic French dish that translates to "pot on the fire" or "pot in the fire." The dish consists of simmered meat, vegetables, and herbs, resulting in a flavorful and nourishing meal. Pot-au-Feu showcases the essence of French cuisine — warm, comforting, and full of flavor.

>> **Spanakopita:** Spanakopita is a delicious and popular Greek dish that features spinach and feta cheese enclosed in crispy, flaky phyllo pastry. The thin phyllo pastry becomes golden and crispy when baked in the oven.

Paella

PREP TIME: 20 MIN | **COOK TIME: 45 MIN** | **YIELD: 6 SERVINGS**

INGREDIENTS

¼ cup olive oil

1 cup chicken breast, diced

1 teaspoon saffron

1 cup onion, diced

1 cup tomato, diced

1 cup carrots, diced

12 young okra, whole

1 quart chicken stock

1 bay leaf

2 whole cloves

2 sprigs of thyme

Two 7-ounce fish fillets, cubed

¼ cup sliced green onions

¼ cup chopped parsley

1 tablespoon lime juice

Salt and pepper

2 cups long grain rice

1 cup bay scallops

1 cup small shrimp, peeled and deveined

DIRECTIONS

1 In a 15-inch cast-iron skillet, heat the olive oil over medium-high heat.

2 Add the chicken and sauté until lightly browned, about 7 minutes. Remove the chicken from the pan and keep warm.

3 Add the saffron, onions, tomato, and carrots. Sauté for 10 minutes or until the vegetables are wilted. Add the okra, chicken stock, bay leaf, cloves, and thyme. Bring the mixture to a rolling boil, stirring occasionally, and reduce the heat to simmer.

4 Add the fish, chicken, green onions, parsley, and lime juice. Season to taste using salt and pepper. Stir in the rice into the seafood mixture. Cover and simmer for 10 minutes.

5 Stir in the shrimp and scallops, cover, and cook for and additional 10 to 15 minutes until the rice is tender and the shrimp and scallops are cooked through. Remove the bay leaf before serving.

PER SERVING: *Calories 526 (From Fat 130); Fat 14g (Saturated 3g); Cholesterol 99mg; Sodium 952mg; Carbohydrate 62g (Dietary Fiber 3g); Protein 34g.*

Cassoulet

INGREDIENTS

4 tablespoons olive oil

1 pound lamb shoulder, medium diced

1 pound pork shoulder, medium diced

Salt and pepper, to taste

2 onions, small diced

4 garlic cloves, minced

2 tablespoons tomato paste

4 Roma tomatoes, small diced

1 teaspoon sugar

1 pound dry white beans, great northern, presoaked over night

2 quarts chicken stock

4 sprigs thyme

2 bay leaves

3 sprigs parsley, separate leaves (mince) from stems (reserve)

3 slices bacon, medium diced

2 cups panko breadcrumbs

1 lemon zest

DIRECTIONS

1 Preheat your Dutch oven with the olive oil over medium heat for about 2 minutes. Preheat your oven to 375 degrees. On a baking tray season the lamb and pork with salt and pepper on both sides and then add them both to the Dutch oven and cook until brown on all sides, about 5 to 7 minutes. Set on a clean baking tray.

2 In the same Dutch oven, sauté the onions for about 5 minutes or until they start to brown. Add the garlic and cook for about 1 minute. Add the tomato paste, tomatoes, and sugar and mix well. Allow the tomatoes to cook until they start to brown, about 8 minutes.

3 Return the protein to the Dutch oven and add the beans; mix well. Add about 2 cups of chicken stock and deglaze the bottom of the pan. Add enough stock to cover all the protein, about 8 cups. Add the thyme, bay leaves, and parsley stems, and then cover and place in the oven. Stew for 1 hour.

4 While the cassoulet is cooking, preheat a 10-inch cast-iron skillet over medium heat for about 2 minutes and then add the bacon, letting it render, until golden brown. Add the panko breadcrumbs and season with salt and pepper. Allow the panko to absorb the bacon fat and cook until golden brown. Turn off the heat, add minced parsley and lemon zest, and mix well. Reserve.

5 Remove the lid of the stew and mix well. Add the panko mixture, allowing it to cook for an additional 30 minutes. Remove from the oven when finished and take out the thyme, parsley stems, and bay leaves. Allow the stew to cool for about 10 minutes.

PER SERVING: *Calories 727 (From Fat 245); Fat 27g (Saturated 8g); Cholesterol 92mg; Sodium 814mg; Carbohydrate 72g (Dietary Fiber 14g); Protein 48g.*

Pot-au-Feu

PREP TIME: 10 MIN | COOK TIME: 1 HR 40 MIN | YIELD: 4 SERVINGS

INGREDIENTS

4 tablespoons olive oil

1 pound beef shank with bone if possible

Salt and pepper to taste

2 onions, medium diced

2 carrots, medium diced

1 leek, medium diced

2 stalks celery, medium diced

4 cloves garlic, minced

2 tablespoons tomato paste

2 Roma tomatoes, small diced (optional)

4 cups stock (add more if needed)

1 teaspoon sugar

3 sprigs parsley, separate leaves (mince) from stems (reserve)

4 sprigs thyme

2 bay leaves

½ pound pee wee potatoes

DIRECTIONS

1 Preheat your Dutch oven with 4 tablespoons of olive oil over medium heat for about 2 minutes. At the same time preheat your oven to 375 degrees.

2 Season the beef shank with salt and pepper on both sides on a baking tray. Add the shank to the hot oil and sear until brown on both sides, about 5 minutes on each side. Remove the shank and place on a clean baking tray.

3 Add the onions and carrots, allowing to brown for about 8 minutes. Add the leek and celery and cook for about 5 minutes, making sure they don't turn brown. Add the garlic and cook for 1 minute. Add the tomato paste, tomatoes (optional), and sugar and mix all well. If you add the tomatoes, cook them until they start to brown, about 8 minutes.

4 Return the shank and mix well. Add 1 quart stock (or enough to cover the protein), parsley stems, thyme, and bay leaves. Season with salt and pepper. Cover and place in the oven for 45 minutes.

5 Remove the lid and mix in the potatoes. Place the Dutch oven back in the oven and cook for an additional 15 minutes, or until the potatoes are soft. Remove the parsley stems, thyme, bay leaves, and the bone. Allow to cool for about 10 minutes before serving.

VARY IT! You can use baby Dutch potatoes — small ones whole, bigger ones halved.

PER SERVING: *Calories 420 (From Fat 167); Fat 19g (Saturated 3g); Cholesterol 44mg; Sodium 554mg; Carbohydrate 33g (Dietary Fiber 6g); Protein 31g.*

Spanakopita

PREP TIME: 30 MIN	COOK TIME: 25 MIN	YIELD: 8 SERVINGS

INGREDIENTS

2 tablespoons olive oil

1 cup onion, minced

2 cloves garlic, minced

2 cups frozen spinach, chopped

1 cup feta cheese, broken into small pieces

½ cup Parmesan cheese, grated

½ cup dill, chopped

1 lemon, zest only

⅛ teaspoon nutmeg

2 tablespoons pine nuts, toasted, chopped

Salt and pepper to taste

1 egg, lightly beaten

½ stick butter

1 pack phyllo dough sheets (defrosted)

DIRECTIONS

1 Preheat a cast-iron skillet with olive oil over medium heat for about 1 minute. At the same time preheat your oven to 375 degrees.

2 Add the onions, cooking for about 3 minutes. Add garlic and cook for 1 minute. Add spinach and allow the mixture to cook until dry, about 5 to 7 minutes. Remove the skillet from heat, allowing to cool for about 5 minutes. Add the feta cheese, Parmesan cheese, dill, lemon zest, nutmeg, and pine nuts. Mix well. Taste and adjust seasoning. Add egg and mix well. Melt the butter in a small pan over medium heat.

3 Set the phyllo on a clean surface and cover with either a damp towel or plastic wrap when you're not using it to avoid drying out. Lay out one sheet of phyllo and brush with melted butter. Place another sheet on top. Next cut the dough vertically into about 3-inch-wide strips.

4 Add 1 tablespoon of the spinach mixture about 1 inch from the end of the dough. Starting at the corner, fold the dough over the spinach mixture to form a triangle shape. Repeat the process until you've used all the dough. Repeat the process until you've used up all of the spinach mixture.

5 Arrange the triangles on a cast-iron griddle (flat side) and place in the oven. Bake for 15 minutes or until golden brown. Remove from the oven and serve warm.

NOTE: The microwave is a great tool for melting butter. Just be careful of your microwave's temperature to avoid splatter.

PER SERVING: *Calories 297 (From Fat 172); Fat 19g (Saturated 9g); Cholesterol 64mg; Sodium 535mg; Carbohydrate 22g (Dietary Fiber 2g); Protein 10g.*

Adding Some Oceania to Your Cooking

The beautiful region of Oceania encompasses the islands of the Pacific Ocean and is divided into four subregions: Melanesia, Micronesia, Polynesia, and Australasia. The region's indigenous cultures have developed unique culinary practices over thousands of years, incorporating local ingredients and traditional cooking methods. Here are some recipes from Oceania you can try:

>> **Aussie Meat Pie:** Australian meat pie also known as Aussie Pie is popular among locals and tourist. It's a must-have at Aussie football matches (that's soccer to you Americans).

>> **Coconut Curry:** This curry is a flavorful and aromatic sauce made with various spices, vegetables, and/or meat.

>> **Coconut Bread Rolls:** Coconut Bread Rolls are a delicious and sweet bread treat that incorporate the tropical flavor of coconut. Whether you enjoy them for breakfast, as a snack, or as part of a meal, they're a delightful fusion of coconut flavor and bread.

Aussie Meat Pie

PREP TIME: 15 MIN + COOLING TIME	COOK TIME: 2 HRS	YIELD: 8 SERVINGS

INGREDIENTS

1 pound beef sirloin tips or bottom sirloin, small diced

1 tablespoons flour

½ teaspoon salt

½ teaspoon pepper

2 tablespoons olive oil

1 onion, small diced

1 carrot, small diced

4 ounces button mushrooms, small diced

2 cloves garlic, minced

2 teaspoons tomato paste

1 tablespoon cider vinegar

1 tablespoon Worcestershire sauce

1 quart beef stock

One 9-inch pie crust

1 puff pastry sheet

1 egg

DIRECTIONS

1 In a medium bowl, mix well the sirloin, flour, salt, and pepper. Preheat your Dutch oven with olive oil over medium heat for about 2 minutes. Evenly disperse the sirloin mixture into the pot, allowing it to sear for 2 to 3 minutes on each side until brown, about 5 minutes.

2 After the meat is caramelized, add the onions, carrots, and mushrooms. Cook for about 3 to 5 minutes or until brown. Then add the garlic and cook for another minute. Mix well.

3 Move all the ingredients to one side of the pot and add the tomato paste, cooking for 1 to 2 minutes. Add the vinegar and Worcestershire sauce, using it to deglaze the bottom of the pan. Add the beef stock and cover with a lid. Allow the sirloin to braise for 45 minutes.

4 Remove the lid and cook for an additional 30 minutes. If your liquid is cooking too fast, turn your heat down, and add another 1 to 2 cups of stock or water. Make sure you're stirring about every 2 minutes to prevent sticking at the bottom of the pot. Remove from the heat. Cool, cover, and refrigerate for at least 1 hour.

5 Preheat the oven to 350 degrees. Using a slotted spoon, add about 1½ cups of beef mixture to your pie crust — if your shell is larger, you might need to add a bit more. Cover the filled crust with your puff pastry sheet. Push down on the edges of the crust with a fork or your fingers along the edges to ensure your slides are sealed. Use a knife to trim the excess puff pastry so it's the same size as the pie.

6 In a small bowl mix the egg well. Brush the top of the pie with egg wash — don't forget to hit the sides. Using a small knife, go in about 1 inch from the edge and make about 4 slits around the pie evenly.

(continued)

7 Place the pie in the oven for 25 to 35 minutes or until golden brown. Remove and serve.

TIP: Don't overcrowd the pan when adding the sirloin (in Step 1). If you're using a smaller pan, divide the beef and cook in separate batches.

TIP: To speed up the cooking process, you can place your cooked meat on a tray in the freezer.

NOTE: Deglazing is the process of incorporating the contracted flavor at the bottom of the pan into your liquid.

PER SERVING: *Calories 388 (From Fat 199); Fat 22g (Saturated 5g); Cholesterol 51mg; Sodium 602mg; Carbohydrate 28g (Dietary Fiber 2g); Protein 19g.*

🍅 Coconut Curry

PREP TIME: 10 MIN	COOK TIME: 35 MIN	YIELD: 4 SERVINGS

INGREDIENTS

1 onion, julienned

1 teaspoon fennel seed, ground

1 teaspoon cumin seed, ground

½ teaspoon mustard seed, ground

½ teaspoon turmeric

1 tablespoon curry powder

2 tablespoons coconut oil or olive oil

2 cloves garlic, minced

1 teaspoon ginger, minced

2 russet potatoes, peeled and small diced

1 cup coconut milk

1 cinnamon stick

Salt and pepper to taste

¼ cup cilantro, chopped

1 cup steamed rice

DIRECTIONS

1 Using a Dutch oven or a 10-inch cast-iron skillet, preheat over medium heat for about 1 minute.

2 Add the onions to the dry pan and allow the fennel seed, cumin seed, mustard seed, turmeric, and curry powder to toast for about 2 to 3 minutes or until fragrant and the onions start to brown. Add the oil, garlic, and ginger and cook for about 1 to 2 minutes.

3 Add the potatoes, coconut milk, and cinnamon stick and mix well. Adjust the seasoning with salt and pepper to taste. Bring the mixture to a simmer and cook for about 20 to 25 minutes, until the potatoes are fork tender. Adjust the seasoning if necessary. Finish with cilantro. Serve with a side of steamed white rice.

PER SERVING: *Calories 395 (From Fat 172); Fat 0g (Saturated 12g); Cholesterol 0mg; Sodium 24mg; Carbohydrate 52g (Dietary Fiber 3g); Protein 7g.*

☙ Coconut Bread Rolls

PREP TIME: 30 MIN + 1 TO 2 HRS PROOFING	COOK TIME: 20 MIN	YIELD: 12 SERVINGS

INGREDIENTS

3 tablespoons water, warm

2¼ teaspoons dry yeast

¾ cup regular canned coconut milk (warm)

4 tablespoons butter, melted

1 teaspoon vanilla extract

¼ cup coconut sugar or granulated sugar

1 teaspoon salt

2 whole eggs

¼ cup coconut powdered milk or dry milk

3½ cups all-purpose flour

2 tablespoons coconut milk

1 tablespoon coconut sugar

DIRECTIONS

1 In a small bowl, combine the warm water and yeast and allow it to sit for about 5 minutes or until it starts to bubble.

2 In a mixing bowl, add the coconut milk, melted butter, vanilla, sugar, and salt. Mix until combined, and all is dissolved. Whisk in the eggs and powdered milk and mix well. Add the yeast mixture to the mixing bowl and mix for about 2 minutes on medium speed.

3 Using the hook attachment, set the mixer to medium-low and add 1 cup of flour at a time slowly. After adding flour, turn off the mixer and scrape down the sides. Turn the mixer back on and repeat the process until you've added all the flour and a soft dough forms. Mix for an additional 5 minutes or so.

4 Place the dough in a greased bowl and cover. Set the bowl in a warm area (like the center of the stove) and allow the dough to rise for about 1 to 2 hours or until it doubles. After it does, preheat your oven to 350 degrees and punch the dough down and return it to the floured surface. Divide the dough into 12 equal pieces and shape each piece into a ball.

5 Using a square 12-inch cast-iron skillet, add your dough (it's okay if the rolls touch). Using a small bowl, mix the coconut milk and coconut sugar. Brush the tops of each ball with coconut milk and finish with coconut sugar.

6 Place in the preheated oven and cook for 20 to 25 minutes or until golden brown. Allow the pan to cool for about 10 minutes before serving. Move to a cooling rack to prevent the bottom from getting soggy.

PER SERVING: *Calories 247 (From Fat 84); Fat 9g (Saturated 6g); Cholesterol 48mg; Sodium 246mg; Carbohydrate 35g (Dietary Fiber 1g); Protein 6g.*

5

The Part of Tens

IN THIS PART . . .

Discover some important do's and don'ts to treat your cast iron with TLC.

Find out some helpful tips to ensure that your cast-iron dishes are a hit.

Chapter **25**

Ten Do's and Don'ts to Make Your Cast Iron Last Longer

You're serious about your investment in quality cookware. After all, you've spent your hard-earned money to purchase some cast iron and you want to protect that investment. This chapter sets some boundaries to help make your cast-iron journey a little easier.

Do Reseason After Each Use

You know that you need to season cast iron before you use it the first time. (If that's news to you, head to Chapter 3 to find out why preseasoning is important and for instruction on how to do it.) Reseasoning your pans *after* each use is also important. The reason is that each time that you clean your cast iron, you remove a little seasoning. If you clean your cast iron enough times without reseasoning, the pans will lose the patina that makes them nonstick, and the metal will become vulnerable to rust.

Fortunately, reseasoning isn't nuclear physics. After you clean and dry your pan, simply wipe a thin coat of vegetable oil over the pan's surface.

Don't Put Cold Water in a Hot Pan

All metals are susceptible to *thermal shock*, a large and rapid change in temperature. If you put a cold pan on a hot burner, a hot pan under cold running water, or subject your cookware to any other combination of extreme and sudden temperature differences, you run the risk of warping or even breaking it.

TECHNICAL STUFF

Whether a pan is hot or cold depends on how quickly the molecules in the metal are moving. Cold molecules move slowly; hot molecules move quickly. The hotter the pan, the quicker the molecules move and all the more haphazardly; the colder the pan, the more sluggish they are. Force an instant temperature change and the molecules don't have time to transition from one state to another. The result? The metal equivalent of a human hissy fit.

The key is *gradual* temperature change. Pouring batter into a hot pan is safe. Putting a room temperature pan into a warm oven? Safe. Taking a pan from your refrigerator and putting it in a cold oven and preheating both together? Safe. Remember. Easy does it.

Don't Use Soap

For a society that has practically made *antibacterial* the new religion of clean, the idea of not using any soap at all sounds practically heretical. But you don't need soap to clean cast iron and using it can break down the seasoning.

REMEMBER

The only time that you need soap is when your pan is brand-spanking new and you have to wash it before you season it. (See Chapter 3 for details.) Beyond that, you don't need much cleaning paraphernalia — just hot water and a stiff-bristled brush. Some people don't even use water. If they have a cast-iron pan that they reserve solely for breads, for example, they simply wipe it out with a paper towel to clean it. (Not using soap doesn't present a health hazard. When you cook with cast iron, the pan gets hot enough to kill any germs on its surface.)

If you absolutely, positively can't stop yourself from sticking your cast iron in a sink full of soapy water, go ahead, but use mild soap and remember that

>> You'll need to season your pan more frequently — maybe even after every use.

>> Bringing out your cast iron's patina — a cook's dream — is going to take you longer. To find out about patina and why your success as a cast-iron cook is important, head to Chapter 1.

Don't Stick It in the Dishwasher

If soap is bad for cast iron (see the previous section), running it through the dishwasher is practically the kiss of death. First, dishwashing detergents are more abrasive than dish soap and cause more damage to the seasoning. Second, in a dishwasher, water bombards your cast iron from every angle. Third, dishes essentially air-dry in a dishwasher, which means that the water that bombarded your pan stays on it until it finally evaporates. (Check out the next section.)

REMEMBER

If convenience is your excuse for putting your cast iron in the dishwasher, think about how inconvenient sanding off rust spots and then reseasoning your pan is. Two minutes of hand cleaning is nothing compared to the toil required to resurrect a prized piece of cast iron.

Do Keep Water Away

Water is one of cast iron's enemies. One of your prime objectives as a cast-iron cook is to expose it to the least amount of water as possible in the least time. To minimize exposure to water, follow these suggestions:

>> Wipe your cast iron dry immediately after you clean it. To make sure that all the moisture is gone, put your cast iron in a warm oven or on a warm burner for a couple of minutes.

>> Other pans are better for water-intensive cooking, so don't use your cast iron as a boiler or steamer — at least not until it's well seasoned. Then, too, be sure to put a nice coat of vegetable oil on the inside of your cast iron.

>> If you live in a humid environment, put a crumpled-up paper towel into the pan before you store it and leave the cover off or ajar.

You can find more tips for caring for your cast iron in Chapter 4.

Do Use It Often

Unlike other cookware, cast iron actually gets better the more that you use it. Every time you cook with it, you're enhancing the pan's cooking properties. You can see this improvement as its color darkens. New cast iron is a gunmetal gray color and porous; old cast iron is black and satiny smooth. (In days gone by, cast iron, new or old, was referred to as *black iron* because of the black color that cast iron took on as it aged.)

The black, satiny patina is the result of seasoning — layer upon layer of seasoning — that comes from using, reusing, and caring for your cast iron. The *only* way to get this black, satiny patina is to use the pan often. Preseasoned cast iron, which comes from the factory already seasoned and ready to use, gives you a head start on this process, but even these pans don't compare to old, well-used cast-iron pans.

TIP

When you're breaking in a new pan, be sure to cook fatty foods the first few times. Sausage, bacon, hamburgers, macaroni, and cheese — any dish with a high-fat content deepens the initial seasoning. After the pan is nicely cured, however, you can cook anything you want in it. So do!

Do Store It Appropriately

Cast iron doesn't require much care in the storage department. You can keep it in a cupboard, or you can hang it on a wall or from an overhead pan rack if you're so inclined. Just make sure that it's anchored well to the wall.

The most important storage directive is to make sure that, wherever you store your cast iron, the area is cool and dry. You don't want to hang cast iron, even purely decorative cast iron, on the wall above your stove, for example, because of the steam that rises from the stovetop. If you're stacking your cast iron, make sure that you leave the covers off or ajar so that air can circulate to keep moisture from forming.

For additional information about caring for your cast iron, head to Chapter 4.

Do Avoid Cooking Acidic and Alkaline Foods at First

Certain foods — acidic foods, such as tomatoes and citrus products and alkaline foods, such as beans — can react to the iron in your pan. When your pan is new and before it's had a chance to develop the protective patina, such a reaction isn't particularly good for the pan (these foods can pit the surface), and it's disaster for your meal, which will end up tasting less like the food and more like the pan. (If you can't see why this is bad, lick your cast iron for a quick taste.)

This doesn't mean that you can *never* cook these foods in cast iron. Chili is a cast-iron favorite, as are old-fashioned green beans. It just means that the pan should be well seasoned before you do so. The seasoning protects the metal and the flavor of your food.

Do Appreciate Its True Value

In some families, the cast iron is passed down through generations as a valued family heirloom — even though most cast iron isn't worth a significant amount of money and, heaven knows, isn't particularly pretty. Cast iron is a treasure because it brings to mind good times, good food, and family. So when you cook with your cast iron, have fun.

If you enjoy cooking in it and you enjoy what you cook, these old, black-iron pans can appreciate in value far beyond their market value, their cooking properties, and all the other practical reasons people use them. Then you'll have a pan that not only *can* last generations but *will* last generations.

Do Use It the Way It's Intended

One of my favorite ways to use my cast iron is for searing and sautéing. The thickness of the cast iron creates an almost perfect heat distribution, allowing you to get a beautiful sear on your protein. When sautéing, you can go from the refrigerator directly to the pan and not have to worry about the cold vegetables cooling down your pan, thanks to its ability to hold heat. Other great cooking methods include baking, braising, and of course, pan-frying.

Chapter **26**

Ten Tips for Surefire Success

Baking is more than a science. When baking, some things have to be measured — for example, the baking powder, eggs, or the amount of liquid-to-flour ratios. But when it comes to cooking, you have way more flexibility. Much of cast-iron cooking is about *feeling.* Many old-school cast-iron cooks don't even measure. They judge quantities by a dollop of this, a dab of that, a pinch here, or a sprinkle there. If you're cooking with an auntie or grandma, you may hear things like "just until," as in "just until the smell burns the back of your nose" or "just until the spoon leaves a trail when you stir the batter." Cooking wasn't about precision. It was about being descriptive enough to get the results you want.

Times have changed, and so has the perception of food. Nowadays, people live in a digital world where digital scales are a common household item, and recipes can be accessed on your tablet, cellphone, or heck, read to you by your AI device! Each recipe in this book is designed to inspire you to think differently about food, how it cooks, and, most importantly, how it tastes. This chapter focuses on ten tips about helping you cook great food for you and the people who matter most in your life.

Seasoning and Reseasoning

I can't say this strongly enough: Any cast iron you cook in has to be seasoned. An unseasoned cast-iron pan is a disaster in the kitchen. Food sticks, it burns, and it just doesn't taste good. Seasoning eliminates these problems: It makes the surface nonstick and ensures that your food doesn't taste like metal. It also protects the pan from rust.

As the seasoning deepens, as it will over time, the pan's cooking characteristics become that much greater and more desirable. So season your new pan and then reseason your pan again after every use by wiping a thin coat of vegetable oil on the inside of it. If your pan shows signs that the seasoning is breaking down, you'll want to reseason it in the oven. Chapter 3 tells you everything that you need to know about seasoning your cast iron.

TIP

You can buy preseasoned cast iron now. This preseasoning takes care of the initial seasoning for you, but you still need to reseason your pans after using them.

Preheating Your Cast Iron

Cast iron is an efficient heat conductor. After it reaches the given temperature, the whole pan — bottom, side, and even the handle — is at that temperature. This is one of the great characteristics of cast iron because it means that the heat distribution is even and that hot spots, the bane of every cook, don't exist.

TIP

It also means that, for most recipes, you need to allow the pan to preheat completely before you add your food. This is especially important for baked dishes, such as cakes and cornbreads; dishes that rely on consistent oil temperatures, such as seared proteins; and recipes that require a quick application of high heat, such as steaks or pan-seared tofu. The preheated pan gives your baked goods a nicer crust, it keeps your fried foods from absorbing too much oil and getting greasy, and it seals in the juices of seared meats without overcooking them.

Using the Right Size Cast Iron

You can make any recipe in just about any cast-iron pan. This versatility means that you don't need many cast-iron pans — one or two is usually sufficient — but it also means that you have to be willing to adjust the recipe as necessary to accommodate cooking times and cooking methods.

REMEMBER

If you don't have the pans you need and don't have a suitable substitute, adjust the cooking times or the preparation method. Cornbread that you put in a skillet takes longer to cook than cornbread made in a loaf pan, for example. Similarly, if you have only shallow pans, stick to searing or pan-frying. Chapter 5 explains the difference between a pan-fry and a deep-fry.

Controlling Your Temperature

Cast iron conducts heat well, so you'll want to control the cooking temperature. You need to keep cast iron's heating characteristics in mind as you set and adjust temperatures:

>> With cast iron, you often don't need to use temperatures as high as those specified in recipes that aren't designed with cast iron in mind. So start out at the temperature the recipe states but always be willing to adjust the heat downward.

>> If you're using an electric range, remember that turning off the burner isn't enough to stop the cooking process. You also need to remove the cast-iron pan from the burner; otherwise, even though the burner's off, your dish will continue to cook.

You can read about the heating characteristics of cast iron and how to adjust temperatures accordingly in Chapter 5.

Modifying Cooking Times

When you cook in cast iron, the actual cooking times may be slightly less than that specified in your recipes. As you cook, don't rely solely on your kitchen timer; look for other signs of doneness.

TIP

When you roast meat, for example, use a meat thermometer. If you're baking a cake or quick bread, test for doneness with a cake tester or toothpick. Yeast breads sound hollow when you thump them. Meat should be at appropriate internal temperatures: Poultry should register 170 to 185 degrees, pork should come in at 170 degrees, and beef should tip the scales at 140 to 170 degrees. Head to Chapter 5 for more tips on testing for doneness.

Coating with Oil or Cooking Spray

Until your cast iron has a dark, satiny patina, some foods may stick. (See Chapter 1 for a description and illustration of what the patina looks like.) For that reason, always use a little bit of oil or cooking spray to ensure a nonstick surface. This advice can even benefit those folks whose pans are well seasoned, because, in addition to making food release easily, the oil or cooking spray also adds flavor.

Cooking with Quality Cast Iron

The quality of your cast iron matters. Quality affects not only how long the pan lasts — poorer quality cast iron is brittle and prone to warping or breaking — but also how well it takes seasoning and what its cooking characteristics are. Some of the characteristics of top grade cast iron are as follows:

>> **It has a finer grain and is easier to season.** This is important for producing a nonstick surface and eliminating the possibility of rust.

>> **The metal has a uniform thickness.** This is important because it makes for even heating and reduces the likelihood of hot spots that can burn or scorch your food. Uniform thickness also reduces the likelihood of the pan warping because of temperature changes.

You can find more information about how to judge the quality of cast iron and the implications quality has to cooking and safety in Chapter 2.

Using Quality Ingredients

What you cook with is as important as what you cook *in*. When you're planning your menu, choose ingredients that will enhance rather than detract from your dish. A great roast, for example, starts out as a bright red, well-marbled piece of meat. Similarly, unless a recipe calls specifically for canned or frozen vegetables, opt for fresh for optimal flavor.

TIP

Sometimes, the best ingredient for the task at hand isn't the freshest, prettiest, most expensive, and so on. The ripest fruit — even overripe fruit that you'd be tempted to throw away if you were just going to eat it on its own — is often the best choice for fruit desserts and fruit breads.

Sticking Around

Obviously, if you're deep-frying, pan-frying, simmering, sautéing, searing, grilling, and so on, you need to be near your stove. But even recipes slow-cooked in cast iron need some attention. You may not need to be in the room standing watch over the stove, but you need to be nearby. You may have to check the simmering liquid to make sure it doesn't steam away, or maybe the recipe requires that you periodically rearrange the ingredients to ensure that everything cooks evenly. Roasting is probably the most hands-off cast-iron cooking technique, and even that path requires you to be around if you want to baste.

Remembering That It's Just Food

On your cast-iron journey, you're going to have some highs and some lows. In those moments when it doesn't work out, don't forget to give yourself grace. Use the experience as a learning opportunity; don't be afraid to try again. It's in those moments where you truly grow and learn. In the heat of success, embrace it, and share it with the people that matter most to you. Always remember food is a connector and can break down many barriers with just one dish.

Appendix

Metric Conversion Guide

The recipes in this book weren't developed or tested using metric measurements. There may be some variation in quality when converting to metric units.

TABLE A-1

Common Abbreviations

Abbreviation(s)	What It Stands For
cm	Centimeter
C., c.	Cup
G, g	Gram
kg	Kilogram
L, l	Liter
lb.	Pound
mL, ml	Milliliter
oz.	Ounce
pt.	Pint
t., tsp.	Teaspoon
T., Tb., Tbsp.	Tablespoon

TABLE A-2

Volume

U.S. Units	Canadian Metric	Australian Metric
¼ teaspoon	1 milliliter	1 milliliter
½ teaspoon	2 milliliters	2 milliliters
1 teaspoon	5 milliliters	5 milliliters
1 tablespoon	15 milliliters	20 milliliters
¼ cup	50 milliliters	60 milliliters
⅓ cup	75 milliliters	80 milliliters
½ cup	125 milliliters	125 milliliters
⅔ cup	150 milliliters	170 milliliters
¾ cup	175 milliliters	190 milliliters
1 cup	250 milliliters	250 milliliters
1 quart	1 liter	1 liter
1½ quarts	1.5 liters	1.5 liters
2 quarts	2 liters	2 liters
2½ quarts	2.5 liters	2.5 liters
3 quarts	3 liters	3 liters
4 quarts (1 gallon)	4 liters	4 liters

TABLE A-3

Weight

U.S. Units	Canadian Metric	Australian Metric
1 ounce	30 grams	30 grams
2 ounces	55 grams	60 grams
3 ounces	85 grams	90 grams
4 ounces (¼ pound)	115 grams	125 grams
8 ounces (½ pound)	225 grams	225 grams
16 ounces (1 pound)	455 grams	500 grams (½ kilogram)

TABLE A-4

Length

Inches	Centimeters
0.5	1.5
1	2.5
2	5.0
3	7.5
4	10.0
5	12.5
6	15.0
7	17.5
8	20.5
9	23.0
10	25.5
11	28.0
12	30.5

TABLE A-5

Temperature (Degrees)

Fahrenheit	Celsius
32	0
212	100
250	120
275	140
300	150
325	160
350	180
375	190
400	200
425	220
450	230
475	240
500	260

Index

V

value, of cast iron, 363

vanilla extract, for cakes, 124

variety, of cast iron, 15–16, 21

Vatapá recipe, 336

Veal Scallopini with Mushroom Sauce recipe, 160

vegetable broth/stock
  about, 198
  Acorn Squash and Cranberries, 230
  Cajun Shrimp and Okra Gumbo, 153
  Cioppino, 194
  Cumin and Hot Honey-Glazed Carrots, 219
  Curry Tofu with Mustard Greens, 152
  Jollof Rice, 339
  Louisiana Seafood Gumbo, 193
  Potjiekos, 338
  Sautéed Shrimp and Okra, 205
  Steamed Clams with Lemon and Garlic, 195
  Stewed Chickpeas, 209
  Three-Bean Succotash, 210
  Vatapá, 336
  White Bean and Swiss Chard Soup, 227

vegetables. See also specific vegetables
  about, 107, 201–202, 206, 215–216, 220, 224, 229
  beans, 109
  Chicken Potpie, 171
  corn, 110–111
  fall, 224
  green tomatoes, 112
  okra, 111
  potatoes, 108
  preparing, 113
  protein in, 108
  as side dishes, 206, 229
  spring, 216

squash, 109–110

summer, 220

turnip greens, 111–112

venison, in Hunters' Venison Bourguignon, 303

vermouth
  Arroz con Pollo, 327
  Chicken Picata, 178

versatility, of cast iron, 15–16, 21

Vibrio vulnificus, 99

volume conversions, 372

W

Wagner, 26

Wagner Manufacturing Company, 35

walnuts
  Double Cherry Tea Cake, 281
  Old-Time Banana Bread, 271

Warning icon, 5

water, on cast iron, 361

weight conversions, 372

wether conditions, campfires and, 135

White Bean and Swiss Chard Soup recipe, 227

white beans
  about, 109
  Cassoulet, 349
  Three-Bean Succotash, 210
  White Bean and Swiss Chard Soup, 227

white cornmeal, 116

white fish, in Caribbean Escovitch Fish, 329

white roux, 105

white shrimp, 94

white wine
  Arroz con Pollo, 327
  Chicken Picata, 178
  Cioppino, 194
  Marvelous Fajita Marinade, 321

Pheasant Faisan, 182

Seafood Chowder, 192

Spinach and Artichoke Dip, 312

Steamed Clams with Lemon and Garlic, 195

whole-wheat flour, for biscuits, 119

width of sides, for evaluating quality, 32

winter squash, 110

wire brush, 48

Wiri Wiri peppers, in Chicken Marinade, 333–334

World Health Organization (WHO), 16

Y

Yankee Cornbread recipe, 241

yeast
  Ambasha (Sweet Flatbread), 342
  Beignets, 290
  Coconut Bread Rolls, 356
  Quick Pizza Dough, 256
  Savory Dill Bread, 252
  Sheepherders Bread, 254
  Spoon Rolls, 251

yeast breads, 120, 253

yellow beets, in Thyme-Scented Root Vegetables, 212

yellow cake mix, in Almost Pumpkin Pie, 307

yellow cornmeal, 116

yellow squash, in Summer Squash Casserole, 203

Z

zucchini
  Calabasa Skillet Souffle, 330
  Dutch Oven Veggies, 297
  Potjiekos, 338
  Summer Squash Casserole, 203

About the Author

Antwon Brinson is an American chef, motivational speaker, and entrepreneur with numerous accolades, including the prestigious 2023 John F. Bell Sr. Vanguard Award. He's widely recognized for his participation as a contestant on HBO's popular show, *The Big Brunch,* and is known for his culinary expertise, charismatic personality, and his commitment to making a difference in the lives of others. Through his company, he offers programs like the Phoenix program, dedicated to assisting inmates in their preparation for successful culinary careers. His passion for cooking, motivation, and entrepreneurship all contribute to his widespread appeal and make him a beloved figure in the industry.

Dedication

To my mom, Mary, thank you for being an example, not just to me but to all the foster kids you dedicated your life to raising. The legacy of your work lives on through me. I am grateful.

To my wife, Margaret, thank you for giving me the time and space to become the man I am today. Your sacrifices and unwavering support give me the strength and inspiration to reach new heights every day. I am thankful.

To my amazing sons, Dominique, Khiam, and Emery, thank you for choosing me as your dad. Your honest feedback, good and bad, has been invaluable. You are my greatest motivation and source of joy. I love you guys.

Author Acknowledgments

I express my heartfelt gratitude to the following individuals: Jennifer, a valued member of my editing team. Your unwavering belief and support throughout this entire process have been invaluable; thank you for this amazing opportunity. Chad, my main editor, it has been an absolute pleasure collaborating with you. I am grateful for your insightful feedback and clear direction.

To my dear friend Catie from HBO's *The Big Brunch*, thank you for your unwavering commitment to this project. I truly appreciate you, homie. Kori, my dear friend and talented photographer, I am grateful for your willingness to capture this historic moment; having you as part of the team brings me immense joy. Lastly, I thank everyone on the Wiley team, from the editors to the recipe testers; without your contributions, this project wouldn't have been completed.

Publisher's Acknowledgments

Senior Acquisitions Editor: Jennifer Yee

Senior Managing Editor: Kristie Pyles

Project Editor and Copy Editor: Chad R. Sievers

Technical Editor: Catie Randazzo

Recipe Tester and Nutritional Analyst:
Rachel Nix

Production Editor: Saikarthick Kumarasamy

Photographer: Courtesy of Kori Price

Dummies is the global leader in the reference category and one of the most trusted and highly regarded brands in the world. No longer just focused on books, customers now have access to the dummies content they need in the format they want. Together we'll craft a solution that engages your customers, stands out from the competition, and helps you meet your goals.

Advertising & Sponsorships

Connect with an engaged audience on a powerful multimedia site, and position your message alongside expert how-to content. Dummies.com is a one-stop shop for free, online information and know-how curated by a team of experts.

- Targeted ads
- Video
- Email Marketing
- Microsites
- Sweepstakes sponsorship

20 MILLION PAGE VIEWS
EVERY SINGLE MONTH

15 MILLION UNIQUE
VISITORS PER MONTH

43% OF ALL VISITORS ACCESS THE SITE
VIA THEIR MOBILE DEVICES

700,000 NEWSLETTER SUBSCRIPTIONS
TO THE INBOXES OF
300,000 UNIQUE INDIVIDUALS EVERY WEEK

PERSONAL ENRICHMENT

Staying Sharp

9781119187790
USA $26.00
CAN $31.99
UK £19.99

Facebook
Carolyn Abram

9781119179030
USA $21.99
CAN $25.99
UK £16.99

Guitar
Mark Phillips
Jon Chappell

9781119293354
USA $24.99
CAN $29.99
UK £17.99

Investing
Eric Tyson, MBA

9781119293347
USA $22.99
CAN $27.99
UK £16.99

Beekeeping
Howland Blackiston

9781119310068
USA $22.99
CAN $27.99
UK £16.99

Digital Photography
Julie Adair King

9781119235606
USA $24.99
CAN $29.99
UK £17.99

Meditation
Stephan Bodian

9781119251163
USA $24.99
CAN $29.99
UK £17.99

Pregnancy

9781119235491
USA $26.99
CAN $31.99
UK £19.99

Samsung Galaxy S7
Bill Hughes

9781119279952
USA $24.99
CAN $29.99
UK £17.99

iPhone
Edward C. Baig
Bob "Dr. Mac" LeVitus

9781119283133
USA $24.99
CAN $29.99
UK £17.99

Crocheting
Karen Manthey
Susan Brittain

9781119287117
USA $24.99
CAN $29.99
UK £16.99

Nutrition
Carol Ann Rinzler

9781119130246
USA $22.99
CAN $27.99
UK £16.99

PROFESSIONAL DEVELOPMENT

Windows 10
Andy Rathbone

9781119311041
USA $24.99
CAN $29.99
UK £17.99

AutoCAD
Bill Fane

9781119255796
USA $39.99
CAN $47.99
UK £27.99

Excel 2016
Greg Harvey, PhD

9781119293439
USA $26.99
CAN $31.99
UK £19.99

QuickBooks 2017
Stephen L. Nelson, MBA,
CPA, MS in Taxation

9781119281467
USA $26.99
CAN $31.99
UK £19.99

macOS Sierra
Bob "Dr. Mac" LeVitus

9781119280651
USA $29.99
CAN $35.99
UK £21.99

LinkedIn
Joel Elad, MBAs

9781119251132
USA $24.99
CAN $29.99
UK £17.99

Windows 10
Woody Leonhard

9781119310563
USA $34.00
CAN $41.99
UK £24.99

SharePoint 2016
Rosemarie Withee
Ken Withee

9781119181705
USA $29.99
CAN $35.99
UK £21.99

Fundamental Analysis
Matt Krantz

9781119263593
USA $26.99
CAN $31.99
UK £19.99

Networking
Doug Lowe

9781119257769
USA $29.99
CAN $35.99
UK £21.99

Office 2016
Wallace Wang

9781119293477
USA $26.99
CAN $31.99
UK £19.99

Office 365
Rosemarie Withee
Ken Withee
Jennifer Reed

9781119265313
USA $24.99
CAN $29.99
UK £17.99

Salesforce.com
Liz Kao
Jon Paz

9781119239314
USA $29.99
CAN $35.99
UK £21.99

Coding
Nikhil Abraham

9781119293323
USA $29.99
CAN $35.99
UK £21.99

dummies.com

dummies®
A Wiley Brand